Sue Elliott is the

James Fox

James Fox was born in 1935 and was one of the youngest pupils at the British Memorial School when the community was evacuated from Ypres in May 1940. After serving in the RAF, he worked for NATO and then as Editor-in-Chief for Magnum Photos in New York and Paris. An accomplished photographer himself, he has published several volumes of photography. He lives in Paris.

Praise for *The Children Who Fought Hitler*:

'Excellent book' *Daily Express*

'A history book with a twist, homemade bombs, protecting royalty, freeing prisoners of war . . . you name it these kids did it, [an] astonishing story' *News of the World*

'Fascinating' *Best of British*

'Extraordinary' *Sunday Express*

'It's hard to come up with new, untold stories about World War Two, but this book succeeds in just that . . . [Sue Elliott and James Fox] have retraced all the individual stories with impressive detail and moving candour' *Military Illustrated*

Also by Sue Elliott

Love Child

Also by James Fox

Ringside
James A. Fox

The Children
Who Fought Hitler

A British Outpost in Europe

SUE ELLIOTT WITH JAMES FOX

JOHN MURRAY

First published in Great Britain in 2009 by John Murray (Publishers)
An Hachette UK Company

First published in paperback in 2010

1

A CIP catalogue record for this title is available from the British Library

ISBN 978-1-84854-087-3

Typeset in Bembo by Servis Filmsetting Ltd, Stockport, Cheshire

Printed and bound by Clays Ltd, St Ives plc

John Murray policy is to use papers that are natural, renewable and recyclable products and made
from wood grown in sustainable forests. The logging and manufacturing processes are expected to
conform to the environmental regulations of the country of origin.

John Murray (Publishers)
338 Euston Road
London NW1 3BH

www.johnmurray.co.uk

Dedicated to the memory of
John Thomas Frederick (Jack) Fox
and to the men of the Imperial War Graves Commission
who suffered or died as a result of internment
1940–1945

Remember me,
'Tis all I ask.
But should remembrance prove a task
Forget me.

Entry in Florence Clarke's autograph book
14 November 1919

Contents

Introduction

O N A FRESH afternoon in May 2001 a group of fifty or so elderly people gather in the playground of what used to be a school. The building – solid, grey brick, with high casement windows and an arched entrance – could pass for any pre-war primary. But this isn't a London suburb or an English provincial town. This is Ieper in Belgium, better known in Britain by its French name, Ypres. The First World War Tommies called it Wipers.

They are here because seventy years ago or more they went to the school this used to be: the British Memorial School, Ypres. Almost all of them have travelled long distances and made a special effort to be here. This is not a regular event: many are seeing each other for the first time since May 1940. Some of the men are wearing medals, regimental ties and badges. An elegant woman has the Croix de Guerre pinned to her coat. There are shouts of recognition and emotional embraces. Wives and husbands are introduced. Life stories over six decades of war and peace are exchanged.

First, the formalities. Mr Luc Dehaene the burgomaster welcomes them back to West Flanders. Then the man who has brought them all together, James Fox, says how pleased he is to see them. This is an important and emotional day for Jimmy Fox; he has spent years tracing those who, like him and his four older sisters, were pupils at the Memorial School during its brief but influential life.

After the speeches, they move inside to what, in their day, was the main classroom. Now carpeted and comfortably furnished, it looks very different from how they remember it. But the ornate oak book-case donated by a Sheffield benefactor in 1939 is still there and so is the board bearing the names of the 342 Old Etonians in whose memory the school was built.

Over cups of tea, they look at old photographs of themselves in school scenes long past: boys in short trousers stand to attention and salute the Union flag; girls in white frocks with flower garlands in their hair dance round a maypole; a fresh-faced Britannia holds court with her cardboard shield and trident. Memories flow of schooldays much like those of thousands of other British children of the period.

The black-and-white images speak of an ordered world of certainty and benign authority, of close family and a supportive community. For the moment, the former pupils relive childhoods remembered as happy, safe and carefree. They enjoy the occasion, an opportunity to celebrate friendship, the past, survival. There will be time enough later to recall less comforting memories, of the chaos that began soon after these photographs were taken, when the world they knew was tipped upside down.

Jimmy Fox was just starting to make sense of that world in 1940. Ypres was all he had ever known. He was born there to a Belgian mother and a British father in 1935. His father John – known as Jack – was a gardener who tended the graves of the Great War cemeteries that dotted the countryside on this northern section of the old Western Front. Jimmy's large and loving family was part of a British community that had been there since 1919. Growing up in that community in those times didn't seem so special. It was just home.

Now, after a decade of research, Jimmy understands how extraordinary it was. The 2001 reunion was just the first milestone in a mission to find out more about the community he was forced to leave as a young child in 1940. Since then he has traced many more surviving children of the British families of Ypres, recording their stories and copying the photographs in their family albums. By capturing their memories of youth – idyllic, heroic and tragic – Jimmy has uncovered a bigger and more affecting story than anyone could have imagined.

They didn't know it at the time, but growing up in their peculiarly British outpost in Europe prepared these children for the fight of their lives. They were tested as no child in Britain was tested. Proximity to danger made them even more determined to defend the mother country – and to reclaim their adopted homeland from the oppressors who had forced them out.

I

Back from the Dead

We had seen other ruined towns, but none like this . . . Ypres has been bombarded to death.

Edith Wharton, *Fighting France, From Dunkerque to Belfort*, 1915

A T THE END of the First World War Ypres was an unearthly place. Once home to 20,000 people, the only things that lived here now were weeds and rats. Of the fine medieval town hardly a building remained upright: its Gothic cathedral was rubble and the belfry of its magnificent thirteenth-century Cloth Hall reduced to a battered stump. In the snowy winter of 1918–19, it was said that a man on horseback could see from one side of the town to the other. Four years of almost constant shelling had reduced it from an affluent backwater to a ghostly wasteland.

Pat Beauchamp, a British nurse with the First Aid Nursing Yeomanry (FANY), came back after the Armistice to find pathos, horror and the bizarre among the ruins:

I was surprised to see anything at all of the once beautiful Cloth Hall. We took some snaps of the remains. A lot of discoloured bones were lying about among the debris disinterred from the cemetery by the bombardments. Heaps of powdered bricks were all that remained of many of the houses. The town gasometer had evidently been blown completely into the air; what was left of it was perched on its head in a drunken fashion.

This unhappy fate was due to an accident of military geography. Ypres had the misfortune to be at the centre of a 'salient', an arc of defensive lines that bulge out into enemy territory. In the static battle of entrenched positions that characterised the war in Flanders after the autumn of 1914, the ancient town found itself at the most vulnerable northern point of the Western Front, with the front line never more than a few kilometres away. When the Germans took the surrounding ridges to the south and east the following year, they used their strategic advantage and superior firepower to pour shells into the town below. 'What Germany could not seize she destroyed,' wrote one British campaign general later. The few remaining citizens who had survived the intensive bombardment of what became known as the First Battle of Ypres, the freezing winter of 1914–15, and the outbreaks of typhus that followed, finally abandoned their cellar refuges under British orders to evacuate.

Among the refugees were Charlotte Dunn's mother and grandparents. Charlotte is now in her nineties and has lived in south-east England since 1940, but she has never lost her lilting Flemish accent or the belief that Belgium is her true home. She and her twin brother were born to the sound of shellfire in January 1918 in Boeschepe on the French border.

My mother and my grandparents had to leave Ypres because there was so much bombing. In 1915 they went over the border, just into France and they were there in an old farm. My grandfather used to go out with the wheelbarrow and see if he could pick a mattress or something up, you know, because their house was burnt down by the Germans and they had nothing. My mother and my grandmother used to do washing for the British soldiers. Covered in little insects, lice or something, she said the clothes were. They used to come past the little farm twice a week to go to the trenches and my grandmother would make coffee for them. It was winter and my mother had nothing, so she pinched this soldier's socks. When he came for his washing he saw her wearing them, and that's how my mother and father met.

As the residents moved out, the military moved in, making mess rooms in the cellars, a main dressing station beneath the old prison, and more than nine hundred dugouts in the seventeenth-century ramparts around the town and on its most exposed flank by the old Menin Gate. For the rest of the war, no one lived here except thousands of soldiers in their temporary underground shelters. Under almost continuous shellfire, it was a transit point where battalions mustered to go up to the front line, and to where they returned, exhausted and depleted. Troops from many nations passed through Ypres but it was the British and Empire forces based here who became most associated with the defence of the town and its Salient. Here, through the years of continual bombardment, three intensive battles and a final push, all the vile ingredients of trench warfare – gas, mud, vermin, foul weather, shellfire and snipers' bullets – combined in a toxic brew.

Having a practically identical experience on the other side of no-man's-land were the German troops, one of whom was a young infantryman in the 16th Bavarian Reserve Regiment, Adolf Hitler. Hitler's part in the First Battle of Ypres earned him the Iron Cross, Second Class. His regiment suffered heavy losses there but returned to the Salient in 1917 and again just before the Armistice in 1918 where Hitler was temporarily blinded in a British mustard gas attack. Another world away, on his triumphant return to Ypres in June 1940, he made a point of visiting the German war cemetery at Langemark, five kilometres away, to pay homage to the young men who didn't survive to see the rise and catastrophic impact of his Third Reich.

Chemical weapons were used by both sides in the Great War but their first major deployment – in the Second Battle of Ypres – heralded a barbaric new development in modern warfare. As the Germans unleashed almost 6,000 cylinders of chlorine gas into the south-westerly breeze on a fine day in April 1915, the effect on the enemy front line was as swift as it was horribly effective. War correspondent Philip Gibbs reported that men came staggering back to Ypres through the Lille and Menin gates with 'some foul spell upon them', gasping for breath, vomiting and then falling unconscious. Gas attacks killed few outright, but the temporary effects were devastating and a lifetime of respiratory problems often followed.

The Third Battle of Ypres produced one of the Great War's most resonant place-names, a name that sounds to English ears very like the Valley of Death. Passchendaele, a hamlet to the north-east of Ypres, already wrecked by this stage of the war, was the focus of a battle that ranks alongside the Somme and Verdun for its death toll and its ultimate futility. The battle was fought in the late summer and autumn of 1917 in the wettest weather for seventy years. Conditions were appalling and losses on both sides the worst of the whole campaign. The British Expeditionary Force (BEF) suffered a quarter of a million casualties; the Germans more. In November the Canadians finally took the shattered village of Passchendaele but it was lost again a few months later in the great German offensive of spring 1918 when the Salient shrank to within spitting distance of Ypres itself.

During this time, some way back from the front line, Jimmy Fox's father Jack was loading and firing 12-inch howitzers.

Dad had signed up with the Royal Garrison Artillery in 1912 and was posted to Hong Kong. When he came to France in 1915 he was working on the heavy guns. He'd tell me much later how the 12-inch guns would be mounted on railway carriages and move along the line. These were the weapons of mass destruction of their time and he must have caused hundreds of deaths with them. No wonder he never wanted to talk about it.

But this war of attrition was already drawing to a close. The spring offensive had exhausted German resources and will, the Americans had come into the war, and the tide had turned against the aggressor.

Though the Allies held Ypres and much of its Salient with a bitter determination, the human cost was unconscionable. The effort of defending this small patch of low-lying farmland cost the lives of 250,000 men from Britain and her Empire – mainly Australians, Canadians and from what is now the Indian subcontinent – a quarter of the total lost in the war. Many could not be identified. Of others there were no remains at all; they became 'the missing' with no known grave. The civilian dead were never properly counted; their remains still lay among the rubble.

At the time it seemed a price worth paying. Ypres had symbolic as well as strategic importance: less than 50 kilometres from Calais, with waterlogged land in between, it was the last bastion before the Channel ports. If Ypres was lost, the Bosche would be at the threshold of the British Empire. On this patch of the Western Front, the war was about more than saving plucky little Belgium from the rapacious Hun. For Britons, especially those in the comfort and safety of their homes, the defence of Ypres and the defence of the realm had become synonymous.

When the shelling finally stopped in October 1918, the boggy and bloodied Salient, with its hundreds of makeshift graveyards and ghostly ruins, assumed a spiritual, almost mystical, importance. It became 'the immortal Salient', a place of inexpressible tragedy but also a potent symbol of heroic sacrifice. This patina of sanctity eased broken hearts and troubled consciences; it yoked the unprecedented slaughter to a cause higher even than King and Country.

Sir William Pulteney, a lieutenant general in the Ypres campaign who later became a key figure in the life of the British colony there, chose *The Immortal Salient* as the title of a battlefield guide he wrote for the Ypres League after the war. Here he summed up this curious mix of grief and jingoism: '. . . our Dead lie here, the history of our manhood's great day lives here'. Rudyard Kipling, who was to play an influential role in the creation of the new war cemeteries, caught the quasi-religious flavour of this post-war reaction to the place when he called Ypres 'the very cathedral of Death'.

The dead certainly vastly outnumbered the living in Ypres by the end of the war. In the blasted battlefields surrounding the town were 200,000 British dead and missing alone. Of those who could be identified, the most fortunate were buried with due ceremony in existing communal cemeteries. The rest lay in crudely marked graves where they fell or in hastily constructed cemeteries near the casualty clearing stations and forward dressing stations, and where fierce skirmishes had taken place – only to risk the further indignity of being blown up repeatedly in subsequent shelling. There were hundreds, perhaps thousands, of bodies and bits of bodies still unburied on the battle-fields, and a vast legion of the missing. It was a place of the Dead.

But it would be the Dead who would rescue Ypres from obli-vion.

In the week of the November 1918 Armistice a small item under the headline 'Visits to Battlefields' appeared in the British press:

> The Press Association is informed by the Secretary to Messrs Thomas Cook & Son that they already have their arrangements in a practically complete form for visits to the various battlefields by those who have lost relatives and friends in the War. 'Of course', said the Secretary, 'it is a little too early to state definitely what we shall do, as it depends on the facilities which can be afforded by the railway and the number of motors placed at our disposal by the authorities. We have, however, a considerable staff of our own serving at the front and when they are at liberty we shall be able to grapple with the matter in a most expeditious manner.'

Battlefield tourism had begun, and with it a fierce debate about whether this meant salvation or sacrilege for Ypres.

Despite its lunar appearance and the final exodus of its residents in 1915, Ypres had never been a ghost town. Throughout the war it was not only full of troops, it also attracted a steady stream of jour-nalists, commentators and writers, fascinated by the romantic grand-eur of its ruins and the horror of the surrounding conflict. Arthur Conan Doyle wrote in 1916 (admittedly while there was still some-thing left of them), '. . . we marvelled at the beauty of the smashed cathedral and the tottering Cloth Hall beside it. Surely at their best they could not have looked more wonderful than now.' American novelist Edith Wharton, working as a volunteer with refugees in France, visited in 1915 after the First Battle of Ypres: 'The singular distinction of the city is that it is destroyed but not abased. The walls of the cathedral, the long bulk of the Cloth Hall, still lift themselves above the market place with a majesty that seems to silence compassion.'

As the town was gradually reduced to rubble over the course of the war, the appetite at home for descriptions of 'the tragedy of Ypres' grew more ravenous. Born of pity, personal loss or plain morbid curiosity, this unlikely market was soon to be translated into a booming tourist business. The novelist Arnold Bennett had predicted this with eerie accuracy in 1915 in his account of the early stages of the war, *Over There: War Scenes on the Western Front*:

> The immediate future of Ypres, after the war, is plain. It will instantly become one of the show places of the world. Hotels will appear out of the ground, guides and touts will pullulate at the railway station, the tour of the ruins will be mapped out, and the tourists and globetrotters of the whole planet will follow that tour in batches like staring sheep. Much money will be amassed by a few persons out of the exhibition of misfortune and woe. A sinister fate for a community! Nevertheless, the thing must come to pass, and it is well that it should come to pass. The greater the number of people who see Ypres for themselves, the greater the hope for mankind.

As 1919 dawned, ruined Ypres started to become quite a busy place. Determined former residents were already drifting back, Charlotte Dunn's grandfather among them, even before the Armistice was signed, to start again on the site of their old homes, living in cellars and shelters made from sheets of corrugated iron, salvaged timber and the detritus of war that littered the place. There were still plenty of soldiers about: demobilisation was slow and since the end of hostilities, in theory at least, they had more time for entertainment. Temporary clapboard shops, cafés and hotels soon appeared in the spaces cleared of rubble, to cater for the military and to accommodate the increasing numbers of civilian visitors coming to see the battlefields and graveyards.

But the Salient was still a lethal place. As well as the general debris of war, Ypres was surrounded by collapsed trenches, water-filled craters, unexploded ordnance and the rotting remains of horses and men. Though battlefield clearance (a hygienic name for a dreadful job carried out by the Chinese Labour Corps) had started, visitors were not yet allowed anywhere near them, unless with special dispensation from, and under supervision by, the Army. Money and contacts worked wonders, however, and no one could stop the most determined grieving relative intent on finding the last resting place of a loved one.

John Parminter's uncle, Captain Percy Douglas Parminter, whom John always knew as Uncle PD, worked for the Directorate of Graves Registration and Enquiries in Ypres in 1919 while he was waiting to be demobbed. This precursor to the Imperial War Graves Commission (IWGC) was set up to record burials and help relatives trace graves. Writing more than forty years later about the state of the battlefields, he recalled:

> It was dangerous enough for those of us accustomed to warfare and to have allowed civilians to wander around on their own would have been asking for trouble. I have vivid recollections of passing a Chinese Labour Corps camp engaged in clearance work not far from 'Shrapnel Corner' just outside of Ypres one evening in 1919. Some of them had got hold of a box of live Mills bombs [grenades] and were having a private war on their own with them. Several were wounded and one killed before they could be stopped.

In the town, conditions weren't much healthier. The ruins were infested with rats, 'some as big as cats', there was no sanitation and everything – including water – had to be brought in daily. The rich could afford to stay away for the time being. Those with large businesses cut their losses, selling their ruined premises off cheaply. No one yet knew if compensation would be available. But the enterprising Flemish were no strangers to hard work and they seized the chance to reclaim their home town.

Returning residents and those from further afield saw another kind of opportunity and soon cashed in to meet the needs of the new influx of visitors. Eighteen-year-old Germaine Vercruysse and her parents set about clearing debris from the site of their old business in the market square and erected the first temporary hotel-restaurant in a wooden hut. They called it the British Tavern and Germaine later married

Uncle PD. Following their example, other places of rest and refreshment sprang up with reassuringly familiar names: the Victoria Palace, the Splendid, and Skindles, after the fashionable Thames-side watering hole of the time. Humbler establishments, small bars or *estaminets* were created from former dugouts and ex-army huts. Souvenir sellers touted their wares among the ruins. Ypres was starting to take on the character of a frontier town: gaudy, permissive and slightly dangerous.

This development was noted with extreme distaste by British commentators, especially those who'd had personal experience of the war in Flanders. The 'well known War Correspondent and Artist' Julius M. Price fulminated in a 1919 periodical:

> I was in Ypres last week and was inexpressibly shocked to note the desecration that is going on there in the shape of wooden 'hotels', restaurants and cafés, which are springing up rapidly in the midst of the ruins . . . The whole place positively teems with memories, and there is not a corner of this soil but where British blood has been shed. When, therefore, one's musings are disturbed by the strident blast of a motor-horn and a luxurious touring car, crowded with smart sight-seers, hurtles past – or one comes across the newly-erected restaurants and cafés alongside ruins, under which, maybe, gallant men lost their lives, one has the feeling that it is all wrong – and positively indecent . . . Ypres and the Salient to-day are but a vast British sepulchre, and should be respected as such.

Presumably Mr Price arrived in Ypres by magic and went unrefreshed for the duration of his visit. His outrage has a whiff of hypocrisy. After all, he was a sightseer like everyone else.

Meanwhile the debate about the future of the town was being conducted at a national political level. With an arrogance that seems breathtaking from this distance, the recently appointed British Secretary of State for War, Winston Churchill, seriously suggested that Belgium should hand over the town to the British so that it could be preserved in its ruined state as 'holy ground' in memory of the sacrifice of the victor's war dead.

'A more sacred place for the British race does not exist in the world,' he told the newly established Imperial War Graves Commission, of which he was now Chairman. He instructed his Vice Chairman, Fabian Ware, to find ways of opening negotiations with the Belgian government. In this, Churchill was at one with his generals and the mourning public he represented: he had commanded a battalion at Ploegsteert in 1916 and he understood just how far the agony of Ypres had gripped the public imagination. To Britons at home and to the thousands of British troops who had survived their service on the Salient, Ypres was already theirs in spirit, if not in law. They believed they had every right to feel proprietorial.

Unsurprisingly, the Belgians had other ideas. As early as 1916, the town architect Jules Coomans had official approval in principle from the burgomaster to rebuild Ypres in its medieval likeness, reconstructing the major buildings exactly as they had been. Coomans had more than a passing professional interest in this plan. Before the war he had overseen a major twenty-year restoration project of all the town's most historic buildings. This was all but complete in 1914, just as the first German howitzers were taking aim at his handiwork.

In parallel, a much more radical plan by the government-appointed architect Eugène Dhuicque proposed a completely new town on the site. To satisfy British sensibilities and their demands for a sacred site, the ruins of the cathedral and the Cloth Hall and their surrounding houses would be preserved as a park with a 'zone of silence' in the centre. To protect them from souvenir seekers and further encroachment by temporary buildings, the ruins now had a cordon sanitaire – a rather puny wire fence patrolled by a teenage guard. More effective, certainly more striking, a wooden board in English by order of the town mayor warned:

THIS IS HOLY GROUND
NO STONE OF THIS FABRIC MAY BE TAKEN AWAY
IT IS A HERITAGE FOR ALL CIVILISED PEOPLES

At the end of February 1919, Churchill tried again. He wrote to Fabian Ware:

What have you been doing about my suggestion for acquiring Ypres as a British mausoleum, and what steps do you recommend me to take to bring this idea into actual operation? A letter should surely be written to the Belgian Government asking on what terms they would give or sell the ruins of the town to us.

Ware prevaricated, conscious of the practical difficulties of displacing so many people from their homes in a country already ravaged by war. In any case, things were moving too quickly. Within weeks the Belgian government, through the King Albert Refugee Relief Fund, was erecting temporary homes for former residents on the town's biggest open space, the Plaine d'Amour. These weather-board huts with corrugated-iron roofs had no running water, but they were better than a rat-infested ruin or a damp dugout. Charlotte Dunn's grandparents moved in to one of them and were allotted a small piece of land, a goat, a couple of chickens and some rabbits. While Charlotte's father was travelling back and forth to the UK, awaiting demobilisation, the family lived here for some of the time. A precious photograph from the early 1920s shows Charlotte and her twin brother, Priestley, outside their grandparents' hut, posing proudly with their livestock.

By July 1919 the offer of financial incentives to return and the promise of war damages opened the way for an influx of returnees. Churchill's vision of keeping Ypres for the Dead was being overtaken by events.

Realising that the town was being rapidly reclaimed under their noses, the British compromised and fell in with the Belgian government's plan for a smaller memorial park based on the Cloth Hall ruins. But the locals weren't happy. Relations between independent-minded Flemish-speaking West Flanders and French-speaking Brussels were traditionally cool. The citizens of Ypres protested vehemently against the Brussels-imposed plan; they wanted their 'old' town back. The government, squeezed between pressure from the British to whom they felt a great debt of gratitude, and the citizens whose town after all this was, postponed a decision. Finally, in 1921, amid much grumbling and disappointment from the generals and ex-servicemen's organisations at home, Britain gave up any claim to 'holy ground' and settled instead on the idea of a purpose-built memorial.

This was the right decision. The new monument would have a much greater impact on the future importance and prosperity of Ypres than any fenced-off ruin or 'zone of silence'. It was to be erected on the shell-blown ramparts at the town's most infamous and symbolic entrance – the Menin Gate.

Within a couple of years of the end of the war Ypres was booming. By 1922, rebuilding to Coomans' master plan was well under way and the town teemed with five thousand labourers, builders and architects, spawning more new businesses set up to serve them. Work was plentiful and so were the opportunities for leisure – extended since the introduction of a 48-hour working week the previous year.

The social fabric of Ypres was under reconstruction too: new clubs and societies were formed – many of them by and for ex-servicemen – and the traditional processions, fairs and festivals soon started up again. As early as 1919 the St Peter's Fair resumed with a cycle race starting outside the wreck of the former post office and the Kattenfest, the famous Cats Festival where symbolic cats are thrown from buildings to ward off evil spirits, was reinstated in 1921.

The population had already rapidly expanded from a handful of plucky returnees in the autumn of 1918 to six thousand by the end of 1920. Now it was boosted, not only by those involved in rebuilding work, but by a significant community of British ex-servicemen. Demobbed, and many now with Belgian wives and girlfriends, they were a vital part of Ypres' reincarnation as a tourist attraction and place of pilgrimage.

After demobilisation Captain P. D. Parminter and his brother bought an ex-army hospital hut by the railway station and established an upmarket taxi and charabanc company offering personally conducted tours 'to the elite', as his nephew John describes them, 'Lords, and those with money, and people who could travel'. To prove it, John still has a handwritten letter on Kensington Palace notepaper from Queen Mary's younger brother, the Earl of Athlone:

I have much pleasure in recommending the 'Wipers Auto Service' to anyone who desires to visit the various battle sectors. During a stay of four days, Princess Alice and I used one of the excellent cars driven by Mr Parminter, who knows the battlefields well.

But for anyone, peer or pauper, getting around the Salient was a problem initially. As Uncle PD recalled:

Transport difficulties were immense in those early days . . . North and west all rail communications had been completely destroyed. Roads to the west were usable – the main supply route to the Ypres Salient through Poperinghe and Vlamertinghe having been raised in long sections and strengthened by the Royal Engineers to carry heavy traffic and shell holes rapidly filled in again after a bombardment. Most others around Ypres had been blown out of existence, and it was a long time before any motor transport could be used.

As soon as roads became passable, other British ex-servicemen started taxi and tour companies, often buying up ex-army vehicles. It was an obvious choice for a post-war small business: they had detailed knowledge of the terrain and the battles that had taken place there, and could spice up any tour with spine-chilling personal anecdotes; they spoke the same language as the visitors, and could count on their sympathy and respect. Dozens of small firms sprang up and, as contemporary photographs show, pullulated round the station just as Arnold Bennett had predicted.

One ambitious tour operator was Leo Murphy, a regular soldier who first came to Flanders at the start of the war with the 1st Battalion the Queen's Royal Regiment and established his British Touring Information Bureau in 1919. But he was best known for his famous Ypres Salient War Museum, the largest collection of war materials in private hands in the world until the outbreak of the Second World War. His son Francis is ninety and nearly blind now, but still manages to show off his father's extensive collection of photos and memorabilia from the post-war days in Ypres.

He had several businesses; one was as a tour operator. He organised for ex-servicemen to come over and visit Belgium, Holland and France on a seven-day tour. They'd cross by boat to Ostend and he'd have luxury coaches to meet them and take them to these countries. When I was seventeen, eighteen, I'd go with them as a kind of tour guide. We also had a shop, run by my mother, that sold lace and souvenirs, but his biggest thing was the museum. He used to say to the British soldiers, 'Mention any small weapon or any weapon you like, or any article – even a horse's gas mask – and I'll show you one, it's all here!'

Francis points out one of his father's favourite exhibits. It sounds unlikely but there is a photograph to prove it: a German gas shell with a smaller British shell embedded in the middle of it. Neither had exploded but apparently the contents leached out, gassing all the Germans within striking distance.

Leo Murphy had a distinguished war record, winning the Croix de Guerre and the Medaille Militaire for organising the civilian evacuation of Béthune under heavy fire in 1915.

Father organised the evacuation of the population and the transport to get them away. And whilst he was going through this town which was being shelled and bombed like mad, he heard voices in a bombed house and dug down to the cellar and rescued a man, his wife and daughter. And he married the daughter – my mother!

Leo was a gifted linguist and spoke six languages, a facility that found him in intelligence work later in the war. His family originated from County Cork (Ireland was part of the United Kingdom until 1922) and he was intensely patriotic.

Father had the biggest Union flag he could buy. God knows how many yards long it was – at least three yards long and one and a half wide and it flew outside our house, over the shop, day and night. In fact people would call on us thinking we were the British Consulate! They'd ask for advice and we'd give it to them! Of course we explained we weren't the Consulate, we were just business people.

As well as making a large contribution to post-war civic life in Ypres – there are dozens of photographs of him accompanying visiting dignitaries – Murphy and his family worked hard in all their enterprises. Francis remembers that, though the peak season ran from Whitsun to the end of August, the shop stayed open all year and they would open the museum on demand.

> If tourists rang the bell and wanted to see the museum at seven o'clock in the morning, we would get up and open up. Or at eleven o'clock at night because they were leaving early the next morning, and said could they see the museum and see my mother's shop, because they wanted to go back with souvenirs of hand-made lace . . . so yes, we would open up.

Murphy knew his market and he gave them exactly what they wanted: safe exposure to the horrible hardware and curios of war; tours of where it all happened from the security of a charabanc; and a nice bit of lace and some postcards to take home as mementos. Because, though many of his customers were war veterans, many more were women – the mothers, wives, sisters and fiancées of the dead.

Transport problems and the scarcity of comfortable accommodation notwithstanding, visitors started arriving in Ypres in large numbers. They came in two forms: the battlefield tourists and the pilgrims. The distinction between them sometimes blurred, but those who came to mourn and remember the dead usually had very different needs and motivations from the merely curious. They, and more particularly those expressing views on their behalf, found the sightseers and the commercialisation of the battlefields 'business' abhorrent.

A piece in the *Daily Express* in September 1919 was typical of many. The writer expected Ypres to be full of pious pilgrims but instead he found 'morbid seekers after sensation. Vandals. Ghouls of the battlefield.' A slightly later piece in the magazine of the Ypres

League, the *Ypres Times*, was obviously meant to be dismissive but strikes us now (with the addition of a rebuilt Cloth Hall and air-conditioned coaches) as a fair description of any First World War battlefield tour today:

> In they come with a rattle and a clatter through the Menin Gate, all packed together in huge char-a-bancs, and after a raucous-voiced guide has pointed out the very obvious Cloth Hall ruins, they are whirled away to one of the show places, perhaps Hill 60, and when they get back home they think they have seen Ypres and the Salient, and perhaps begin to wonder what all the fuss is about.

So much was written during the course of the war about its terrible cost and impact in the Ypres Salient – much of it in floridly patriotic terms – that there was intense public interest in coming to see these sights as soon as the Armistice was signed. Interest was served and fuelled by those staples of the modern tourist trade, the guidebook and the package tour. Michelin started publishing battlefield guides while the war was still in progress and dozens more were produced in English between 1919 and 1921. By 1919, Thomas Cook was already offering two levels of battlefield tour: a luxury package at thirty-five guineas (£36.75) and a more modest option at nine and a half guineas (about £10). Other British travel agencies were quick to jump on the bandwagon. A battlefields tour was sold as a convenient and educational side-trip for visitors staying in the coastal resorts between Ostend and Le Touquet, just as today it is an optional adjunct to a three-day city break in Lille or Bruges.

From the Ypres end, small operators like Leo Murphy offered a local, more tailored, and more personal service. Once there, independent travellers could make use of facilities like Captain Parminter's Wipers Autos and the comforts – under a corrugated-iron roof – of the Hôtel de la Gare run by his sister-in-law, John's mother Simone.

Foreign travel had started to take off before the war but mass tourism was still to come; travel remained pretty much the preserve of the comfortable and leisured classes. Paid holidays were not the norm for working people and the average industrial wage of around £3 a week meant that a few days in Belgium – even if it was to see the final resting place of a husband or son – was well out of reach for the majority. So the commercial end of the market served those who could afford both the time and the money.

Disliked as they were by those who, wanting to protect the sanctity and 'immortality' of the Salient, disparaged their lack of reverence and their ostentatious spending habits, these early battlefield tourists were vital to Ypres' – and Belgium's – fragile re-emerging economy. Importantly for the nascent British colony, they also helped sustain the growing number of families headed by British ex-servicemen who had decided to make their new lives there.

Ironically, all the doubtless heartfelt but nevertheless highly emotive journalism about the Salient's sacred soil and its symbolic importance as 'the place of sacrifice of the best of England's sons' (as one writer put it in 1915) not only helped brand Ypres as a pilgrimage destination for the bereaved; it also attracted those who perhaps didn't have a 'proper' reason to go, but who wanted to associate themselves with the mass outpouring of grief after the war. This was a time when nations and communities as well as individuals felt a huge sense of loss, a painful hurt seeking resolution in some kind of healing gesture or action. In that sense, they were all pilgrims. They were all looking for meaning in a disaster unprecedented, incomprehensible, in its scale and human cost.

The ex-serviceman was another kind of pilgrim, returning to honour fallen comrades, to commemorate the efforts of his regiment or battalion and – less consciously perhaps – to rekindle the intensity of feeling and kinship forged on the battlefield in the limbo of the post-war world. Together, the bereaved, the war veteran and the non-combatant seeking vicarious war thrills made a volatile and sometimes inharmonious mix. The 'real' pilgrim, however, was distinguishable by a sole and determined purpose: to find the grave of a loved one or, if there was no grave to find, to inhabit the landscape where he had spent his final weeks. This was no excuse for the adventure of foreign travel; it was an emotional journey that the mourner felt impelled to make, a 'sacred quest'.

The Revd. Philip (Tubby) Clayton founded Talbot House, the servicemen's refuge in nearby Poperinghe that inspired the international voluntary service organisation Toc H. Clayton knew about the lives of soldiers in war. Afterwards he wrote feelingly about the burden of the pilgrim's journey and the promise of relief it held:

> As you go, sadly proud, about the Ypres countryside, you will feel that you are in a land given over utterly to hatred . . . You will feel held down by the horror of it all, submerged in a dark atmosphere of mud and murder, groping in a grim underworld of demented passion. The whole place is like the crater of a volcano, with the lava scarcely cool. Into this your love thrusts you upon your sacred quest, that you may know at least where they had laid him.

This appeared in *The Pilgrim's Guide to the Ypres Salient* published by Talbot House in May 1920. 'Compiled, written and illustrated gratuitously' by ex-servicemen, it aimed to give 'those who desire to visit the Graves and Battlefields a dependable and comprehensive Guide to their actions from the moment when they decide to undertake the journey until the moment when they once again set foot in England'. Unlike any Michelin guide, it gave frank appraisals of the available accommodation (Ypriana – 'cheerful, clean, cooking good'; Splendid – 'rather expensive', and somewhat unnecessarily, Hôtel de la Gare – 'opposite Station') and pointed out cheap options ('Situated outside the Menin Gate there are several restaurants newly built of wood, which have rooms to let from 5 to 10F per night'). It was informative, too, for those who could afford to be choosy. Among the advertisements for 'Battlefield tours de Luxe: personally conducted tours by ex-officers in high class motor cars', the *Manchester Guardian* and a four-page spread on Rolls-Royce cars, appears a note: 'Ypres is a more convenient centre than Poperinghe for visiting the Salient. But those who look for a higher standard of comfort than can be found in its wooden buildings, would do well to take rooms at Skindles Hotel, Poperinghe.'

Most importantly, given that the overwhelming majority of the dead and missing were from the industrial and agricultural classes, and a war widow's pension was far less than the average weekly wage, the *Guide* gave information about the growing number of organisations offering low-cost accommodation and subsidised travel for pilgrims of limited means.

The YMCA was among the first to offer basic accommodation for pilgrims in Ypres, opening its forty-bed hostel in August 1919. The Church Army wasn't far behind: the *Guide* notes that it has 'a similar scheme under consideration. Particulars can be obtained from Mr Screech, Church Army Hut, near the Prison, Ypres'. The St Barnabas Society, funded by private donations and set up in 1919 to help relatives visit war graves, established hostels in Calais, Boulogne and nearby Hazebrouck, each with its own chapel for private prayer. 'They provide a sympathetic home atmosphere for all those visiting graves', the *Guide* notes approvingly, 'and are entirely free from the Tourist Agent element'. A valued service for women travelling alone or perhaps in small groups was the availability of a St Barnabas 'lady worker' to meet them at Ostend and escort them to their accommodation – an early and benevolent incarnation of the holiday rep.

Ex-servicemen's organisations too – the British Legion and the Ypres League – organised pilgrimages for considerably less than the cost of a commercial tour. With second- or third-class travel, hostel or small hotel accommodation and no profit margin, these brought a visit to the battlefields within reach for many: one in 1920 offered travel and two days board in Ypres for £3 11s 6d (about £3.60). A number of free places were available to the most deserving, allowing some of the poorest to make the trip. A grateful widow, Lillian Payton, wrote to the Ypres League in 1926: 'I enclose a photo which I took of our "little bit of England", and the memory of our visit to Ypres and the motto of the League will remain with us always.' Alongside the letter, published in the *Ypres Times*, is a touching picture of her son Bertie, in his school uniform, cap in hand, by his father's grave. Ever alive to the power of an emotive image, the League made good use of this later in a rather different piece of propaganda.

They came at first as individuals and in small informal groups, then the pilgrims started to arrive in bigger, organised parties throughout the 1920s. The largest was led by the British Legion in August 1928 when 11,000 ex-servicemen and their families visited Ypres and the Western Front, led by Edward, Prince of Wales, and Prince Charles of Belgium.

Why did they come in such numbers to such a benighted place? They were looking for comfort, a way to come to terms with the unbearable pain of a violent parting from a lover, son or best friend. They craved that elusive message of hope sought by all war-bereaved: that the sacrifice hadn't been in vain. Above all they were looking for a permanent marker that would provide public recognition and private solace. A name carved in stone in a quiet and beautiful place that looked a little like home.

Now the men who had known Flanders fields only too well during 1914–18 returned to Ypres to start the task of burying and memorialising the dead. The work of the Imperial War Graves Commission began in earnest.

2

Builders of Silent Cities

We are the Dead. Short days ago
We lived, felt dawn, saw sunset glow,
Loved and were loved, and now we lie
In Flanders fields.

John McCrae, 1872–1918

THE BRITISH CAME to Ypres because of the Dead. First, the mourners and then the men who came to make the cemeteries.

When the mourners started coming, even the biggest cemeteries were rudimentary and temporary-looking. Most weren't really cemeteries at all, perhaps just an outcrop of crude crosses on the edge of a water-filled crater in a muddy field. By the end of the war there were hundreds of these hurriedly made graveyards on the Ypres Salient, often dug in darkness or in the mists of early morning, sometimes under shellfire, men buried with as much solemnity as haste allowed. Others, to be discovered perhaps many decades later, lay with limbs intertwined in unidentified mass graves where they were interred by the enemy after a major offensive. Many weren't buried at all but still lay out in the fields and in the trenches where they fell. Hardest for their bereaved to bear, of thousands there was no trace at all. They had been blown to oblivion as they died, before they could be buried, or as they lay in their graves.

For those fortunate enough to have a marked grave to survive the duration, even here there was pathetic disarray. On his first visit to the battlefields in 1917, the architect Edwin Lutyens discovered a desolate new universe. He saw scattered graveyards – many inaccessible because nearby roads had been completely destroyed – 'and then a ribbon of isolated graves like a milky way across miles of country, where men were tucked in where they fell . . . For miles these graves occur, from single graves to close-packed areas of thousands, on every sort of site and in every sort of position.'

By the beginning of 1919, as mourners poured not only into the Ypres Salient but to other battle sites along the Western Front, there was intense pressure to bring order to this chaos and to give practical expression to the eulogies to the war dead that the public were so used to hearing from their political and military masters. This task, previously unimaginable in its scale and sensitivity, fell to a small organisation that had been in operation for less than two years. In its early days it faced formidable practical and political obstacles and scorching criticism for its radical policies. The objective was doubly delicate: to satisfy the needs of hundreds of thousands of families in mourning, but also to create a vast memorial overseas that would in perpetuity reflect the values of the nation that built it. Even trickier, it had to pay proper tribute to its war dead without glorifying war itself.

In this daunting task the new Imperial War Graves Commission had two vital assets: a leader of energy and vision and a workforce of exceptional dedication.

Fabian Ware was already too old, at forty-five, for active service in 1914. An educationalist and colonial administrator in South Africa who went on to edit a national newspaper, the *Morning Post*, Ware had already distinguished himself in a variety of fields, picking up useful contacts and diplomacy skills along the way. More importantly, perhaps, he had formed a view of Britain's leadership role in the world that did not hark back to the Edwardian legacy of Empire. He believed that cooperation and partnership among equals achieved more than the imposition of the will of the strongest. He was a patriot, but also a forward thinker.

As soon as war was declared Ware volunteered his services to the British Red Cross. In September 1914 he found himself in Lille in charge of a 'mobile unit', a motley collection of volunteers and their cars who moved around forward areas – and occasionally behind enemy lines – to pick up the wounded, give emergency first aid and transport them to field hospitals. It was while performing this service for French soldiers in the early months of the war that Ware grew increasingly concerned about the fate of the British dead. He noticed the hastily made burial grounds, how the rain and wind soon obliterated the inscriptions on the temporary wooden crosses, and how there seemed to be no system in place for recording the location of graves and who occupied them, so that relatives could find them later.

Ware quietly expanded the work of his unit, with support from the Red Cross, to seek out, record, and mark British graves using imprinted zinc strips on tarred wooden crosses that wouldn't rot in the wet. To find graves often scattered over a wide area of countryside, his men used an informal network of local contacts – with priests and children proving the best informants. One of his team wrote of his satisfaction at doing this early work:

> It frequently requires considerable patience and some skill as an amateur detective to find the grave of some poor fellow who has been shot in some out of the way turnip field and hurriedly buried, but I feel my modest efforts amply rewarded when I return a day or two later with a wooden cross with a neat inscription and plant it at the head of his grave, for I have the proud satisfaction of knowing that I have done some slight honour to one brave man who has died for his country.

Despite initial opposition from the Army, who were responsible for battlefield burials, Ware used his powers of persuasion and the evidence of a difficult job being well done to convince the Adjutant General of the British Expeditionary Force, General Macready, that this work should be put on a more formal footing. By the spring of 1915 Ware's mobile unit had assumed official responsibility for this work, together with a title, the Graves Registration Commission. By October over 30,000 graves had been identified and recorded in France and Belgium, and its work was transferred from the auspices of the Red Cross to the Army.

Ware's helpers were all still volunteers with no army rank or pay structure, but the vital nature of their work for morale at the front and at home was soon grasped at the highest level in the military command. General Haig reported to the War Office:

> It is fully recognised that the work of the organisation is of purely sentimental value, and that it does not directly contribute to the successful termination of the war. It has, however, an extraordinary moral value to the troops in the field as well as to the relatives and friends of the dead at home. The mere fact that these officers visit day after day the cemeteries close behind the trenches, fully exposed to shell and rifle fire, accurately to record not only the names of the dead but also the exact place of burial, has a symbolic value to the men that it would be difficult to exaggerate.

Ware's work received further recognition when, in spring 1916, his organisation was re-designated as the Directorate of Graves Registration and Enquiries and its officers given commissions; Ware himself became a lieutenant colonel. It was now a fully-fledged part of the Army. By May he reported that 50,000 graves had been registered, 5,000 enquiries answered, 2,500 photographs of graves supplied to relatives and 200 prospective permanent cemetery sites selected. But Ware knew that these efforts, essential as they were, could only be the beginning of the much larger operation ahead.

He began preparing for the future. In 1915, in an early gesture of generosity and solidarity, France had passed a law that granted Britain land in perpetuity for war cemeteries. Ware now worked hard with colleagues to persuade the Belgian government – in exile and with most of its land occupied by Germany – to do the same, with delicate negotiations coming to fruition in 1917. He courted influential figures in the arts and architecture who he thought could help him achieve his vision of simple, beautiful and elegant cemeteries that would be a credit to the war dead and to Britain. It is likely that he first met the most distinguished architect of the day, Edwin Lutyens, through their mutual contact with Alfred, Lord Milner, with whom Ware had worked in South Africa. Lutyens was impressed, finding

Ware 'a most excellent fellow and very keen to do the right thing without fear or favour of the present sentiment. With a preference for the most permanent and perfect.'

Efforts were started to make the temporary cemeteries less bleak and unwelcoming. Horticultural advice was sought from the Royal Botanic Gardens at Kew and an expert toured thirty-seven cemeteries in France, reporting back on suitable plants and shrubs for the conditions he found there. Simple planting schemes – grass and annuals – were started in the larger cemeteries in forward areas where they had an uplifting effect on the troops: 'They cheer our men who are constant visitors to our cemeteries and who frequently pass them when on the march,' wrote the Kew adviser, Arthur Hill. By the autumn of 1917 there were four plant nurseries supplying the cemeteries of the Western Front and a substantial gardening contingent consisting of men unfit for military service and women from Queen Mary's Auxiliary Army Corps. The Army wouldn't pay for plants, tools and transport, so these were funded by the Red Cross.

When the horticultural work began in 1916 the war was still only at its mid-point, with the bloodbaths of the Somme and Passchendaele yet to come. Nevertheless the toll continued to mount, and with it the workload of keeping track of the dead and missing. Ware was constantly in the field, directing and observing. But he also had his sights firmly on arrangements for carrying the work forward on a permanent basis as soon as hostilities ended. Fearing a free-for-all once the Army relinquished control after the war, he started lobbying for an 'imperial commission' to care for soldiers' graves and to take charge of permanent memorials in their honour.

As Ware saw it, the task of burying the war dead was fraught with problems that had to be overcome before his vision of a 'permanent and perfect' memorial could be realised. One of the first difficulties to arise was bodies going AWOL. For reasons of practicality and economy (but also ethics) the Army had banned the exhumation and repatriation of remains early on in the war. However, families with money and influence were often determined to 'bring their men home' for private burial and there were those in France and Belgium only too willing to provide this service for a fee. In some cases private enterprise wasn't necessary. In 1915 the body of a British officer, a grandson of Prime Minister William Gladstone, was dug up under fire and transported to England 'in obedience to pressure from a very high quarter'. A number of similar instances were reported, though no record of illegal repatriations was kept. Once the war was over, the Army's writ would no longer run; families could demand that their dead be disinterred and returned to them. By the end of 1918, requests for repatriation were running at the rate of ninety a week. The possibility of burial apartheid – officers brought home, men buried abroad – was real.

Then there was the question of the erection of private memorials in war cemeteries. The Victorians had made the commemoration of the dead something of a fetish and this had only accentuated the traditional link with wealth, class and social rank: the wealthier and more important the family, the bigger and more ostentatious the physical manifestation of their grief. Classical pillars with weeping maidens, angels, cherubs and crosses of all dimensions made many civil cemeteries a restless jumble of masonry. Rank bought prominence. Cemeteries for the military, in which rank is all, could go the same way.

Not uppermost in the minds of grieving British families, but of concern to Ware, was the fact that thousands of those who fought and died for the Empire were not Christians at all but Hindus, Muslims, Sikhs, Buddhists or Jews. The symbols of Christianity taken for granted as fitting funerary emblems in Britain wouldn't do for them. Would this difference relegate them to some non-Christian corner or accord them lesser tribute? It was a distinct possibility.

Ware had clear and forthright views on these matters that flowed from his fundamental belief that the war dead should be treated equally and with integrity. He knew from his extensive contacts with serving officers and ordinary soldiers that their desire, consistent with military tradition, was to be buried where they fought and died, side by side. Repatriation served the wishes of the living, not the dead; it was divisive, creating a geographical and symbolic distinction between rich and poor, officers and men. The integrity of a war cemetery would be compromised if some of the dead were removed for burial in churchyards and civil cemeteries at home. Ware believed that everyone who had died in the service of their country and Empire should merit equal treatment in death, regardless of military or civilian rank, race or creed. This meant no individual memorials and no territorial divisions by rank. It also suggested not a cross at the head of every grave but a simple uniform stone.

These views, formulated during the course of his early work, were to become foundation principles for the new permanent war graves commission Ware was now determined to bring to birth. The first step was made in March 1916 with the appointment of an advisory body, the National Committee for the Care of Soldiers' Graves, with Edward, Prince of Wales (later to abdicate as King Edward VIII), as its President. By the start of 1917 Ware's vision for a new permanent commission, independent of government and the military, 'an equal partnership of nations' within the Empire, as the Commission's official historian Philip Longworth describes it in *The Unending Vigil*, began to take shape.

Ware persuaded the Prince of Wales to suggest such a body, constituted under Royal Charter, to Prime Minister Lloyd George. Despite objections that the work should be undertaken 'in-house' by the Department of Works, over the following months Ware argued his case convincingly that only an independent body under the Crown could adequately represent the views and wishes of the Dominions within the British Empire. After extensive negotiations and consultations, on 21 May 1917 the Royal Charter was signed and the Imperial War Graves Commission (IWGC) came into being. The Prince of Wales was to be its President, the Secretary of State for War its Chairman, with representatives from the colonies, Dominions and India and up to eight other Commissioners to be appointed. Fabian Ware was made Vice Chairman, effectively its chief executive officer.

The Commission now had exclusive responsibility for the graves of members of the Imperial Forces who had died 'while on active service whether on sea or land'. It could acquire land in Britain and abroad, erect memorials (and, importantly, prevent others from doing so in its cemeteries), arrange burials, make cemeteries and 'plant trees, shrubs and flowers therein'. It would also take over the work of the

Army Registration and Enquiries Directorate, though this carried on in parallel under Ware's direction until 1920.

The Charter wasn't just about practicalities. As the first body of its kind to embrace countries of the British Empire in an equal partnership, the Commission had a remit that enshrined Ware's cherished principles of unity and cooperation, albeit couched in the stylised language of imperialism. By honouring the war dead, the new Commission was charged to 'keep alive the ideals for the maintenance and defence of which they have laid down their lives, to strengthen the bonds of union between all classes and races in Our Dominions, and to promote a feeling of common citizenship and of loyalty and devotion to Us and to the Empire of which they are subjects'.

This gave Ware, his Commissioners and colleagues the authority and independence they needed to start their monumental task. The year 1917 was significant for the foundation of two institutions born of the Great War that have quietly informed – and reformed – the public's view of war ever since. The Imperial War Graves Commission is one. The Imperial War Museum is the other.

Of those who sat round the table at the first meeting of the new Commission in November 1917, one was uniquely qualified for the role. Rudyard Kipling, creator of *Kim*, 'If . . .' and the *Just So Stories*, was the most popular writer of the day and a bellwether of public sentiment. He knew what the country was thinking and he both led and reflected contemporary taste for works that celebrated Britain's military and Imperial achievements. But he was more than a purveyor of patriotic writings. He was the first Englishman to win the Nobel Prize for Literature and he had already refused a knighthood and the position of Poet Laureate. To this record as a public figure he added another, less welcome, qualification.

Two years before, in 1915, Kipling and his American wife Carrie had lost their eighteen-year-old only son following the Battle of Loos, just outside Lille. John, known as Jack, was one of the hundreds of thousands of 'missing' with no known grave. Since receiving news of their son's disappearance, the distraught couple had spent much of their time touring the military hospitals and graveyards of northern

France, hoping to find out what had happened to him. In his poem 'My Boy Jack' Kipling wrote of their sad quest:

> 'Have you news of my boy Jack?'
>   *Not this tide.*
> 'When d'you think that he'll come back?'
>   *Not with this wind blowing, and this tide . . .*

The loss was especially bitter because Kipling had used his influence to secure Jack a commission with the Irish Guards despite the fact that he had failed a medical: severe short-sightedness disqualified him from active service.

Kipling wasn't the only bereaved parent on the Commission, but he was the only one with an ability to translate his personal grief into public epitaphs that would serve the dead of two world wars. A common feature of all but the smallest British and Commonwealth military cemeteries is Edwin Lutyens' 'Stone of Remembrance', which he originally proposed as 'a great fair stone of fine proportions, 12 feet in length, lying raised upon three steps', that would bear 'some fine thought or words of sacred dedication'. Kipling supplied those words, adapting an Old Testament verse to read: *Their Name Liveth For Evermore.* He also solved two literary conundrums for the Commission: how to inscribe the headstones of those who couldn't be identified, and how to convey in a dignified way that the contents of a grave had been destroyed by shelling. For the latter he suggested the powerful *Their Glory Shall Not Be Blotted Out.* For unidentified graves he came up with three short but affecting words: *Known Unto God.*

If Kipling's attachment to the work of the IWGC was emotional as well as practical, it also informed and inspired his writing. His short story 'The Gardener', published in *McCall's* magazine in 1925, touched a chord with its many women readers. They could identify with Helen's pilgrimage to the Flanders grave of her 'nephew' (in fact, as we learn, her illegitimate son). Critics of the time and later commentators alike were intrigued; it had elements of ghost story, mystery and religious allegory. The gardener at the fictional Hagenzeele Third Cemetery who leads Helen to her son's grave makes a brief but highly symbolic appearance. Even on the most superficial reading, he has a Christ-like compassion and leads the way not just to the grave, Kipling suggests, but to Helen's redemption and to the unburdening of her grief.

This sounds overwrought to modern sensibilities, but Kipling knew his stuff, both as a bereaved parent and as a professional IWGC adviser. He had been in dozens of such cemeteries and had talked to the gardeners there. The story had such impact at the time perhaps because it struck readers with what we now call 'emotional truth' – it captured the complex feelings and experiences of those who came to the war cemeteries in a way that no press report ever could. It also showed how far the IWGC had come in the public imagination since its inception in 1917.

Kipling died in 1936 without ever finding out what had happened to his son. In 1992, the Commonwealth War Graves Commission identified the grave of an unknown Irish Guards lieutenant as being that of John Kipling, though this was later challenged by two battle-field historians. Whether or not Kipling's boy Jack is still missing, the legacy he inspired lives on in every British war cemetery in 134 countries.

As soon as the Imperial War Graves Commission became a reality in 1917, it adopted Ware's principles of equality and integrity into its early planning. However, the battle to convince the public that these would best serve their war dead was only just beginning.

Expectations of the new organisation were high and there was pressure to share its plans for cemeteries and memorials with the public as soon as possible. But there were important decisions to be made, not least on the form the cemeteries should take, and on this there was disagreement among those advising Ware: the architects Edwin Lutyens and Herbert Baker, and the Directors of the national art collections. Though Ware – and now the Commission – was committed to the principle of 'no distinction between officer and men lying in the same cemeteries in the form or nature of the memorials', they had to decide how the principle was to be realised in practice.

Sir Frederick Kenyon, Director of the British Museum, was appointed to chair an advisory committee that would come up with practical proposals, and he duly reported early in 1918. His recommendations formed the basis for how British war cemeteries look today. He believed that, although they should not be 'gloomy places, it is right that the fact that they are cemeteries . . . should be evident at first sight'. He rejected the idea of a memorial 'park' with a single abstract form on which the names of the dead were inscribed, instead opting for 'rows of headstones, of a uniform height and width, the graves themselves being levelled to a flat surface and planted with turf and flowers'. These would 'carry on the military idea, giving the appearance as of a battalion on parade', but each headstone would bear details of the deceased, a regimental badge and a short inscription supplied by the next of kin (though 'the effusions of the mortuary mason, the sentimental versifier, or the crank' would be filtered out). He also proposed – and this was to be both controversial and would tie up much effort in the first years of operation – that the smallest cemeteries and the isolated graves should be concentrated into larger sites.

Over the following months, crucial decisions were made about the size and proportions of the headstone, the lettering to be used, what badges and emblems were acceptable (regiments, military and support organisations like the Red Cross and YMCA) and what were not (the Boy Scouts, Harrow School, the Red Hand of Ulster and the Union Jack). Two monuments would be installed in all but the smallest cemeteries: Lutyens' 'Stone of Remembrance', and Sir Reginald Blomfield's 'Cross of Sacrifice', a classically proportioned stone cross with a sword inset. Lutyens, Blomfield and Herbert Baker were each commissioned to design an experimental cemetery. Matters of taste, aesthetics and practicality were carefully balanced to achieve the most pleasing but also the most cost-effective result. By the end of its first year of operation, the Commission had made significant progress and felt confident in publishing *The Graves of the Fallen*, an illustrated summary of its main decisions written by Kipling, early in 1919.

Though response was muted at first, a virulent press campaign, led by the *Spectator* and the *Daily Mail*, soon ensued, accusing the

Commission of riding roughshod over the wishes of Britain's bereaved families. This unleashed a public reaction that had been brewing for some time. Relatives of officers objected to the principle of uniformity and didn't see why they shouldn't put up their own memorial if they could afford to. They didn't like the idea of an 'unchristian' headstone and demanded a cross. They wanted the ban on repatriation of bodies lifted so that they could bring their loved ones home for burial. And those content with graves abroad fiercely objected to the idea that bodies in isolated graves or tiny cemeteries should be exhumed and 'concentrated' into much larger ones.

Well-organised opposition to the Commission's plans gained a head of steam. There were angry advertisements accusing the Commission of tyranny. A War Graves Appeal Committee was set up to lobby MPs. The choice of Kipling as creator of epitaphs was attacked because he was 'not a known religious man'. An 8,000-name petition to the Prince of Wales pleaded for the replacement of the headstone by a cross. Views were heartfelt: 'It is only through the hope of the Cross that most of us are able to carry on the life from which all the sunshine seems to have gone, and to deny us the emblem of that strength and hope adds heavily to the burden of our sorrow,' wrote one campaigner. But conceding to them would compromise the Commission's scheme for clean lines and a uniform look to the cemeteries. Besides, contracts with monumental masons for thousands of headstones were already sealed. A paper circulated to the House of Commons by MP William Burdett-Coutts put the situation grimly but realistically: 'the whole work on this great Imperial and National Memorial is now paralysed by this fatal atmosphere of doubt'.

The debate split along class and party lines, with trade unionists and ex-servicemen's organisations strongly supportive of the Commission's equitable approach, and those with most to lose from the withdrawal of what they saw as their inalienable right to 'do as he likes with his own dead' ranged in staunch opposition. The mass of ordinary people who had fought and lost loved ones in the war were most likely to support the Commission's plans, but the least likely to have their voices heard.

After rumbling on for more than a year, matters came to a head in a House of Commons debate in May 1920. The Commission's case was admirably served by Burdett-Coutts, who started by quoting from a letter from Kipling:

> . . . *we shall never have any grave to go to. Our boy was missing at Loos. The ground is of course battered and mined past all hope of any trace being recovered. I wish some of the people who are making this trouble realised how more than fortunate they are to have a name on a headstone in a known place.*

Emotional appeals were made by both sides in intemperate exchanges. Finally Winston Churchill, as Secretary of State for War and Chairman of the Commission – despite worrying Ware with some earlier equivocation – closed the debate with typically robust rhetoric. The Commission's cemeteries, he said,

> . . . will be entirely different from the ordinary cemeteries which mark the resting place of those who pass out in the common flow of human fate from year to year. They will be supported and sustained by the wealth of this great nation and Empire, as long as we remain a great nation and Empire, and there is no reason at all why, in periods as remote from our own as we ourselves are from the Tudors, the graveyards . . . of this Great War shall not remain an abiding and supreme memorial to the efforts and the glory of the British Army, and the sacrifices made in the great cause.

The matter wasn't put to a vote. The Commission had survived a serious challenge to its plans and working principles. Ware's vision could now proceed unimpeded.

Six months later, just before Armistice Day 1920, the remains of an unknown British combatant were exhumed from a grave in the Ypres Salient, one of four unidentifiable bodies taken from each of the major battlefields of the Western Front to an Army HQ outside Saint-Pol near Arras. Here one was chosen at random. The others were reinterred in an anonymous grave – according to one account, 'in a shell hole on the road to Albert'. The selected remains were borne with great ceremony to London where their final resting place became the Tomb of the Unknown Warrior in Westminster Abbey. This symbolic homecoming produced a huge and unexpected catharsis for a nation still in mourning, a counterpoint to the quieter but no less heroic efforts to memorialise the dead in foreign fields.

Despite the political ructions at home, these efforts had never stopped. In fact, 1919 was a year of intense activity as the work of burying the dead was finally relinquished by the Army. It was also the year that the men who were to form the heart of the British community in Ypres first started arriving to begin their labours.

Jimmy Fox's father Jack had spent the war firing howitzers into the German lines with the 41st Heavy Artillery Group. Still waiting for demobilisation in 1919, he was recruited into a special Labour Corps to begin the huge task of 'concentration' – moving 160,000 isolated graves in the chaos of the battlefields of France and Flanders to make larger, permanent cemeteries. And the even more distasteful task of gathering up and burying the thousands of disintegrating bodies still scattered over, and just beneath, the land.

Technically, burials were still the responsibility of the Army, working with and through the Directorate of Graves Registration and Enquiries. The Commission could only take over the cemeteries once concentration was complete. Fabian Ware straddled both organisations, but he hadn't nearly enough manpower to carry out this daunting task. The Directorate had five hundred men but Ware needed thousands. His request for a specialised burial corps had twice been turned down by the War Office. Now the situation was desperate; pilgrims were starting to flood into the Ypres Salient and the other battlefield areas. They would be shocked and distressed to find so many graves and graveyards in disarray, not to mention the possibility of coming across unburied corpses. This reflected badly on the British government and was a potential public relations disaster for the new Commission. Ware made direct appeals to the Cabinet. As a result, a Labour Corps of 15,000 men recruited by the Army, to be enticed by an extra two shillings and sixpence – about £20 in today's values – a day on top of their service pay, was agreed. They would form the Exhumation Companies and Graves Concentration Units that would do the job.

Recruitment started in the spring of 1919 but it wasn't straightforward. After three months, only 4,347 men had started work in France and Belgium. Not only was it a particularly unattractive job; with demobilisation still in train there was a general shortage of manpower immediately after the war, even though those men who had been demobbed were anxious to return to employment. The male working population had been decimated and what little labour was available was in demand on the land, in factories and for reconstruction projects.

It is likely that Jack Fox was one of those first volunteers. Though his service record shows that he did not join the IWGC as a gardener-labourer until May 1920, there is a photograph of him at work in an early British military cemetery in 1919. This is Haringhe, usually known as Bandaghem, one of three that served the hospitals and casualty clearing stations around the railhead at Proven, to the west of Ypres. The Tommies, who couldn't cope with Flemish place-names and favoured gallows humour, dubbed them Bandaghem, Mendinghem and Dozinghem. Here he is with a fellow worker, sleeves rolled up, among the graves. Rudimentary planting is in evidence; the rows of dark wooden crosses are fronted by low flowerbeds and unkempt grass. The crosses are mostly small and uniform, but a few stand out – bigger, white, in distinctive designs. One grave even has low railings round it. Individual memorials have obviously crept in here, confirming Ware's fears of untidy lines and unequal treatment.

Jack never talked to his children about his concentration work, not even to his son Jimmy. Jimmy's sister Betty, the youngest of Jack's four daughters, was particularly close to her father and spent a lot of time in the cemeteries where he worked as she was growing up. Knowing him as she did, she believes he felt a debt of gratitude for being spared. Though he had a dirty and dangerous job on the heavy guns, he was never in the front line and came through the war physically unscathed. He wanted to honour those who hadn't been so lucky.

Unlike them, Jack had a long and fruitful life; he died in 1974 at the age of eighty-three. Betty remembers just one occasion when he did talk:

> We were living in Bonn, and Dad visited. He wasn't really a drinking man. We were having a dinner party and he had a couple of brandies after dinner and he started to talk about the war . . . I signalled to people not to move because he was starting to talk about things he'd never spoken about before. He talked and talked and talked. About picking up bits of bodies in sacks, how they had to try and find anything that might identify the bits they'd found, with someone there taking down notes of it all as they went. Awful. The next day he seemed to regret it. 'I talk too much,' he said to me.

The work was certainly unsavoury. Exhumation companies went on to sections of battlefield marked out with tape in a grid pattern to search for remains. The same section would be scoured over and over again, as remains gradually started working their way to the surface. On the first trawl there would be obvious markers such as rifles or helmets on stakes but there were other tell-tale signs: grass of an unnaturally vivid green, greenish-black water in puddles and shell holes, and small bones brought to the surface by rats. Then the digging would start. Remains, when found, were put on sacking soaked with cresol, a fierce chemical disinfectant and deodoriser. Any identifying materials – identity discs, scraps of uniform, badges and buttons, surviving personal effects, even teeth – were retrieved and recorded before the remains were taken to one of the large concentration cemeteries like Tyne Cot, Poelkapelle or Cement House, where burials were still taking place. If remains yielded no identification, the grave would bear Kipling's poignant inscription, *A Soldier of the Great War, Known Unto God*.

Some of the men working in the early cemeteries told upsetting stories of desperate relatives. Robert Rolfe's father, Howard, had a visitor while he was working among the wooden crosses.

> It must have been about 1920 when they were still sorting things out. A man came up, a Canadian, looking for a grave. Dad

looked it up and took him to the grave. This chap pulled out a revolver and said: 'Start digging, I'll give you a pound for every square inch of khaki.' He wanted the uniform. Poor man, he was deranged – it was his only son. Dad said, 'OK, guv'nor, but I need to go and get my tools.' Of course he didn't go back. If you look at those headstones now, apart from those Known Unto God, so many of them were sixteen, seventeen, eighteen. Terrible.

Concentration and retrieval work continued. By May 1920 almost 130,000 bodies had been reinterred and the Commission had taken over 788 cemeteries in France alone. But there were many more to come; bodies were still being found and brought for burial, a process that continues today. In the same month that Jack Fox was formally recruited, there were already more than four hundred gardeners working in France and Belgium and twenty more were being sent out every week. Even this was insufficient and the Commission had to consider using local labour and women to plug the gap. But local living conditions were unsuitable, it was thought, for women. And the Commission was reluctant to abandon its policy of employing British – and wherever possible ex-Service – labour, despite Treasury objections that local labour would be cheaper.

As the Commission gradually built an infrastructure in London, France and Belgium, begging and borrowing materials to start with, the work of creating permanent cemeteries began in earnest. The 'experimental' cemeteries, all in France and all, as it turned out, designed by Reginald Blomfield, were completed in 1920. *The Times*, in a piece in September of that year, was ecstatic, declaring Blomfield's efforts at Forceville 'the most perfect, the noblest, the most classically beautiful memorial that any loving heart or any proud nation could desire to their heroes fallen in a foreign land'.

Given that the Commission had had such a mauling from the press only months before, this was a significant turnaround. The report continued:

Picture this strangely stirring place. A lawn enclosed of close clipped turf, banded across with line on line of flowers, and linked by these bands of flowers, uncrowded, at stately intervals, stand in soldierly ranks the white headstones. And while they form as perfect, as orderly a whole as any regiment on parade, yet they do not shoulder each other. Every one is set apart in flowers, every one casts its shade upon a gracious space of green. Each one, so stern in outline, is most rich in surface, for the crest of the regiment stands out with bold and arresting distinction above the strongly incised names . . . It is the simplest, it is the grandest place I ever saw.

The ranks of shining Portland stone, softened by green turf and familiar English cottage garden plants, with the imposing Cross of Sacrifice and Stone of Remembrance enclosed by a low wall and hedging, made for a cemetery different from any seen before, and one with a particularly calming and uplifting atmosphere. Not gloomy, not jumbled, but a clean and striking whole. Ware's vision realised.

Translating this template to hundreds of other cemeteries was another matter. Before real gardening could start, there was much hard labour. Charlotte and Priestley Dunn, born outside Ypres to the sound of shellfire in 1918, had led an itinerant life until their father finally decided to settle there with his Flemish wife in the early 1920s. Priestley remembers:

Though my grandparents were still living in a hut in Ypres and the same prospect faced us once my father was demobbed, I think my mother and her parents persuaded him that life wasn't all that bad, so finally we settled down in Ypres. But in Ypres there was no work. The Imperial War Graves Commission was just starting up and former soldiers were offered jobs. Initially it had a big camp near Ypres train station not far from the Skindles Hotel and a huge operation was under way. Dad got a job of unloading headstones for the cemeteries that had arrived from England by train. There was this huge marshalling yard by the station where the stones were unloaded on to ex-Army lorries from the '14–18 war. Father spent three or four years unloading the heavy gravestones from the trains on to the trucks. My mother said that when he came home his back was raw flesh, but he wouldn't give it up.

George Simpson's father – also called George – joined the IWGC, like many others, in 1920. He was an ex-serviceman who had served in Mesopotamia (now Iraq). He had no background in horticulture but George says, 'I think he quite liked the idea of going to France to look after the war graves.' After working for the Commission in Calais, where he met his French wife, he moved to Hazebrouck in the Ypres area and worked on the early stages of what would become the biggest concentration cemetery of them all, Tyne Cot, with 12,000 graves, more than 8,000 of which are unidentified.

Hazebrouck is a considerable distance from where Tyne Cot, the main repository for the dead of Passchendaele, was under construction. George's younger sister Rosemary describes the primitive accommodation: 'Dad lived on the site in an old tin shed – just a ditch with a bit of corrugated-iron sheet over the top'. George remembers much of what his father told him about the creation of the biggest Commonwealth war cemetery in the world, and the labour this entailed:

> You can imagine what it was like before it was started. Everything had to be imported, brought to the actual site. The earth came from Holland, the stones for the outside wall came from Italy – the workforce were actually Italians, to build the wall. Dad was saying, the topsoil came by rail from Holland to Zonnebeke, and from Zonnebeke it had to be wheelbarrowed to Tyne Cot [a distance of about five kilometres]. Because it would take them a month of Sundays to get it done, they found a disused German field train, on a little narrow gauge track, so they laid that out from the station to Tyne Cot. Instead of wheelbarrows, they just loaded up these trucks and pushed them, so that saved quite a bit of time.

George's father 'lived and breathed Tyne Cot', so it must have been particularly disappointing for him to miss the visit of King George V in 1922. The King and Queen Mary were on a pilgrimage of their own to the cemeteries of France and Flanders, a decision that did much to boost the reputation of the Commission and the morale of the gardeners. At Tyne Cot on 10 May the King inspected a long line of gardeners from a strip of specially laid turf. George Simpson senior should have been there but this was the day his son George decided to arrive in the world, so he was with his wife and new baby instead. To mark the two auspicious occasions, he planted the strip of royally trodden turf in their garden in Hazebrouck.

Tyne Cot gets its name from a barn that stood near the level crossing on the Passchendaele–Broodseinde road. The Northumberland Fusiliers named it 'Tyne Cottage', a handy moniker for a landmark and a reminder of home. The Salient was full of them: Hyde Park Corner, Willesden Junction, Regent Street, Pall Mall and Peckham – but also Purgatory and Hell Fire Corner. Unfathomable French and Flemish place-names were anglicised: Wytschaete became White Sheets and Ypres Wipers. Even today the British head of the Ypres office of the Commonweath War Graves Commission refers to the Hooge Crater cemetery as 'Huge Crater' and Ploegsteert as 'Plug Street'.

For some time, many cemeteries were in transition between the temporary and the permanent. In his story 'The Gardener', which culminates in a large concentration cemetery, Kipling describes how they looked to the visitor at this stage:

> The place was still in the making, and stood some five or six feet above the metalled road, which it flanked for hundreds of yards. Culverts across a deep ditch served for entrances through the unfinished boundary wall. [Helen] climbed a few wooden faced earthen steps and then met the entire crowded level of the thing in one held breath . . . All she saw was a merciless sea of black crosses, bearing little strips of stamped tin at all angles across their faces. She could distinguish no order or arrangement in their mass; nothing but a waist-high wilderness as of weeds stricken dead, rushing at her . . . A great distance away there was a line of whiteness. It proved to be a block of some two or three hundred graves whose headstones had already been set, whose flowers were planted out, and whose new-sown grass showed green.

By 1922 the Commission had finished 132 cemeteries in France and Belgium, with another 285 under construction, and employed 876 gardeners in the two countries – the lion's share of its 1,300-plus complement. Two hundred Crosses of Sacrifice had been erected and 40,000 headstones shipped, with half of them installed. Whether they were finished or not, they all received visitors. During the previous summer Kipling had inspected thirty temporary cemeteries between Ypres, Amiens and Rouen. At Rouen he noted 'the extraordinary beauty of the cemetery and great care that the attendants had taken of it, and the almost heartbroken thankfulness of the relatives of the dead who were there'.

Some of these visits would stay long in the memory of the early gardeners. As for the gardener in Kipling's short story, it was a part of their duties to help visitors find graves. Grateful pilgrims would often try and press money on gardeners who had assisted them but they weren't allowed to accept it. Betty Parker's father Charlie worked in another of the great concentration cemeteries, Lijssenthoek, just outside Poperinghe. Much later he wrote about an incident in 1923, which he said he would never forget.

The foreman was on a fortnight's leave and I was in charge. I saw a lady hesitating by the entrance gates. I enquired if I could help. She handed me a note of a location of a grave. It was difficult for a stranger to find one grave in over ten thousand. I led the lady to the grave and started to leave. She said, 'Wait a minute, would you please read the inscription on the stone? My eyesight isn't very good.' I said, 'Certainly. On the top is the Australian National Badge, then the regimental number, Sgt – and the name – of the Australian Army. Died of wounds – and the date – and his age. Below, the Cross. Then the verse, "Peace, Perfect Peace"'. The lady said, 'That is correct.' She put her hand on the stone and said, 'This is my day. This is my only son. Now I can go home and die happy.' She said she had sailed from Australia and was now going home. She asked for a little soil from the grave and I scooped up a bit which she put in an envelope with a twig from a Polyantha rose growing on the grave. She offered me something, which I refused, this being the rules of the Commission. She asked my name as I led her back to the entrance.

After a time my wife received a registered envelope. Inside was a thin gold chain with a golden sovereign attached. This was from the Australian lady. My wife sent her heartfelt thanks. About two years later I received a letter from the lady's niece saying that she had passed away.

There must have been many such stories. At last Fabian Ware could be sure that his vision was the right one. More importantly, it was now clear that the public thought so too.

3

Sunshine and Shadows

Every Armistice Day we had our parades and we marched through the town, proud, and the Belgian people used to watch us and clap. You know, I thought I was the Queen sometimes!
Charlotte Dunn, born 1918, daughter of an IWGC
gardener

CHURCHILL MAY HAVE been denied his sacred ruins, but Britain gained a valuable living asset: a colony of expatriates who were rebuilding Ypres, not as a lifeless shrine but as a welcoming place of pilgrimage.

Over the five years since the end of the war the colony had rapidly expanded: by 1926, those of British descent in Ypres alone numbered almost five hundred. Others lived in surrounding towns and villages, and scores of British men had started families with French and Belgian women. By then Ypres was a changed place. After the immediate post-war years of rapid reconstruction, the face of the town had been transformed. To the British ex-serviceman, 'their' Ypres had undergone a phoenix-like resurrection:

We picture the Ypres of war − ruin − desolation − emptiness. We step from the train to a brightly new and very complete town. We make our way through the streets to the central Place, and here a square of hotels, shops, houses stare across with strange incongruity to a mutilated thing rising stark and jagged against the sky. The ghostly witness, the symbol of all that has drawn us here, the ruined belfry tower rising from the ruins at its foot. This is Ypres to-day, a new venture, a newness of bricks and mortar clustered about this monument of a beautiful culture in the past, of unparalleled heroism in our day.

By 1925, when this was written for *The Immortal Salient*, Ypres was indeed a 'new venture'. Buildings were miraculously back in place, more or less as they had been before 1914. Only on closer inspection was the artifice revealed: building dates on fine Flemish façades read not 1622 but 1922, and their brickwork looked strangely clean and unmarked by time. Work on rebuilding St Martin's Cathedral was well under way, though it was to be another three years before the decision was made to rebuild the Cloth Hall.

Not everyone was delighted with the new Ypres or its residents' efforts to return to the normality they had known. An ex-serviceman on a pilgrimage was shocked by the 'hideous' reappearance of the annual fair in the marketplace: 'To the present inhabitants it is probably the outstanding event of the year but I cannot think of Ypres as anything but a glorious sepulchre of our wonderful dead, wherein such revelry is sacrilege'. Old soldiers saw their precious memories being swept away with the remnants of the ruined town: 'We knew Ypres as a ghastly place and shell-torn rubble, a place where murder came from the skies at all angles and it was that Ypres to which our sacred memories cling – not the present Ypres of red-tiled buildings and ghastly yellow bricks!'

But the moment for preserving Ypres as a 'cathedral of death' had long passed and life had to go on. Since the end of the war, reconstruction, tourism and mass pilgrimages had revitalised the place, attracting new money, new visitors and new residents. By the end of the decade it would be almost back to its pre-war population, though half of these people would be newcomers. A small but influential part of the influx were the British, ex-servicemen like the Parminter brothers and Leo Murphy, who had fought in Flanders, met their wives here, and who were now settled with homes, families and thriving small businesses. Ypres' first cinema was started by Captain Leonard Knox, formerly of the Royal Army Service Corps (RASC), who also ran the Shannon Hotel and a battlefield taxi business with his French wife and his sister Hester. The newcomers weren't all servicing the tourist trade: two started a milk round with an army surplus truck and another set up a pig farm on the outskirts of town. But far greater in number than the small entrepreneurs were the men employed by the Imperial War Graves Commission to create the constellation of cemeteries now scattered throughout the old Salient.

Like Jack Fox, some were already here in 1919 doing the early concentration, preparation and planting work. Many more came over the next five years to transform the temporary cemeteries into pristine permanence.

At first the workers' living conditions were rough. The lucky ones had billets with families in the surrounding towns and villages where there were still homes intact. Most lived in former army barracks or in huts, tents and caravans in IWGC 'camps' near big cemeteries out in the countryside. Here they had packing cases for furniture, blankets for carpets and nothing to do in the evenings. The least lucky had to live more or less rough on site, like George Simpson's father at Tyne Cot. Some were formed into mobile gardening parties, known as 'travelling circuses'. These small itinerant groups would spend a week at a time away from base, tending the most outlying cemeteries, returning to camp at the end of a week, usually via every bar along the way.

These were not family-friendly conditions, so in the early years the majority of the Commission's employees – and therefore the British community – were young single men, recently demobbed from war service. Their work was depressing, their workplaces isolated, and the Flanders winters bleak, so it wasn't surprising that they let rip on their visits to town. Uncle PD was among those who took a robust view:

. . . wherever in the world a community of British people is established, they bring their customs and traditions with them, and the British at Ypres were no exception during these years. A bit wilder perhaps than they would have been elsewhere, but things in Ypres were a bit wild then in the early 1920s . . . and if some of our lads on occasions celebrated rather unwisely when off-duty, who can blame them? They had survived the slaughter of four years of war and were back again in the terrible Salient with their friends and the memory of their quarter of a million comrades lying in the cemeteries around the town, and where for the Grace of God they would have been themselves. The reaction was understandable.

But there were married men with families coming to Belgium too, and conditions weren't much better for them. Arthur Jones' father arrived in Ypres to work for the IWGC with his English second wife and three young children:

My father was captured on the Somme in 1917. He came back in 1918, buried his first wife and married her sister Minnie. They came to Ypres in 1922 with his children from his first marriage and they all lived in a little wooden caravan with an IWGC badge on the outside, with a tent alongside it. There was no housing for the men and their families. They went from tent, to caravan, and then finally to a larger wooden hut.

Even as late as 1925 IWGC families were being housed in temporary accommodation. Louise Francis' father was a sergeant major in the Royal Horse Artillery when he met a young French girl during the war. They married in 1919 and Louise was born the following year. He joined the IWGC in 1921 and they moved from Albert, near the old Somme battlefields, to Ypres a few years later.

I remember arriving in Ypres. We went into this awful wooden bungalow near the river. I remember my mother being very upset. It was a dreadful place. Because we were near the moat, the ramparts, there were rats about. It was primitive, very difficult for her with two young children.

Betty Parker's parents took the harsh conditions stoically. Before the war they had both worked in service in Somerset, he as a gardener, she as a maid. He'd had an uneventful war in India with the Somerset Light Infantry, and after demob started work for the IWGC at Lijssenthoek cemetery. Betty, their second child, was born in 1925:

> I arrived in the world in a hut with a dirt floor in the middle of a field just outside Poperinghe. It was very hard at first. Mum woke up one time – she used to have a bit of chocolate by the side of the bed – and there was this rat gnawing on the chocolate. And it was so cold, when she went for a bucket of water from the standpipe [some distance away], by the time she'd got it back it was frozen over. They were hard times, but there you are, they got through it. Mum and Dad never ever made a fuss. They knew how to cope.

Lillian Wilkins' parents were both English, but they were destined to meet in the ruins of Ypres in 1920. Her mother – also Lillian but known as Lily – was apprenticed at fourteen to a court dressmaker in London. Here she became friends with another young apprentice, Jeanne Faes, the daughter of Belgian refugees. Jeanne's parents owned the Trumpet restaurant in Ypres' market square. The first months of the war were just about bearable for the Faes family, but after the November 1914 bombardment they fled to Britain and settled in London for the duration.

> When the war finished and the Faes family went back to Ypres, my mother was invited to go and stay with them in the Trumpet [then a temporary building], and lo and behold there were two soldiers in lodgement with the Faes family. So consequently, my mother was polite and they were all there together and my father said: 'Would you care for me to write to you?' and my mother said: 'No, I don't think so.' Well, the following year Mother receives another invitation to go out to Ypres and lo and behold, my father and his friend Fred Prince are still there, and a correspondence starts up . . .

After a traditional courtship, Lily married Harry Wilkins in 1923 and Jeanne Faes married Fred Prince the following year. Lillian was born in 1924 and her sister Joyce arrived five years later. The Princes had two children, Robert and Joan, and a lifelong friendship between the two families was forged. Harry Wilkins and Fred Prince joined the Imperial War Graves Commission as soon as they were demobbed and worked together reburying the dead in the new cemeteries around Ypres. Harry had come through the war 'without a scratch'. He never talked about it, and Lillian doesn't even know what regiment he served with, but she knows that he was devoted to his work as a gardener–caretaker and later as a head gardener in Flanders: 'It was his whole life, being out there'.

The British colony quickly expanded as work on the cemeteries gained pace. As more of the men brought out wives from home or married local women, and the nature of the work moved on from construction and planting to maintenance, the balance of the colony changed. The riotous young men went home or settled down to married life. Of the seventy-six British men living in Ypres in 1920, only sixteen were married, eleven of them to French or Belgian women. By 1926 – one of the peak years for the colony with 285 British 'heads of household' – almost half were married, with roughly equal numbers of British and local wives, and the all-British families had 131 children between them. More Commission families, like the Parkers, lived in Poperinghe, Zonnebeke, Kemmel and other nearby towns and villages where a British war cemetery was never far away.

Poperinghe, fifteen kilometres due west of Ypres, had a significant British population. During the war it was the behind-the-lines rest centre affectionately known to British troops as 'Pop'. Here they spent their time off from the trenches in its bars and brothels, and here the Revd. Tubby Clayton offered recreation of a more wholesome kind at the servicemen's refuge, Talbot House. Just out of firing range, Poperinghe escaped the damage inflicted on Ypres and carried on more or less regardless throughout the war. Afterwards its proximity to the large concentration cemetery at Lijssenthoek meant that it soon became second only to Ypres as a home for IWGC employees.

Caroline Duponselle served in the bar of her parents' hotel in Poperinghe and this is probably where she first met Larry Madden. Madden was a young Irish-Australian who had lied about his age and signed up for the Australian Imperial Force (AIF) just before his seventeenth birthday. He arrived in Flanders in 1917. Young and feckless and already too fond of a drink, he was not considered a good match for Caroline, but they married after the war and their only child, Elaine, was born in 1923. The Duponselles were a large, hard-working Belgian family; the hospitality trade was their life and many of Elaine's nine aunts and uncles worked in the business:

> They had quite a large hotel for Poperinghe in those days. It had about eighteen bedrooms and a cinema and what they called a brasserie – kind of a big pub. And there was a restaurant that was quite well-known because my grandmother was an excellent cook. So my grandfather was in the brasserie, my grandmother was in the kitchen, there were two aunts serving in the restaurant and others helping my grandfather. My Uncle Charles – the oldest one – ran the cinema. He went to Brussels every Friday to bring back the films for the week. And the younger one was running the projector. Simone, my youngest aunt, was only a year older than I was.

Belgian parents kept their children close. Though the British were welcome in Flanders, parents were reluctant to see their daughters move away with new husbands and they applied pressure – incentives as well as threats – on young couples to stay locally. After their marriage, Caroline's father bought the Hotel Majestic in Ypres for her to run. Larry, having done concentration work while still in the AIF, formally joined the IWGC as a Field Assistant in 1922. By the mid-1920s the reconstruction boom in Ypres was over, the cemeteries were all but finished, and secure employment was hard to find. For British men who had married local girls but who perhaps had only rudimentary French or Flemish or who hadn't bothered to learn any at all, the Commission was the obvious, if not the only, potential employer.

After the war Jack Fox cleared bodies from the battlefields and dug graves for them in the new concentration cemeteries. Off-duty he courted Rachel Dumortier, a daughter of the Belgian family he lodged with. They were engaged to be married but then Rachel died, it was said, after being hit on the side of the head by a snowball.

Jack transferred his affections to the eldest daughter, Adrienne, and they were married in November 1919. Like other Flanders brides, on their wedding day twenty-year-old Adrienne wore a dark dress, a long lace veil and a corsage of glass stones.

Many of these unions proved long and contented marriages and produced large, tight-knit families. Some, where domestic problems were aggravated by cultural differences, were less happy. The children of these troubled marriages felt conflict keenly, even if they only recognised its causes much later in their lives.

Stephen Grady's father, also Stephen, met and married a French girl, Berthe, in Armentières in 1917. After the war he joined the IWGC as a gardener and the couple settled in Nieppe, on the border with Belgium. Stephen, born in May 1925, was the second of their four children. Though they enjoyed a free-range childhood in the French countryside, life at home was more difficult. Their mother became an invalid, blinded by cataracts by the time she was thirty. In retrospect, Stephen sees the fault lines in his parents' relationship.

> I think it was a bad marriage and he didn't like the French. He was there against his will. In those days you got married and put up with it. She was Catholic of course, we all were except Dad. All her life she tried to get him to convert, without any success. And because she was blind she was over-Catholic. We were in church all the time.

On the surface at least, life got better and better for the British colony. Families moved out of temporary accommodation as more houses became available for sale and rent. Commission wages weren't generous but staff were paid in sterling and the favourable exchange rate (especially after the collapse of confidence in the franc in 1926) meant that the British were almost twice as well off as their Belgian peers. Those who grew up there knew they were fortunate: 'We were rich. The British in Ypres were rich. We were up, up, up. And we were proud'; 'Ypres was a lovely place for the English between the wars. We didn't have to worry about anything. We wanted for nothing'.

officers; head gardeners the NCOs; gardeners and everyone below them the ranks. Though they all came together for the big set-piece events – Armistice parades, the Christmas parties and trips to the seaside – there were inevitable social and cultural divisions. British wives socialised with each other according to their husbands' rank and, though there was more cross-cultural neighbourliness in the outlying towns and villages where there were fewer British families than in Ypres, the British and local women tended to socialise separately.

Social divisions weren't absolute. In some cases the status of the wife determined the circles they moved in. Nina Pitt was born in Ypres in 1922, while her family was still living in Captain Knox's Shannon Hotel. Her parents met in Flanders when her father was in the Royal Engineers and her mother was in the Women's Auxiliary Army Corps (WAAC). Before the war, Florence Clarke was a cultured woman who spoke fluent French and taught English and History. Her wartime album – an old quarto-size army record book – records visits with friends to ruined French and Flemish towns. There are photos of early cemeteries and of couples cuddling in overgrown shell holes. Here too is the comically inverted gasometer that attracted FANY Pat Beauchamp's attention in Ypres in 1919.

Florence and William Pitt married in 1920 and brought up five children in Ypres. William became a driver for the IWGC, taking equipment to cemeteries. After starting off in the Shannon Hotel, the Pitts lived a comfortable life in a rebuilt Flemish house where the children played whist in the back room while the parents played bridge with their friends in the parlour. Nina remembers her mother never doing housework: 'There was so much poverty, anyone who earned a bit of money would employ someone to help them out.' Unlike the English, for whom staff meant status, Belgian wives frowned on paid help. Homemaking was their job and theirs alone.

Unless they were involved in the family business, like Elaine Madden's mother in her hotel or Francis Murphy's mother in her lace and souvenir shop, the mothers of the British colony didn't work outside the home. Families of four or more children were common. Howard and Edna Rolfe were probably exceptional: nine of their ten children were born while they were in Ypres. Mothers looked after their families, visited each other's homes and, if they were British, organised tea parties. Commission families were often clustered together in the same streets: the Fox family was one of fourteen living on the Chaussée de Bruges.

Jimmy's mother was a keen knitter and her children display a range of ingeniously hand-knitted garments in their photographs. Other mothers were trained seamstresses or at least competent home dress-makers and so made most of their children's clothes. Betty Parker's mother, furious that the nuns at her daughter's convent school kept letting down the hems of her tunic ('You could go to school without knickers, but woe betide you if your dress was too short'), knitted her a tunic to thwart their efforts.

The farmland around Ypres was productive and the town had good shops and an excellent market. There are fond memories of Dunn's patisserie and its strawberry ice cream, and 'a little English shop' that imported goods especially for the British: Ovaltine, Shippam's fish paste and Typhoo tea. In mixed marriages wives kept a traditional table. Sidney Harper's French mother was a chef and he still misses her food. There were other delights too:

I remember as a kid, my grandfather would keep pigs, you wouldn't take them to the slaughterhouse, you'd kill them yourself. I'd bring the buckets to collect all the blood so that my grandmother could make the black pudding and you've never tasted black pudding like it. Unbelievable. I wish I had the recipe now, I'd make a fortune. Then I used to play with the pig's bladder as a football.

In the Fox family Adrienne did the cooking, but Betty remembers her father taking over for his specialities, Christmas dinner and steamed puddings:

Although our mother was Belgian, we children were all brought up with a great respect for the English traditions. To me the English shop was very big and posh; it was there that we bought things like Tate & Lyle Golden Syrup. Dad used this to make us real puddings cooked in a cloth on our big stove. We never left the table hungry, but we didn't buy a lot of ingredients in the shop as Father had an allotment where he grew everything. Sometimes I went with Mother to the main market in the square in front of the Cloth Hall. On the food stalls it was customary to taste samples and I got used to these 'tasties'. Once I picked up a smooth white sweetie from a stall selling clothes pegs and washing soap and popped it in my mouth. It soon came out again – it was a mothball!

As most of the fathers were gardeners by trade, they worked their own gardens and allotments to produce food for their families and competed with each other in the annual British Legion flower and produce show. At home they read English newspapers delivered a day after publication – the *Daily Express,* the *Daily Telegraph* and the *News of the World* – and listened to BBC radio from London on bulky headphones. Dorothy Charlton's father went one better:

He fitted up – that's when they had the 'cat's whiskers' – a wireless in every bedroom and we all had earphones for our beds, so we could listen in bed to anything special. We were the first house in Poelkapelle to have a radio in a cabinet. It was called a Cambridge and it was American and they queued up with the priest outside the house to come and listen to it. Everybody came through to the back – my father put it in the kitchen so that people in the village could come and listen to Henry Hall and his dance band.

Radio not only offered intriguing new technology, it promised an instant link with home. Bob Simmons' father was quick to see its business potential. After driving field ambulances in Flanders during the war, he married a local girl and studied radio at French night school while running a garage business. He opened the first radio shop in Ypres in 1925 and probably sold Dorothy's father his Cambridge cabinet. He was also a radio ham.

One of my first memories was of being ill with earache and going downstairs to the kitchen and lying on the couch behind my father while he was talking to people all over the world on his amateur radio transmitter. He called me 'the junior op' and he used to release the canary from the cage and I remember looking at this canary, worried that it might get electrocuted by the high tension coils!

Languages spoken at home depended on the nationality of the mother, though English was always a constant as few of the fathers spoke anything else well. In mixed households, where children saw a lot of their maternal grandparents, Flemish was the lingua franca. After nearly seventy years in Britain, Charlotte Dunn sometimes struggles to express herself in English. She admits: 'Even these days I often speak in Flemish to myself.' In the Fox household, Betty and Jimmy say their father insisted on English: 'Though Mother was Belgian, we always spoke English at home – her English sounded like broken Welsh. If she could get away with it she spoke in Flemish if Dad wasn't there, but we'd answer in English.'

Even in all–British households the children would know French or Flemish because these were the languages they were taught in until the British Memorial School opened in 1929, and they were the languages of the streets where they played with local children. Jerry Eaton, one of six brothers whose IWGC gardener father worked in France until Jerry was twelve, 'lived with the French as French' until moving to Ypres; here the boys all continued to speak French among themselves at home, baffling their English parents. Other children, too, found Flemish a useful code when they wanted to outwit Mum and Dad.

There was plenty going on outside the home. A football club, Rémy Sport, recruited at first from the nearby IWGC camp at Rémy railway siding and was soon established on the Belgian FA fixture list. Uncle PD was an early member and recalls pleasant Sunday away matches in neighbouring towns, celebrating their success afterwards with hospitable hosts and their supporters. He also recalled would-be golfers volunteering to clear ground outside the ramparts to create a nine-hole course in the early years following the war. After shifting mounds of war debris and filling in shell holes, the project proved too ambitious but they did manage to make a putting green. The Ypres

British Sports Club rented grounds on the outskirts of town where a cricket pitch was laid and a vital feature of sporting and social life – the Ypres Cricket Club – was formed. Matches against the British colony in Brussels and other teams of IWGC men were favourite summertime fixtures and the 1936 Jubilee Cup tournament was a big occasion.

The children of the colony, like Lillian Wilkins, recall a social whirl of 'whist drives and parties and dances. It was lovely, it really was.' The whist drives were held at the British Legion Club, a regular haunt for the ex-servicemen of the IWGC with its bar and billiard room, and the dances were in the large hall at the Ypriana Hotel. Here, too, there were annual Christmas parties where all the Commission families from Ypres and outlying districts came for a splendid tea, games and 'really good stuff' from Father Christmas – played by a senior official from the IWGC area office. In the summer there were outings to the coast at La Panne, and some families even ran to renting a holiday home there for a week or two during the summer. Commission employees also enjoyed paid leave so that they could visit the UK at least once a year.

The British Legion was a linchpin of the community, with its club for the men and its programme of events that regularly brought the British community together. It also contributed to the town's prosperity during the 1920s through its large-scale pilgrimages from Britain. Founded in 1921 by Earl Haig to keep the flame of remembrance alive and to represent the peacetime interests of ex-servicemen, the British Legion established a branch in Ypres almost immediately and quickly attracted over a hundred members. For IWGC gardeners, many of them former regular soldiers, 'the Legion' was an essential part of their post-war lives, linking past and present, work and leisure.

There were other networks for the men. Elaine Madden remembers a 'secret room' in her mother's hotel in Ypres, where men in strange costumes held mysterious gatherings: 'It was a big room on the first floor behind a gate. My father was one of them and I asked him what it was about. He said it was some kind of Lodge but it was a secret and I shouldn't talk about it or ask questions because it was none of my business.' The Builders of the Silent Cities Lodge was established in 1922, inspired by Rudyard Kipling's description of IWGC workers and intended as a kind of craft guild for them. Priestley Dunn was a long-standing member of the Number 12 Lodge, and later became its Master. There are still Silent Cities Lodges in Flanders though their members, like the majority of staff now working for the Commission there, are Belgian.

The Royal Antedeluvian Order of Buffaloes also had a Lodge in Ypres, where Nina Pitt's father was a Brother. Nina still has a photo of their 1928 Christmas party, held at Skindles Hotel. Thirty or so children are gathered with their parents in front of the Christmas tree, Union Jack in evidence in the background.

Whenever groups of British visitors came to Ypres there were welcome receptions in local hotels to which everyone in the colony was invited, and large-scale pilgrimages were the occasion for special celebrations. Charlotte Dunn, whose father was 'a big Legion man' and the standard-bearer for the Ypres branch, remembers the curious combination of revelry and remembrance that characterised the town in the inter-war period:

> It was lovely. Always something to do. Always something going on because of the parties coming over. When they came, we used to have a special evening ball, just for English people. There were two big restaurants in Ypres, the Continental and Skindles, and my Mam and Dad were very friendly with the owners there, so the parties went there and we were always invited. Dinner, then off to the Menin Gate, back home, change and off to the ball. Afterwards, three and four in the morning, there we were arm-in-arm marching through the square – not drunk, no, not like now . . .

The biggest ever British mass pilgrimage was organised by the British Legion and led by Edward, Prince of Wales, in August 1928, when 11,000 people spent five days in the battlefields of France and Flanders. As its first President the Prince had been involved in the IWGC since its earliest days. He came to Flanders often, but there are mixed memories of him. George Simpson's father wasn't impressed:

'Dad said he was a disgrace. He'd just come up from a weekend in Paris apparently, and looked very scruffy.' Louise Francis saw him many times: 'He came to all the big occasions. We all had a crush on him, he was very nice looking, but he was so young, and he was always fidgeting, it must have been so boring for him. To me, he always looked awkward, I felt sorry for him.'

Dorothy Charlton recalls hearing that he had ended up in jail in Ostend one night after an evening's carousing in the casino with Prince Charles of Belgium. She can still recite his anthem ('the national anthem of the Prince of Wales. No English people know it, they're so ignorant about their own history') which the children learned at school and which was printed on a scarf given to her mother:

> *Among our ancient mountains*
> *And from our lovely vales*
> *Oh! Let the prayer re-echo*
> *God Bless the Prince of Wales!*

Pilgrimages were part of everyday life in Ypres, and pilgrims a source of endless fascination for the children. Betty Parker remembers: 'We used to follow them round sometimes, just to be near them. In those days you could always tell the British, the way they were dressed: the flannels, the blazer, almost a uniform.' English women pilgrims, too, stood out in a crowd, but for the wrong reasons: Nina Pitt says they could always pick them out for their clumpy shoes and frumpy clothes. The Belgian children played the same game. John Parminter's wife Nenette grew up in Ypres and remembers following the pilgrims: 'Us children, we wagered against each other whether we recognised if it was an English or a Belgian woman. We laughed at the English women with their sensible shoes and pleated skirts and we thought, the English – they don't know how to dress.'

November 11, Armistice Day, was the most important date in the calendar for British pilgrims and for the British colony. The occasion gained in pomp and importance after the opening of the Menin Gate memorial in July 1927, when there was somewhere of sacred significance to march to. Like Charlotte Dunn and many of the children, Sidney Harper would be there with his father:

> I remember the marches we used to do on Armistice Day. We'd go to St George's Church and then form outside; a big column of all the War Graves Commission people; the kids would follow their fathers. We used to march to the Belgian memorial first and lay a wreath there and then on to the Menin Gate and lay wreaths there. Very serious occasion, we all took it very seriously.

The Menin Gate, Reginald Blomfield's massive 'triumphal arch' begun in 1923, was the inspired alternative to the 'zone of silence' – the proposal to fence off the Cloth Hall ruins as a war memorial. The idea for a purpose-built national monument to the British war dead of Flanders coincided with the Imperial War Graves Commission's decision to commemorate 'the missing' on a single memorial rather than in individual cemeteries; the two came together in the Menin Gate, which bears the names of more than 54,000 casualties without known graves. It dominates the symbolic eastern entrance to the town through which thousands of British Empire troops marched to the trenches, many to their deaths. Its scale, stone construction and classical adornments of funerary urns and lions couchant make a striking contrast with the warm brick Flemish houses that huddle around it on the town side.

On 24 July 1927 all the Commission families in the Ypres area were invited to the official opening by Field Marshal Lord Plumer, in the presence of Albert I, King of the Belgians. The ceremony was considered so significant that it was broadcast live by the BBC and relayed to churches and public places throughout Britain. In his address, Plumer spoke of the special grief borne by those who had 'no grave to visit, no place where they could lay tokens of loving remembrance'. The Menin Gate, he said, was a memorial worthy of those who had no known grave; it would 'give expression to the nation's gratitude for their sacrifice and their sympathy with those who mourned them . . . Now it can be said . . . "He is not missing; he is here".'

When buglers of the Somerset Light Infantry played the Last Post it proved to be the emotional summit of the occasion. The *Daily Mail* captured the moment: 'On this morning, played on the ruined ramparts of Ypres, overlooking the highway that led to death, its haunting sadness was almost unbearable. Tears filled the eyes and sobs caught in the throat. Away over the moat, across the fields to the cemeteries, one heard the sad message of a nation in mourning.' Such was its impact, the playing of the Last Post soon became a nightly ritual at the Menin Gate.

On the afternoon of the same day Plumer had another official duty. It wasn't as grand as opening the Menin Gate, but it had even more significance for the British colony: he laid the foundation stones for their new church and school. As the *Ypres Times* reported:

> The dominant notes of the great ceremony in the morning at the Menin Gate were stateliness and splendour, while the quiet service in the afternoon suggested homeliness and simplicity. It seemed natural after gazing at the mighty memorial with awe and reverence, to turn later to the simple homely thoughts of Church and School. And as the Menin Gate bears testimony to the majesty of sacrifice, so Church and School, when finished, will be mindful of the seed-time of service.

At the close of the ceremony, Plumer was presented with a posy by a little girl. With it was the message: 'From Jeanne Lomas, the first English child to be born in Ypres since the Great War'.

When they describe their childhoods, those who grew up in Ypres say: 'We had total freedom, there was no question of "don't go there, don't do that"'; 'We had a lovely life in Ypres. We were happy, we had freedom'; 'It was a good life, we hadn't got the restrictions we have now'.

Though some parents were strict, most children went about freely on their bikes and *trottinettes* – big scooters with pneumatic tyres – and played with whoever they liked. Growing up among the old battlefields was exciting. On their doorstep was an adventure playground of ruins, abandoned dugouts, overgrown trenches and mysterious metal playthings. A few kilometres outside Ypres, Sanctuary Wood with its old trench network was a favourite spot for blackberrying and picnics, and Hill 60 drew boys on the hunt for war souvenirs.

The battlefields yielded a harvest of rusting ordnance and 'mountains' of old ammunition were left outside farm gates. It was all too tempting: 'We were warned not to touch this stuff, but we did'. Children joined with the locals in a lively trade in salvaged metals. John Gabriel was one of them:

We used to go in old dugouts and find live ammunition and take it apart – take the cordite out of live bullets and put it in a long line and set fire to it, like a fuse. We used to follow the plough and all the little round lead shot came up – the size of a marble and they were what filled the shells. There were thousands and thousands of those – you could pick up bagfuls of them. We used to take them to scrap merchants and get a few francs. We didn't argue how much, we just took what they gave us.

Even Charlotte Dunn couldn't resist joining in, despite her mother's warnings:

'Don't you dare to go in the trenches.' No, Mam, no, we said. All of us, on our bikes, in the trenches, Hill 60, playing wars. Lovely it was, we had a lovely time. And as we got older there was a lot of money to be won. We had a bucket and we'd go in the trenches and all over the battlefields for booty, iron and cartridges, and then we'd take it and this man used to weigh it and buy it, and we'd have francs. Dozens of us with buckets. 'Don't you dare tell your father.' No, Mam.

Occasionally, things went wrong. Arthur Jones was with other British children on Hill 60 one day, looking for bayonets and helmets:

I was about twelve and I went on my bike without telling Dad. There were shells and we would try and knock off the cap and unscrew it, to get the lead cap which was worth something. But we got cured of that when a young lad we were with had a piece of metal in his hand and he said: 'I've got a gold bracelet!' – he was scratching at it and it was yellow. He took it home and was polishing it by the fire in his kitchen when there was an almighty bang. It detonated and the blast took his fingers off. That kept us away from the battlefields for a long time.

The lad was Leslie Rolfe, one of the nine Rolfe children. He lost all his fingers apart from the little finger of his right hand. He was nine years old. His sister Blanche recalls that, when he went back to school, nobody would play with him.

Sometimes there were gruesome finds. Boots with human bones still inside and worse, as Sidney Harper discovered:

At nine or ten, we used to go up to places called Hill 60 and Hill 62, playing in the trenches. They were still there and the duck-boards were still laid, going rotten. I can recall on one occasion running in this trench and a bit of it collapsed on one side and there was this body looking at me with a cup in his hand. I couldn't get away from there quick enough.

The shadow of war was always there and, despite the fun and care-free times, they couldn't avoid the fact that they lived among the dead. Fathers didn't talk to their children in any detail about the war, or their work in the cemeteries. They kept remembrance of the sacrifice alive for bereaved families and for the nation and Empire, but preferred to forget their own wartime experiences. But living with the aftermath of war was part of growing up in Flanders Fields. Charlotte Dunn reflects the experience of many of the children when she says:

My father wasn't a talking man. He had that army thing stuck in him. You know, 'don't ask questions' . . . I was brought up with dead soldiers. I used to go with my grandfather because they had a big piece of land by the canal and they used to find the bodies, after. I was brought up with, how can I say? I was brought up with the cemetery.

Often children visited their fathers at work. Dorothy Charlton went with her sisters to see their father in the cemeteries during the school holidays: 'He would tell us stories about the different regiments. You know, we would see a gravestone and he would say: "He's the son of a famous Scottish comedian". He would tell us the stories of these people. He was quite a raconteur. Some of it, I think, was imagination but nevertheless he told a good story.'

Betty Fox started visiting the cemeteries young. In the family album there is a photograph of her, no more than a toddler in her little summer smock, hair ribbon and baby shoes. She's looking intently at two blooms in her hand. It could be in any back garden, but it's in a cemetery. She's standing between a gardeners' bothy and a rank of identical white headstones fronted by a long flowerbed, looking perfectly happy and at home.

When she was a bit older, she would walk miles to see her father working:

> I followed Dad about everywhere. I must have been a pain in the bum to him! I used the excuse of taking him a flask of tea – he was perfectly capable of taking his own flask, but I liked to take it. To me as a child it wasn't creepy. You didn't trample about or rush around, or pick the flowers. It was almost as if you were working. If people came to visit the graves, you kept away. I always wanted to help Dad and this usually meant raking up the grass and putting it into large carts with rubber tyres. Or just walking alongside him with his lawnmower and then after the freshly cut grass had been stacked up and put in the cart I would ask to sit on top of it as it was taken to the compost heap. And he let me go round and pinch off the dead flowers.

The Menin Gate holds special memories for Betty:

> Dad had turns of duty there, clearing the leaves and the perished wreaths – they were made of real flowers then. I used to go with him of an evening after tea to do this little job. I used to take the ribbons off the old wreaths – they were beautiful ribbons, better than you see today, silky and with the different colours of the

regiments. I would roll them up very neatly and keep them treasured in a little box. I didn't do anything with them, I just collected them . . . He took me up to the roof once. He said, 'Nobody else will be able to show you this', and I held his hand tightly while we looked through the big open portholes at the traffic going through below.

Stephen Grady's father, head gardener for the Steenwerck group of cemeteries around Nieppe, was a reserved man who nevertheless chafed against authority. He didn't talk about the war and Stephen never heard him talk politics, but they often went to the cemeteries together: 'My father had a little saddle on his crossbar and that's the way he used to take me to the cemeteries on a Thursday when there was no school. And I remember he used to say, "If you ever see a car stop, hop over the wall!" He didn't mean visitors, he meant someone from Head Office in Arras.'

Spending time in the 'silent cities' had a lasting and positive impact on many children. Nina Pitt's father was only a driver, but she still: '. . . loved the gardens. I was always tidying up, picking the dead flowers. I always remember the head gardener saying to my father: "Get your girl into Kew Gardens because it's obviously what she likes and enjoys".' She didn't get to Kew, but much later she did take a course in horticulture and floristry.

John Gabriel believes his lifelong love of the countryside springs from the days he spent as a child in outlying cemeteries with his father:

We'd set off in the morning, we had our sandwiches and I had a little square seat on his crossbar, and I sat on there and away we went. We'd be there all day. To keep me occupied he might cut an area of grass and put a sheet down and I'd just lark about in all this grass. I wasn't on my own, I'd be with friends – sons and daughters of other gardeners. The cemeteries were always in the middle of the countryside. I can remember it now, chaffinches and yellowhammers, and they had these little sheds where we ate our sandwiches. Oak Dump was where I liked going best – a very small cemetery, only a hundred graves.

These visits helped children in other ways. Dorothy Cuthbert's father, Herbert, worked at Messines Ridge British Cemetery: 'When I was a little girl my father would take me with him and we'd go round the different graves seeing what they said. That's how I learned the alphabet and how to read words.' Nor was this an experience reserved for children of the British colony. Nenette van Bost's father made sure his children paid their respects:

> We had to go to the cemeteries on our bikes . . . because he felt that all those people had to be honoured. The First World War was still very big in his mind and we had to do our one minute's silence always at the Cross [of Sacrifice]. He never talked about his own experiences – only about the others – and whenever there was a little bit of weed growing there, we had to clean it up. Oh yes, I knew virtually every cemetery around Ypres.

These were idyllic times: free, adventurous and full of friendship within a secure and close community. But there were shadows other than those cast by the Great War.

Home life was less than comfortable for some children. In the light of adult experience, they see now that their parents were struggling in unhappy marriages where differences of religion or culture had become irreconcilable. Some mixed couples parted, but this was the exception in a devoutly Catholic country. Religion was the principal, though not the only, cause of unhappiness. Catholic mothers instilled in their children an almost hysterical fear of Protestant churches, some even telling them that the Devil lived there. When the new Anglican church of St George and the British Memorial School opened at the end of the 1920s, religious differences came to a head in some families.

Dorothy Charlton describes her mother as 'a dreadful woman, a religious fanatic, and a terrible snob', who 'hated everything English', despite marrying an Englishman. Dorothy suspects that she married because she was pregnant and that, bitterly regretting her mistake, she took her guilt and frustration out on her family. She was excessively strict and disapproving, and never forgave her husband for moving

Dorothy and her sister from their boarding convent on the coast to the new British school in Ypres.

Here, one of Dorothy's best friends was Elaine Madden. Elaine didn't have much of a home life either. Her mother, though loving, was always busy working in the hotel while her father was in the bar drinking with his old army pals or at Lodge meetings. She felt she was living in a business rather than a home. Then things got worse. When Elaine was ten, her mother died of septicaemia following a miscarriage; she was thirty-two. Elaine's world, short as it was on love and homely comforts, collapsed completely. The Duponselle family went into deep mourning.

> When my mother died I was obliged to wear black and for the first six weeks I had to wear a long black veil. When I had my first Communion at the cathedral in Ypres I was the only one in black. All the other little girls were in white dresses, dressed up like brides, and there was me in my black veil which went down to the waist.

Worse was to come. Her father's drinking, exacerbated by Caroline's death, was now out of hand. His IWGC records say only that 'his employment ended' in March 1932. Whether he left or was sacked is unclear but Larry Madden, always unreliable, was by now a liability. He was in no position to care for Elaine and he made it clear that he didn't intend to. 'I don't want her', Elaine remembers him saying, 'she looks too much like her mother'. So she was sent to live with her grandparents and extended family at the Palace Hotel in Poperinghe.

Death was a common visitor. Hardly a child in the British colony escaped the experience of a parent, sibling or close friend dying tragically young. Infant mortality was high, health care rudimentary and immunisation rare. Children died of undiagnosed appendicitis, croup epidemics, meningitis and polio. Jack and Adrienne Fox rejoiced at the birth of twin boys in 1935 after four girls – Mariejeanne, Alice, Jacqueline and Betty (their firstborn, a boy, had died in infancy). But the twins struggled for life: Jimmy was tiny, barely tipping the kitchen scales against a kilo bag of sugar; John was born brain-damaged and lived only a matter of months. Adrienne kept a photo of John in his tiny white coffin, together with a lock of his hair, with her until she died in Ypres in 1952.

Although tragedy affected almost every family, growing up in the British colony was, for most, full of the comforting certainties of childhood. As far as the children were concerned, whatever languages they spoke or whoever they played with, they were British and the Ypres Salient was their home. But in more influential quarters, doubts were being raised. Had the community integrated just a bit too comfortably? Was it in danger of losing its British identity and values in the midst of all these 'continental' influences? Some thought so, and intended to do something about it.

4

A Little Sprig of Empire

*There could be no better Memorial to those who gave their lives
for England, than to secure for the British children . . . living in
the Salient, that they be brought up in the faith of their fathers,
and trained in the ideals and loyalties for which so many gave their
lives.*

Ypres League fund-raising flyer, 1925

IN AUGUST 1931, seventeen years after Britain declared war on
Germany, a letter went out to women of means who had perhaps lost husbands and sons in the Ypres Salient, or who might
otherwise be sympathetic to an emotive appeal to their patriotic
values.

Dear Madam,

*To all who, in proud memory and in reverent gratitude, are con-
scious of this solemn anniversary in our Empire's history, we send forth
this message today. Its high purpose is that due honour may be paid to
the Glorious Dead who rest in the Salient they sanctified by their
endurance; its burden is a plea for the funds needed to maintain and
endow the British Settlement established at Ypres in their memory.*

*Seven hundred Britons live about it – most of them are employed
in the care of the war cemeteries – and, but for its existence, they
would be without any link with the homeland, and their children
would grow up lacking any knowledge of their mother tongue.*

*The Settlement, which will be 'for ever England', is doing a work
which is truly national in scope and character. Pilgrims to the battle-*

fields – who at times number nearly 1000 a week – find within its boundaries a very beautiful church and a rest-room for the weary, and the little children of the community – more than 100 of them – going to and from their English school, as though they were in very truth in England . . .

Enclosed with the letter was a leaflet about the British Settlement. On the cover is a touching photograph of a young schoolboy, standing 'in homage' at the foot of a war grave, his cap held reverently at his side.

This is Bertie Payton, the son of the widow who wrote so gratefully to the Ypres League in 1926, thanking them for funding her pilgrimage to her husband's grave. Without knowing this (there is no caption to the photograph) the reader might think that he is one of the 'little children of the community' – the subject of this appeal. The image is perfect because it tells readers everything they need to know about the British in Ypres: they are there because of the war dead, bringing up a new generation of loyal sons and daughters of the Empire. This effective piece of communication crowned more than a decade of campaigning by those who sought, as they saw it, to give the British colony in Ypres permanence, status and purpose.

The colony had grown organically from the work of the Imperial War Graves Commission and from servicing the needs of battlefield tourists and pilgrims. It had played a major role in the town's rehabilitation from the ruins of war and was vital to its continuing prosperity. But it also had intense symbolic and emotional importance, especially for the military men who had led campaigns in Flanders and for whom the Salient remained the sacred site of their greatest triumphs and tragedies. For them, and for the many ex-servicemen at home who still thought of Ypres as 'theirs', the colony's presence was a permanent reminder – together with the magnificent new Menin Gate – of Britain's sacrifice and Belgium's debt. The British in Ypres were a living memorial; while they were a thriving force there, Britain still had a stake in the Salient.

Whether the IWGC gardeners and their families felt the heavy weight of this responsibility is doubtful. The men got on quietly with their jobs and their lives, preferring to look forward rather than back. They took the remembrance aspects of their task seriously – how could they not, given their own war experiences? But they didn't glorify British achievements and they didn't teach their children to. And it wasn't as if the Belgians needed any reminders from Britain about their debt; this was acknowledged freely and in the most practical of ways. Nevertheless, for some, it wasn't enough that the British in Ypres were there to look after cemeteries and welcome pilgrims, in the process helping to restore the fortunes of the town. No, they represented something even more important: the dissemination of British values and prestige abroad, a small, late flowering of the Imperial dream in Europe.

So there were mixed feelings about the ease with which many of the British men had settled into the Flemish community. Relations with the Belgians were more than cordial but intermarriage, particularly in a Catholic country, posed a threat. How British *were* these families? Children born in Belgium of Belgian mothers were technically Belgian by nationality, though their births could be registered with the British Consulate in Brussels and children could choose to be British once they reached the age of majority. Then there were the important cultural questions of language, religion and education: English might be only one – or none – of the languages spoken at home by the children of these families; there were no permanent Protestant churches in Ypres; and they were being taught in Flemish or French in schools where Roman Catholic religious instruction was compulsory. The dilution of British values or, worse, their corruption ('At my convent school history was all about how horrid the English were to Joan of Arc') was a real risk.

It was obvious to those for whom the colony represented more than just an expatriate workforce that it needed bolstering with the permanence of bricks and mortar – institutions that would symbolise and safeguard British cultural and religious traditions. It needed an Anglican church and its own school.

The men most closely associated with the campaign for these institutions were, unsurprisingly, all from the most senior ranks of the military. Field Marshal Sir John Denton Pinkstone French, first Earl of Ypres, was Commander-in-Chief of the British Expeditionary Force at the start of the war until he was replaced by General Sir Douglas Haig at the end of 1915, after rubbing politicians and even his own colleagues up the wrong way. He was then put in charge of the British Home Forces where he led the British suppression of the 1916 Easter Rising in Ireland. He was an experienced but old-fashioned general, easily roused to fury, and he continued to fight a bitter rearguard action against those at home who had forced his departure from the main theatre of war.

In retrospect, his military record looks undistinguished: he oversaw the First and Second Battles of Ypres and made strategic errors. But the immediate post-war mood, though sombre, remained deferential to those in authority. The recriminations came later. After the war Field Marshal French was credited as the principal saviour of Ypres and his title forever linked him with the place. On 4 August 1924, the tenth anniversary of Britain declaring war on Germany, he used the occasion of a pilgrimage to the Salient to make a public appeal for funds for 'an English Church' for Ypres.

If French fronted the campaign, the men doing the legwork were Field Marshal Lord Plumer and General Sir William Pulteney. Both had served in the Salient. Plumer, a cartoonist's dream of a general – squat, bluff and with a huge silver moustache – was in fact a highly competent, well-regarded and popular leader. Known as 'Daddy Plum' by his troops, he was responsible for one of the Allies' few stunning successes, at Messines Ridge in 1917. Pulteney cannot claim credit for any successes, stunning or otherwise. He was described by one senior officer as 'the most completely ignorant General I served under during the war, and that is saying a lot', but he was one of the few commanders not to fall out with Field Marshal French in the early years of the war. He survived the duration without attracting either opprobrium or glory.

The three generals were all founder members of an ex-serviceman's organisation called the Ypres League, started in 1920 by a Canadian, Henry Beckles Willson. Willson, who had served in the Salient as a lieutenant colonel with the Canadian Expeditionary Force, was a journalist and one of the influential commentators who wanted to keep Ypres as a sanctuary of ruins, railing against its 'desecration' by the new tourist industry. He had written that the Salient 'belongs henceforward to history and will for evermore be a sacred place for pilgrims to the graves of the heroic dead'.

Unable to halt the tide of returning residents and the new influx of visitors with rhetoric, he set up the Ypres League as a way of perpetuating the ideal of 'the Immortal Salient' through comrade-ship, remembrance and commemoration, a 'brotherhood of all ranks – British, Belgian, French and American'. The League also had prac-tical objectives: organising pilgrimages and publishing information about the battlefields and cemeteries. Looking back at its work today, there's a strong undercurrent of military moralism. A 1925 recruitment flyer proclaims:

> No cause could be more inspiring that that which com-
> memorates British tenacity, develops comradeship, and helps
> the thousands who have joined the League by cheering words
> and practical deeds. The stupendous effort of the War has
> engendered a lassitude and even pessimism. Perhaps these will
> pass away; indeed, they must. Hundreds of those who have
> joined the League have regained courage and an optimistic
> view.

The League was very well connected: its Patron-in-Chief was the King and the Prince of Wales one of its two royal Patrons. The Earl of Ypres was its President, Lord Plumer of Messines was one of its four distinguished Vice Presidents and Lieutenant General Sir William Pulteney chaired its Executive Committee. The League's 'Representative at Ypres' – the local fixer – was none other than Captain P. D. Parminter.

Though never as large or as influential as the British Legion, and not as representative of the ranks, it had a membership network in the more genteel English towns and cities, in the Dominions, and in New York. The League kept its members informed through a quarterly magazine, the *Ypres Times*, which was also widely read among the British colony. Today it makes fascinating, if excitable, reading with its determinedly upbeat accounts of derring-do on the battlefield, its naked hatred of 'the Bosch' (a name redolent only of kitchen appliances for modern readers), and its appeals for 'stirring narratives of outstanding incidents' for a planned *Ypres Book of Valour*.

The *Ypres Times* perfectly captures a heroic, even jingoistic, view of the war prevalent among the upper officer class in the 1920s before the war poetry of Siegfried Sassoon, Wilfred Owen and what has become known as 'the literature of disillusionment' challenged the prevailing orthodoxy in the last years of that decade. Its rhetoric may now seem unsubtle and anachronistic, but the *Ypres Times* provides a lively chronicle of what was to become the League's main achievement and memorial: the British Settlement.

The idea of an Anglican chapel for the use of visiting pilgrims had been mooted since 1919 – prompting immediate objections from other denominations and faiths. There were other, more practical, objections. A senior IWGC official wrote to Fabian Ware that it would be a much better idea to build a non-denominational chapel as part of plans for the Menin Gate. The alternative being proposed by the League would 'take a lot of money . . . I do not think for a moment a Church of England built at Ypres would serve as useful a purpose and it would very probably sooner or later fall into decay and disuse.'

Nevertheless, at the end of 1924 the Menin Gate architect, Sir Reginald Blomfield, produced a 'Report and Design' for the League with outline plans for an elegant chapel near the ramparts by the Lille Gate, in the same materials as the Menin Gate, small red Belgian brick and Euville stone, at a cost of 'less than £10,000'.

In May 1925 the Earl of Ypres died, giving unexpected impetus to the project. Seizing the opportunity to give the plan a new push, Plumer and Pulteney now proposed that the church should be a national memorial to the Field Marshal: 'What better place could be chosen in which to set up his memorial than the ancient town of Ypres, which by his foresight, his strategy, and his dogged resolution he saved?' Plumer's fund-raising committee set about its task with renewed vigour, placing letters in national newspapers and sending out appeal leaflets to prospective donors. These reveal the real objective of the project:

The Church will be used of course by the thousands of 'Pilgrims' and tourists who pass through the city, but this is by no means the only or the greatest reason for its erection. In connection with the care and upkeep of the British War Cemeteries, there are a large number of British families living in and around Ypres, forming a British Colony of over 600 souls, many of whom are children. Surely it is a national duty to provide for the spiritual care of these who watch over the graves of our dead. There could be no better Memorial to those who gave their lives for England, than to secure for the British children who in consequence are living in the Salient, that they be brought up in the faith of their fathers, and trained in the ideals and loyalties for which so many gave their lives.

But there was a problem: the Lille Gate site was found to be fatally undermined by old wartime dugouts so, through the good offices of the IWGC man on the spot, Captain W. J. Perrott, a new site not far from the Cloth Hall and cathedral was purchased for the equivalent of £875. Blomfield was re-engaged to produce ambitious new plans for a church, a parsonage, a Pilgrims' Hall – and a school.

So far, the old pals' act of military connections through the Ypres League had kick-started the project. Now the old boy network came into play. Both Plumer and Pulteney had gone to Eton College, the English public school that has supplied eighteen British Prime Ministers and the officer class for all its wars from the Crimea to the Falklands. Old Etonians had made a notable sacrifice in the Salient between 1914 and 1918: 342 of its finest had perished there. In October 1926 the College's Provost, Dr Montague Rhodes James – better known as the ghost story writer M. R. James – made an appeal to Etonians, inviting them to raise £1,500 to pay for the building of the school. This would, he said, be a living memorial to 'the unforgotten friends of youth':

> The need for such an institution may possibly not be at once obvious, but it is real and imperative. The children who will be taught there are those belonging to the 200 English residents who are, and will continue to be, engaged in caring for the

graves of the Fallen. They – their children – number at present upwards of 200, and, as things are, they neither learn their native language, nor can they keep in touch with their national Church. It would surely be a very appropriate, effective, and kindly service that Eton would be rendering if it gave them opportunities of doing both these things.

The letter produced results. Within weeks, Pulteney was able to report to Fabian Ware of the IWGC that: 'We have got about £1000 for the School'. The organising committee felt sufficiently confident to start building and to approach the London County Council about supplying teachers, securing two in principle on secondment for a period of four years. Some time later an advertisement appeared in the *LCC Gazette*, for a headmaster for 'Eton School, Ypres' '. . . to take charge of a new school for about 80 children aged 5–14 built in connection with the War Graves Commission. If a married man whose wife is also a teacher is appointed, the latter might be engaged as assistant teacher.' Salaries would be on the standard scale for state schools and 'the cost of quarters and living are very inexpensive'. Details were scant, but times were getting tough in Britain and the prospect must have sounded more attractive than a council school in a London slum. There were more than a hundred applicants.

By the summer of 1927 Pulteney reported progress in the *Ypres Times*. The entire cost of building the school – £1,650 excluding exterior landscaping – had been subscribed 'by Etonians and their relatives'.

In fact, neither Eton nor the IWGC had any direct responsibility for the new school. The 'British Settlement', of which it was part, was a self-governing legal entity granted 'civil personality' status by the Belgian government in 1931 'in remembrance of what we owe to the British nation and in homage to the spirit that inspired the erection of these establishments in the Ypres District'. This bestowed certain privileges and exempted its Trustees from death duties.

Nevertheless, both institutions maintained a close and benevolent interest. Eton's Provost, M. R. James, was a Trustee until his death in

1936 and Eton provided the school's two Treasurers. The first of these, E. L. Vaughan, set up a trust fund in November 1929 in which Etonians – not Eton College – provided £200 a year 'to educate twenty boys'. The Commission was similarly represented on its governing committee, with Sir Fabian and Lady Ware among the permanent members.

From Eton's point of view, however, its namesake in Ypres was always something of a freelance operation initiated by some of its old boys and there was never any firm constitutional link with the College. After its initial effort in raising the cost of the building and setting up the small endowment fund, it seems to have considered its financial responsibilities acquitted. But the school and the British Settlement needed secure ongoing funding and efforts now targeted a much broader range of potential sponsors, including the wealthy ladies and the headmasters of all the public schools, who were urged to take out a subscription for a ten-year period. Lord Plumer even made a BBC broadcast charity appeal. Over the next decade subscribers and donors included the City livery companies, army garrison churches and the King. 'A Friend who desires to remain Anonymous' (but reported in the *Ypres Times* as the Prince of Wales) made a timely donation of £500 in 1929.

Perhaps this explains some doubt about the school's name. The first pupils will say with absolute certainty that they went to 'the Eton Memorial School', but it seems that this was its colloquial name only, useful shorthand and effective for initial fund-raising purposes. Officially, in its early years at least, it went under a variety of other names: the Ypres Memorial School, the Ypres British School, or just the British School. By the time its second headmaster, William Allen, arrived in 1933, it had become sufficiently distanced from Eton to be known henceforward as the British Memorial School, although the *Ypres Times* persisted in calling it the Ypres British School until as late as 1939.

Most of the pupils were the children of IWGC employees, but the Commission – an independent body acting under Royal Charter – was at pains to dissociate itself from the fund-raising efforts. 'The Commission's interest in the School is purely a benevolent one', it wrote to a would-be donor requiring further particulars. In fact, it helped in many practical ways, not least in funding the school to the tune of £500 a year as a contribution towards the education of Commission children.

Those who had been approached to help fund the school could be forgiven for thinking that it was being run by the IWGC, and many enquiries ended up on Fabian Ware's desk. Among the women targeted by the August 1931 fund-raising appeal was a Mrs J. M. Tate of Queensbury Terrace, Hyde Park. She wrote to the IWGC:

> *I have been asked to subscribe to an English School which has been started at Ypres to teach the children of English men employed there . . . If the fathers are there for other employment than tending the cemeteries I should be very glad if you would inform me what this is. I cannot say I feel inclined to educate the children of all and sundry English residents in the Ypres Salient.*

The polite reply informed Mrs Tate that seventy-five children of ex-servicemen gardeners attended at that point and that: 'The Eton School at Ypres is undoubtedly of the very greatest benefit to the children of the Commission's gardeners and the education provided there is in every way excellent.'

In January 1929 Pulteney reported in the *Ypres Times* that the buildings, apart from the Pilgrims' Hall, were all but complete. St George's Memorial Church – decorated and furnished down to its font, windows and bell tower entirely with gifts in memory of fallen men and proud but decimated regiments – was dedicated by the Bishop of Fulham on Palm Sunday, 24 March.

Among the many gifts was a Bible presented by King George V, inscribed in Latin: MORTEM OPPETENTES VITAM MERUERUNT (*Going out to meet death, they earned life*). There were eighty regimental and sixty personal memorials, and 180 chairs donated by individuals and organisations. 'It is impossible not to be interested in the Church and its Memorials,' Pulteney wrote, 'they represent many units and many individuals . . . the dignity of the whole building leaves nothing to be desired.'

The school, dedicated the same day, received its first forty-eight pupils the following month. In the schoolroom a large plaque bore the names of all 342 Etonians who had died in the Salient. Below it read:

THIS SCHOOL IS A MEMORIAL OF THOSE WHOSE
NAMES ARE WRITTEN ABOVE. IT WAS BUILT BY
THEIR BROTHER ETONIANS IN THE YEAR 1928
IN GRATEFUL REMEMBRANCE.

The Times, reporting on the opening of the 'Ypres Memorial School', noted that this 'was a venture of a type which had not before been attempted. It had been made because it was believed that these British subjects, unless educated at an English school, would be lost to England'.

It wasn't long before a Board of Education report was able to quote a visiting pilgrim: 'It is a source of endless wonder and pleasure to Britishers abroad that here in historic Ypres, they should find this vigorous sprig of the Empire'. The colony now had permanent institutions to confirm its position and status in the Belgian community; the British colony was now synonymous with the British Settlement.

For the families of the colony, like Lillian Wilkins', the new buildings quickly became central to their life in Ypres:

> Every Sunday we used to go to the evening service at St George's and then up Elverdingestraat to the newsagents where they would have the English newspapers. Then from there we used to go round the ramparts and listen to the Last Post. And then we'd go to the Princes at the Trumpet and have a drink. That was our Sunday routine for years. My father belonged to the church and Joyce and I were in the choir. Every Sunday, Sunday School and Evensong. Jack Fox – who was in my father's group of gardeners – was in charge of the Sunday School. He was a lovely man . . . And we were very, very proud of our School, and of being British among the Flemish.

At a time when imperialism and passionate nationalism have long been out of fashion, it is difficult to view the achievement of the British Settlement objectively. Yes, it was born of values and principles tarnished by twentieth-century experience. But these men – and the women who handed over their cash – created something important and substantial, not only for their own times but for the tumultuous years that followed. Their physical legacy is a group of fine buildings and a unique and moving memorial in St George's Church. Their human legacy is a cohort of children who experienced an education rich in the values and symbolism of nationhood. They grew into people who knew what they were fighting for.

The *News of the World*, in a fulsome report on the new British School in Ypres, was unwittingly prescient: 'Possessed of . . . a sound English education, these youthful Britons will commence well equipped to fight their battles in the world'.

5

A Very British School

*Who can deny that, but for the Ypres British Memorial School,
the character of these children might not become too merged in the
Continental and, more, lose touch and sympathy with the land of
their fathers, which is their heritage?*

Headmaster's Annual Report, 1937

THE ETON MEMORIAL School as it was known locally – if not
officially – soon developed an ethos as distinctive as that of its
famous namesake. But not without a struggle.

The children of the British colony who first went through its
doors in 1929 had known only French and Flemish schools, where
the heavy emphasis on religious instruction, strict segregation of the
sexes, and 'continental' culture and curriculum couldn't have been
more different from what they were about to experience. Though
some have warm memories of their early years in convent schools,
others haven't forgotten vindictive nuns, uniforms 'like straitjackets'
and 'having to pray eight times a day'.

Dorothy Charlton, whose French mother was intensely religious
and equally protective of her family's social standing, had been sent
to a Catholic boarding school from a young age:

I was four. Both my sister and I were packed off . . . but when the
Eton School was built it was impressed on all the British people
that the children should go there. Much against my mother's will,
we went. My mother was totally against that school – it was a nest
of heathen so-and-so's. It caused quite a stir. You know, it was

considered quite something that we were taken away from this fee-paying school and went to this school for free.

Dorothy was eight when she was moved to the new British school. She and her sister Andria came in by bus from Poelkapelle and were the first to arrive, waiting for the caretaker to come and unlock the gates on the first day. But far from enjoying their brand-new school, they were in for a shock:

> It was dreadful! We couldn't speak the language to start with. I spoke French with my mother, Flemish in the village. In the convent it was French, but we had a teacher who could speak English – a nun who had been in England during the war and she taught us all sorts of English songs and things – but we just repeated them parrot fashion. We knew very little English when the school started. And we had to learn everything all over again – pounds, shillings and pence when we were living with kilos and francs. We were a confused lot really.

Louise Francis was another non-English speaker when she joined the school in 1929, despite having an English father.

> I was in the first class, and I was more than eight years old, but I couldn't speak a word of English. My mother was French and we spoke French at home – even my father, who spoke French very well. I'd already struggled when I had to go to a Flemish school when we moved to Ypres – I could understand it but I never learned to speak it – and then I had to start all over again from scratch at the Eton School. Some of the children were Flemish speaking, others were French speaking and Mr and Mrs Morris had a terrible time trying to get us to speak English.

Harry Morris and his wife Kathleen had been chosen from over a hundred applicants for the posts of head and assistant teacher. They were just starting to realise what they'd taken on. Dorothy remembers them as 'a splendid couple': 'He was an ex-army officer with a gammy leg . . . a gentleman of the first order. And she was a delightful woman; she would have done very well in Victorian England.

She could play the piano and sing. She was airy-fairy but delightful.'

The initial intake of forty-eight quickly grew to seventy-two during the course of that first term, posing an immense challenge for the Morrises and their assistant Kathleen May. The Morrises had come from large inner London schools. What faced them was very different from Fulham or Pimlico, where they had taught before. In Ypres they found something closer to a village school, where children from four to fourteen across the ability range had to be taught an English elementary curriculum in a single schoolroom. And all in a language that was foreign to most of the pupils. As Harry Morris reported at the end of that first term: 'About a quarter of them spoke English fairly well, others spoke a little English with a very strong foreign accent, while the remainder spoke only French or Flemish.' Despite this, his aspirations for the school were already clear: 'The teaching is entirely on British lines, with emphasis on the study of the English language, which has been so sadly lacking in the past . . . Thus these children will grow up quite British in outlook and well able to maintain the spirit of the British Empire.'

If English was a priority, so was discipline. The cane was used frequently on boys and occasionally on girls. One former pupil even described Morris as 'sadistic', recalling that his elder brother had to be taken to the doctor after a beating that bruised his spine. Sidney Harper was taken away from the school for a time after Morris expelled his brother. Corporal punishment was new to them both: 'Cane was forbidden at Belgian schools. They'd grab you by the hair, or the ears, or the cheek or anything, but no cane. We had the cane at the Memorial School.'

George Simpson was seven when he started at the Memorial School – his first. He has never forgotten the bitter injustice of getting 'six of the best' for missing lessons one day. He and two other children had arrived at 8 a.m. as usual, on the local bus from Passchendaele, to find workmen laying slabs in the playground. The workmen told them there was no school that day, so they walked the fourteen kilometres home. The next day when they arrived, Morris refused to believe their story and gave them all a caning.

Devastated by four years of shelling, the medieval town of Ypres in February 1919

Life returns. The Hôtel de la Gare, Ypres, owned after the war by John Parminter's family, patched up to take early visitors in 1919. The temporary Skindles Restaurant is in the background

Five-year-old twins Charlotte and Priestley Dunn with their Flemish mother, grandparents, young neighbour and sundry livestock outside their temporary home in Ypres, 1923. Commission gardeners and their families, like other Ypres residents, had to live in temporary buildings for some years after the 1914–18 war

Jimmy Fox's father Jack (*right*) at work in Haringhe Bandaghem Cemetery in 1919, before the erection of permanent headstones

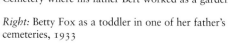

Above: John Gabriel and friends play in Chester Farm Cemetery where his father Bert worked as a gardener

Right: Betty Fox as a toddler in one of her father's cemeteries, 1933

Below: Commission gardeners after a day's work, Reservoir Cemetery, Ypres, 1929. Lillian Wilkins' father Harry is second left, Jimmy Fox's father Jack second right

Above: The Menin Gate was inaugurated on 24 July 1927 by Field Marshal Lord Plumer. The same afternoon, Plumer laid the foundation stone for the 'Ypres Memorial School', part of the new British Settlement

Left: Jimmy's father, Jack Fox (with eldest sister Mariejeanne next to him), and his Sunday-school class at St George's Memorial Church

The British Settlement, as it was known, comprised St George's Memorial Church, the British Memorial School, the Pilgrims' Hall and Presbytery

Empire Day celebrations, 1933. These became a feature of school life in the 1930s, when the children performed drills, patriotic songs and folk dances to an audience of parents and distinguished visitors. Priestley Dunn is holding the Union flag

A birthday party group from the 1930s: Lillian and Joyce Wilkins in matching outfits, Rene Fletcher (*second left*) with necklace, with her mother behind her and Elaine Madden (*second girl from right*)

The Fox family in the autumn of 1939. *Back*: Alice, an aunt, mother Adrienne; *front*: Jacqueline, Betty, father Jack, with Jimmy proudly wearing his British Memorial School cap

The school's second headmaster, William Allen, with his Elders (prefects) in 1936. School Captain Jerry Eaton is seated; Elaine Madden is behind Allen; next to her is Billy Crouch

The senior class at work in March 1940, weeks before the German invasion. In the front row are John Gabriel (*to the right of third headmaster Clifford Yorath*) and Bob Simmons (*right*). Joyce Dawson is in the centre of the second row

British Memorial School pupils visit Bedford House Cemetery, March 1940

Pupils of the British Memorial School in March 1940, shortly before they had to abandon their homes. Jimmy Fox is circled

These were difficult early days; frustration with communication problems inevitably exploded into temper and bad behaviour on both sides. There were problems of success too. Twins Charlotte and Priestley Dunn went to the Memorial School from the first day, but it was soon obvious that with the rapid expansion – ninety-three on the roll by the start of the new school year in September 1929 and with sixteen children turned away – there were already many more pupils than the new building could cope with: 'We must have been about eleven. The school wasn't big enough for us. There was only one classroom and across the road there was a pub and over the pub a big empty hall, so yes, the older ones used to cross the road every morning and go up the stairs.'

As soon as the adjacent Pilgrims' Hall was finished in 1930, the accommodation problem eased and children were able to use this new space as an extra classroom, for practical activities and to house the colony's growing library of English language books. Inevitably for a collection dependent on gifts from Ypres League members, this was heavily weighted towards military subjects and over the years there were constant appeals for more suitable reading matter for children.

The Pilgrims' Hall was a large, pleasant room where, a little later, Mr Godden the caretaker doled out his home-made soup to those who lived too far away to go home for lunch and where the children performed plays and concerts on the small stage. Former pupils in particular remember the impressive dress uniforms of Lord Plumer and Sir William Pulteney in their glass cabinets, and on the end wall a large painting of St George and the dragon. Outside, a small playground enclosed on all sides by the church and the backs of neighbouring houses, with a margin of grass at the far end, provided space for games.

The War Graves Commission was a stalwart supporter of the school from the outset, helping with cash and in kind. It paid for a charabanc to bring in children from outlying villages where there wasn't a bus service and its medical officer, Dr Nan Roberts, gave the children regular health inspections – a benefit unknown in local schools. It contributed substantially to running costs with an annual grant and paid for another assistant teacher to cope with the rising numbers in its first year. The new appointment brought the staff up to four and the number of available places to 120 – though this stretched to a peak of 128 in 1934.

Even with four teachers, this still made for large classes of children of different ages and abilities. Classroom management in such limited accommodation must have presented practical difficulties and the strict discipline was necessary to make the school run smoothly. No wonder early visitors found the children 'exceptionally well-mannered'. After only two terms, Kathleen Morris was able to write to Lady Plumer: '. . . their improvement in general behaviour is almost unbelievable, and best of all, at last they have some idea of what is meant by a "sense of honour"'. The children's command of English was improving too. 'Some are now able to read quite fluently and understand the English books with ease', Morris reported in the *Ypres Times*. 'They are also beginning to write simple English, though the spelling is often startlingly original.'

In June 1930 the first prize-giving was held in the new Pilgrims' Hall, with the architect Sir Reginald Blomfield as guest of honour. Blomfield told the children how, when he first started work on the school, it was planned for just forty pupils and the site was 'a mass of ruins with a stream running through it'. The *Ypres Times* reported that he counselled them:

> . . . to remember always those men to whose memory the school had been built, and to copy their ideals of courage and unselfishness. They should always strive to cultivate the quality of true British sportsmanship – not merely skill, but the will to do their level best for their team. They were very fortunate, living in a foreign country, to have a real British School, and they should try always to show the best qualities of the race to which they belong.

It was the first of many inspiring speeches from a succession of generals, bishops and titled worthies, exhorting pupils to stand tall and do their best for Britain. After a difficult first year, the ethos of the school was already emerging: discipline and obedience, effort and teamwork, loyalty to King, Empire and School. Not so different from Eton itself. Sir William Pulteney reported that the children 'were receiving an English education, and . . . were being brought up as British citizens, to the intense relief of their parents'.

In May 1931 the 'Eton Memorial School, Ypres' underwent a Board of Education inspection. The inspector spent three days in the school and made a detailed report identifying problems and recommending improvements. Some problems were purely practical: a fire risk in the temporary classroom over the garage; desks and toilet seats unsuitable for the smallest children. Others were more fundamental: were the older children being prepared for their working lives – most likely back in Britain – after they left at fourteen? And was enough being done for the brightest? The results of a standard intelligence test given to every pupil over ten 'amply bore out the impression, gained from the response shown in the various classes during the visit, that the School contains a number of very bright children'.

The report is thorough and constructive, crediting the Morrises with having overcome early difficulties: 'They have created an atmosphere of refinement and inculcated habits of industry; they have established friendly relations with the children and obtained the goodwill of the parents; and they have secured . . . marked progress . . . particularly in reading, writing and speaking English.'

The inspector took the trouble to talk to parents and the report reveals a range of aspirations for their offspring: 'Some would like technical training for their boys; for their girls they appeared to have in mind occupations such as . . . a trained nurse, a stewardess, office worker and even a teacher.' These aspirations could only be met if the brightest children were transferred to schools in the UK to complete their education, and if the curriculum for older pupils had a more vocational bias, including 'domestic work and commercial training'. In the following years these and many other recommendations – naps for the infants after lunch, a hot meal for children unable to go home at lunchtime, teaching metric as well as Imperial measures, 'more pictures, illustrations, photographs etc. (particularly of things British)' – were successfully implemented by the Morrises and their successors.

Another striking suggestion, appearing almost as an afterthought under 'Some miscellaneous points', would have a marked impact on the school's reputation in the British colony and on the children's memories in the years to come:

> It might perhaps be found practicable to include in the regular school routine, in addition to concerts, prize-givings and 'open days', the holding of celebrations of anniversaries such as Empire Day and other occasions for corporate and collective activity . . . [to deepen] the significance of the school for both children and parents. They would constitute a real contribution towards the valuable work the school is performing as a centre of British culture and British traditions.

Meanwhile, friendships were forged. The intimate scale of the school allowed children to make friends with others of different ages, and for family groups to stay in close contact so that brothers and sisters could protect younger siblings from bullying and playground mayhem. British families often lived in the same streets so it was natural for 'the big girls' to escort the younger ones: Mariejeanne, the oldest of the Fox girls, called on the Wilkins a few doors down the Chaussée de Bruges to take Lillian to school in her first year.

Elaine Madden was a couple of years younger than her best friends Rene Fletcher and Dorothy Charlton, but that never seemed to make any difference. Elaine and Dorothy, who both had difficult home lives, looked on the Memorial School as something of a refuge and did well there. For Elaine, a bright but lonely child, it provided the friendship, affection and stimulus she craved. Her mother's death had cruelly disrupted the life she'd known in Ypres. Still in deep mourning, she was sent to live with her grandparents in Poperinghe. They took her away from the Memorial School and put her in a boarding convent where she had to wear thick black stockings and a tunic that came down to her ankles. Grief and bewilderment soon turned to rage. 'I think when you lose somebody that you love . . . I mean I was only ten years old, you can't quite realise what death is. You think you've been abandoned. So you really do get mad. I got madder and madder . . .'

Elaine had only been at the convent a few weeks when she took a pair of scissors and cut her hated uniform off at the knees and her black stockings at the ankles, an act of such shocking perversity that her grandparents were told to come and remove her at once. If this was calculated to get her back to her old friends at the Memorial School, it worked. Her best friend Rene was delighted to welcome her back, although she cut a pathetic figure:

Poor little Elaine. I can see her now, this little tiny girl, covered in black. Black all over her face. Dreadful to dress a child like that. But she was always a vivacious little girl and of course when she came back to school it was all bravado: 'Oh, I'm all right', and her arms going like mad, like windmills, and she didn't cry, but I bet she did a lot of crying on the quiet. She was that type of girl.

School was Elaine's solace; she worked hard and did well. The teachers were kind and did their best to help her. Best of all, she looked forward to going to Rene's house:

I loved Rene. They had a lovely home and she used to invite me very often after school to go and have tea or do my home-work with her. Living in a hotel you don't have any kind of private life, everything was for the customers . . . Rene had a brother and she had a sister and she had parents. They had a lovely house, with a lounge and a dining room and a kitchen. Everything I never had. Rene provided the whole life that I thought was the ideal. It felt homely, loving. Her parents were nice and she was one of the sweetest, nicest girls in the school.

As they got older, friendships between boys and girls inevitably took on a different character. Elaine, an attractive girl with a maturity beyond her years, was admired by the girls and fancied by the boys. George Simpson, like many of her male contemporaries, remembers her as 'a cracker' and another contemporary, John Osborne, looks back wistfully: 'You always notice someone who's different to the others. She was very attractive and self-assured. I wanted to get to know her, but I was too shy.' Even younger children recognised that she was different. For Betty Parker she was 'much more grown-up than the others. I was in awe of her. She was a lovely looking girl.' Elaine had many admirers but her heart was reserved for Billy Crouch:

> I was in love with him, or at least I thought I was. He was rich, his father owned a factory in Courtrai and they were moneyed people. We used to play tennis in the school and he was the only one wandering around with three racquets! I remember one day he said: 'Meet me behind the cathedral after school and if you kiss me, I'll give you one of my racquets.' I was so scared that if he kissed me I might have a baby, so I never went. But we did kiss later . . .

George Simpson was a friend of Billy's, with assignations of his own.

> Billy Crouch was very sweet on Elaine. His father had a textile factory that made the material for the poppies. They used to try and bribe her to go behind the buttresses of the Cathedral for a snog. I remember when I was about fourteen, having a little snog with Georgette Piper round the back of St George's Church, because Harry Godden [the caretaker] came up; he must have guessed what was going on and he gave me such a whack round the ear!

Harry and Kathleen Morris finished their four-year baptism of fire in March 1933 and returned to London. As Sir William Pulteney, Secretary to the school Trustees, wrote: 'No two people could have faced the uphill work ahead of them with more courage'. They were pioneers in this small experimental school in a foreign country. They fought the early battles necessary for future success, establishing a sound if rudimentary curriculum, a British ethos, and English as the medium for learning. As the Bishop of London reminded the children in his 1933 address. 'The objects of the School were to teach them the "Three Rs" and to inculcate in their minds a love for England – the country to which they belonged.'

In this, the Morrises had succeeded admirably. Sir William Pulteney must have been well pleased. His co-creator of the British Settlement, Lord Plumer, had died in July 1932, leaving him to carry the banner for the British in Ypres. At the Morrises' last prize-giving, the faithful *Ypres Times* reported:

> Of all those present Sir William Pulteney looked the happiest. He smiled with delight and justifiable satisfaction as the proceedings developed. There is no exaggeration in stating that, but for his tireless energies and almost illimitable influence, there would be to-day no Ypres League, no British Settlement at Ypres and, consequently, no British School there.

For their part, the earliest pupils remember their initial struggle to master the English language, the sometimes harsh discipline, and the unfamiliar Britishness of it all.

By the time the new headmaster, William Allen, arrived with his wife Florence and their young daughter Barbara, the school's ethos was firmly established. Now Allen planned to build on that foundation with his own brand of consolidation and innovation. As he saw it, his job was to raise standards and reinforce the school's image of itself and in the wider community: the British Memorial School would be an institution for pupils, parents and the town of Ypres to be proud of.

When the Allens took over in the summer term of 1933, there were 112 pupils, representing the children of men who had fought in thirty-eight different regiments, corps or services in the Great War, including the Australian Imperial Force and the Canadian Royal Highlanders. Of the total roll, ninety-six children had fathers employed by the Imperial War Graves Commission. Allen, a navy man and active British Legion member, recognised at once the school's unique character and potential: he would make it a showpiece.

He immediately set about making changes modelled on public-school traditions that would improve academic standards, encourage competitive teamwork and engender a sense of pride in his pupils. He introduced a uniform and a two-house system – Plumer (green) and Pulteney (yellow) – to compete at the end of each year for a cup donated by Dowager Lady Plumer. He awarded red buttons every week for achievement and cajoled British public schools and commercial firms into donating end-of-year prizes. Prep sessions and Saturday-morning classes for exam entrants were added to the timetable. School Elders (prefects) and a School Captain were appointed from the top class. A photograph from 1936 shows a serious-looking Jerry Eaton as School Captain, seated beside Allen. Among the six Elders standing behind them are Elaine Madden and Billy Crouch.

Performance and ritual soon became a regular part of school life: 'The Pilgrims' Hall on Friday afternoon', Allen wrote, 'is the venue of enthusiastic youngsters agog with an excitement which finds its vent in a roar of cheers when the victorious House receives its star'. Florence Allen produced dozens of plays and concerts (with costumes created by Lillian Wilkins' mother and her Thursday sewing circle), revealing at times '. . . a quite unexpected display of histrionic talent by some of the older children'. These extracurricular activities took a lot of effort by the teachers and parents but, as Allen observed, they 'give immense pleasure to children and adults of the colony and well repay the hours of rehearsal and extra sewing'. His wife taught the children traditional folk dances and 'probably for the first time in this ancient town' May Day was celebrated in the traditional English manner, with a May Queen elected by ballot and dancing round the maypole, much to the bemusement of Belgian neighbours watching the proceedings from their first-floor windows.

Rene Fletcher was one of the first May Queens and her friend Dorothy can remember exactly what she wore: 'Her mother made her the most beautiful white dress and it had tiers and tiers of lace. She made a beautiful May Queen.' The summer months were particularly busy. May 24 was Empire Day and, as the school inspectors had suggested, a celebratory display of patriotic songs, drill and a salute to the Union flag was the perfect way to bring school, colony and community together. Rene, also an impressive Britannia in the Empire Day celebrations of 1934, recalls: 'We were taught to be proud of Britain. Empire Day was a big thing. They had all the songs, you know, "Land of Hope and Glory", "Jerusalem", and dancing that we were taught by Mrs Allen – a Scottish reel and an Irish jig.'

This was always a memorable occasion for John Gabriel. 'You were all assembled in the playground and the Union Jack would go up and we'd all be standing up straight, and someone would be picked out, perhaps the School Captain or somebody, and he'd come up and salute the flag. And we'd sing patriotic songs like "I Vow to Thee My Country". So we felt very British. Absolutely.'

For Lilly Boucher, one of the six children of the Commission nurseryman William Boucher, it is among the most poignant memories of her schooldays. 'On Empire Day we used to go outside and sing. The Belgian people used to watch out of their windows. The first song was always "Land of Hope and Glory". Father and Mother were there and I will never forget as long as I live, we were singing "Land of Hope and Glory" and great tears were coming down my father's face. I can see it now.'

Whether they were British tourists or VIPs, a steady stream of visitors were encouraged to inspect the school. Leopold III of the Belgians – an Old Etonian – was among the first when he came to Ypres in July 1934, soon after becoming King, to inaugurate the carillon in the Cloth Hall belfry. He was welcomed by fellow Etonian Sir William Pulteney and presented with a bouquet by Barbara Allen, the headmaster's daughter. Then 'the children, assembled in the playground, gave His Majesty three truly British cheers, on his departure for the Menin Gate'. Jerry Eaton was in the inspection line; his abiding memory is of the King's army uniform – and his freckles. A succession of Lords and Ladies, Honourables, colonels and lesser mortals followed, all no doubt thoroughly approving of what they saw.

Allen demanded high standards and is remembered for being strict. He too used the cane – and the threat of it – on both boys and girls. Uniform had to be worn correctly: gymslips and white shantung blouses for the girls, grey trousers, green jerseys trimmed with yellow and a cap badge with the letters BMS for the boys. It was a distinctive outfit that marked them out in the town and so required good behaviour outside the school gates. Boys were expected to raise their caps to adult friends and neighbours, British or Belgian. Around the town the Memorial School children were known as 'Jampotten' by the

Belgian children; they don't know why, their school caps weren't red. Perhaps it was based on a presumed love of bread and jam. They would chant 'Jampotten! Bully Beef!' when the children went by, so it probably went back, as all things in Ypres did, to 1914–18. In retaliation, the tea-drinking British responded: 'Koffeepotten!'

John Parminter's Belgian wife, Nenette, first met him when they were children in Ypres: 'The Belgians used to tease him because they wore this uniform with the funny little caps, which boys in Belgium didn't wear, so we thought it was very, very funny.'

Lillian Wilkins' mother, a professional dressmaker, helped Rene Fletcher's mother make blouses for the girls. Lillian wouldn't dare go to school without the right kit. 'Mr and Mrs Allen were very, very strict. You couldn't go to school with brown stockings on or black stockings with brown shoes because your school shoes were at the mender's . . . Oh, no way! And if whatever I had was different, Mother used to have to send a letter with me. The Allens were very, very strict and very, very nice.' Allen particularly impressed the boys, and is remembered as 'a brilliant teacher'. Jerry Eaton agrees. 'Mr Allen was a man who knew precisely what he wanted and he was a very good disciplinarian and a very good teacher. He did most of the teaching to the upper class and taught us everything. He helped me a lot.'

George Simpson, who received a glowing testimonial from Allen when he left the school in 1936, believes: '. . . he did a pretty marvellous job . . . the curriculum was fantastic – arithmetic and algebra, history and geography. In history you learned your dates, Kings and Queens. Geography was mostly about the Empire. After all, when you looked at it, there wasn't much left on the map after the red bits had been filled in.'

Picking up the inspector's recommendations, Allen soon expanded the curriculum for older children, adding chemistry, cookery and vocational subjects: elementary book-keeping, typing and Pitman's shorthand. He also introduced swimming and tennis in the summer and cross-country runs on Saturday mornings in winter, though '. . . whether for the exercise or the refreshments of which we all partook on our return, the children possibly could provide the answer. If they did nothing else, they helped to augment the friendship between the staff and pupils.'

Extracurricular activities flourished. There was an allotment for the children to learn how to grow vegetables, with competitions for the best runner beans. Letters were exchanged with pen pals in the English-speaking Dominions. The school 'adopted' a tramp steamer as part of an LCC scheme and even organised a trip to Antwerp to meet it, but the SS *Hartismere* had to embark unexpectedly, so they went to the zoo instead. 'An excellent wireless set', paid for by funds raised locally and in Britain, relayed live to the classroom events such as the proclamation of the accession of the new King Edward VIII, as well as BBC broadcasts for schools. Like the British fathers in Belgium, Allen noted in his 1936 Annual Report that 'we regard our set as a link with Home'.

Though he didn't shrink from using the cane, Allen preferred the power of reward and incentive ('The sun shone, the end of term was in sight, and the Cup stood, a glistening urge to all competitors to pull their weight'). Prize-givings during his tenure grew in length and importance, and photos from the period show tables overloaded with bounty. The *Ypres Times*' regular correspondent, Henry Benson MA, observed in 1935: 'I know of no other school which, in proportion to its size, presents so many awards for merit – all of them well worth winning, and some of intrinsic value . . . I venture to hazard that, if a show of hands had been demanded at the conclusion of the proceedings, the "haves" would have outnumbered the "have nots" '. The prizes were sponsored by individuals (Captain Peabody for Progress and Mrs L. K. Briggs of Broadstairs for Ordinary School Work), regiments (the Third Army Corps Prizes), public schools (the Cheltenham College Essay Prize and the Eton Prize for Mathematics) and commercial companies (tennis racquets from Slazenger, pens from the Waterman Pen Company and books from the publisher John Murray).

Many are still treasured possessions. Rene Fletcher wasn't academic but she did win prizes: 'I was never very bright, but I used to get high marks for my writing and for neatness, you know, silly things. But on prize day in my very last year at school I walked off with five prizes and I was thrilled about that. The first prize was for sewing – I'd made a dress – and I've still got the prize.' She also still has the photograph of her fifteen-year-old self with Mr Allen, wearing the dress she made ('She was *the* girl!' says Dorothy Charlton, 'teacher's favourite'). Rene, now ninety, still has the slim leather box containing an ornately tooled manicure set of Sheffield steel. In the lid is a black-edged visiting card that reads: *Ypres British Memorial School. Presented to Irene Fletcher for Needlework. July 1935. With every good wish from Dowager Viscountess Plumer.* Though individual pieces have been well used and the buttonhook is broken, the set – and everything it represents – still means a great deal to her.

Rene's manicure set is not the only British Memorial School prize to have survived and given good service over the years. At the same prize-giving, her friend Dorothy won the Cheltenham College prize for an essay on *The Tempest* – a complete works of Shakespeare:

> My father said we could each take something when we left [Belgium], and I chose my Shakespeare. It was the one thing that I had with me all the time, trekking through . . . wherever I went. I didn't have clean knickers but I had my Shakespeare. I left it with my Commander when I was in the Air Force and transferred . . . it was taken care of and returned to me at the end of the war. And whenever I have a problem, I can open my Shakespeare and it tells me what I want to know. It's like a Bible to me.

Though there were a number of very bright children at the school, the girls weren't encouraged to aspire to higher education or careers in the professions. It would have been unusual if they had; this was, after all, only an elementary school and expectations of girls were generally low at that time. One or two were obviously academic and won scholarships to schools in the UK, but the rest went into domestic service, dressmaking, hairdressing or office work. The Hon. Mrs H. Adeane, a member of the governing committee, is frequently credited in annual reports for her 'very deep interest' in finding the girls employment. Judging by the number who ended up in service, it's possible that she acted as one-woman domestic staff agency on behalf of her titled friends in England.

'Housecraft' was certainly on the curriculum. Betty Fox recalls having to go to the headteacher's home to 'do the dusting and learn domestic service'. Even then she realised 'we were being used, getting you ready for service, that's what it was'. Betty, always interested in food, found her true vocation as a cook.

Dorothy Charlton had higher aspirations, but her ambitions soon came to a crashing halt. 'When I left the Memorial School I wanted to be a nurse, and I could get to be a nurse by coming to England. So I went to a Catholic training school in Letchworth. I lasted less than a year – my mother had me back. Too much freedom in England! After that I just sat at home and embroidered.' But it wasn't all for nothing. Danny Quinn, neighbour and friend of the Charltons in Poelkapelle, remembers that when Dorothy got back, she taught the young people in the village the latest British dance craze, 'The Lambeth Walk'.

Given its origins, the school was always keen to encourage its brightest boys to join the armed forces. By the mid-1930s, with increasing anxiety about German rearmament, there seemed even more reason to prepare pupils for the possibility of another war. In 1936 Allen started a signalling class, 'for boys wishing to enter some branch of His Majesty's Forces'. Here they learned semaphore and Morse, and outside experts were brought in to help. Bob Simmons' father, who had started the first radio shop in Ypres, was one of them:

My father gave us lectures on radio and electricity. He was a very good teacher actually . . . the principles of magnetism, radio and electricity and also, being a ham, he knew Morse. Mr Allen was in the Navy in the First World War and he thought it was important for us to know Morse and semaphore, so my father taught Morse.

During Allen's tenure, three boys went on to the Army Apprentices School in Chepstow, one joined the RAF as a Boy Entrant and George Simpson – unfairly caned for missing a day's school – joined the Army and spent much of his career as a professional soldier, rising to the rank of Major. Donald Eaton joined the Navy as a Signaller (so those semaphore and Morse lessons didn't go amiss) but his brother Jerry had other ambitions. He wanted to fly.

> I always wanted to join the RAF. I used to cycle to French air-fields in the early 'thirties to watch the old flying machines, so I was always very interested. Then the final decision came in 1935 during the Armistice celebrations in Ypres. That year for the first time the RAF sent a detachment. So there they were, marching in their smart blue uniforms and I thought, this is for me!

Allen researched the available options for him: he could join as a Boy Entrant or take an Aircraft Apprenticeship. Jerry was a bright lad and Allen recommended the latter option.

> He arranged for me to sit the entrance exam and got me properly supervised and I took this exam and my father eventually got a letter to say that I was 290-something out of the 1,016 who'd sat it. So I joined the RAF at the start of 1937 and went to Halton Technical Training School. Within a few months I got my first taste of flying in an old biplane, and that was it, I was hooked. But Mr Allen helped me get there.

'After four years' hard work and devoted service' the Allens returned to London in March 1937. There's no doubt that William Allen achieved his goal of making the British Memorial School something of a showpiece. He gave pupils individual help and encouragement and made them all proud of their school and their country. But there are stories other than those told in the self-important annual reports and florid eulogies of the school's many qualities in the *Ypres Times*. William Allen had favourites, especially among the girls; he had 'a roving eye'; his wife was 'horribly jealous of the girls' and was 'an aggressive woman'. Florence Allen, it was said, 'loathed Belgium' and couldn't wait to get back to England. Tittle-tattle perhaps, but the strains of expatriate life were never far from the surface and observant children took notice.

Perhaps the attractions of Ypres had palled for the Allens by 1937. Certainly the headmaster's final report, reprising his many innovations and the school's achievements since his arrival, is terse and presented in the form of a list. He ends the report starkly: 'I think that is all.' If there was a farewell reception and parting gift there is no surviving account of it. The Allens' much-loved assistant, Miss Summers ('a charming, talented and very industrious lady', in the opinion of the *Ypres Times*, who, 'having exploited no eccentric methods . . . leaves behind a record of splendid educational achievement'), certainly got a fulsome send-off and a silver-backed hairbrush for her efforts.

The Allens were succeeded by a 29-year-old Welshman, John Clifford Yorath, and his wife Victoria. Bringing 'the full energy and enthusiasm of youth', the Yoraths' arrival heralded 'a new wave of progress', wrote the *Ypres Times* on an uncharacteristically forward-looking note.

The Yoraths' first challenge was a pleasant one: to organise the colony's celebrations for the Coronation of King George VI and Queen Elizabeth in May 1937. Judged 'an outstanding success' by the *Ypres Times* (by no means an objective observer in such matters), these were attended by 'practically the whole British Community around Ypres, some coming from as far afield as Mons'. The newcomers mounted an impressive programme including a Parade of Shields and a pageant of Kings and Queens of England, 'King Charles II and Henry VIII receiving prolonged applause'.

The only surviving photo of the occasion shows a line of splendidly costumed young monarchs in the school playground, with Elizabeth I and Henry VIII particularly impressive in their padding, flounces and ruffs. Celebrations continued into the afternoon with a 'grand sports meeting', followed by a tea for the children. Then the youngsters 'were shepherded home, tired but happy', carrying their commemorative mugs. Some time later, the new King and Queen sent signed photographs which took their place alongside the dress uniforms in the Pilgrims' Hall.

The life of the school appeared to carry on much as before under the new headmaster. John Osborne is among many who remember Yorath's red hair and precise pronunciation; he was 'a marvellous headteacher', strict but fair, and a star of the colony's cricket team.

He introduced the Union flag to the boys' cap badge – a move much approved of by Henry Benson in the *Ypres Times* – but otherwise it seems that standards on the uniform front had slipped from those upheld so rigorously by Mr and Mrs Allen. By 1938 the school photograph shows few girls in regulation blouses and gymslips and a variety of outfits among the boys.

Discipline, too, may have taken a tumble. Bored during the holidays, a group of older boys – Bob Simmons among them – embarked on a jape that could have ended in disaster. 'We climbed over the gate and somehow broke into the school. We got in and rummaged around a bit, opening a locker and stealing some biscuits. We played with some chemicals and tried to make chlorine gas and that's how the fire started . . . Anyway, the school grass shopped us to Mr Yorath.' After nearly fifty years, Bob refuses to name the informer.

> Yorath had us up before the whole school and offered us a choice between a public caning or forgoing the annual picnic trip. We all chose the caning. Mr Yorath was a self-professed psychologist. Before the punishment he told us a story of how he'd dealt with a gang of tearaways in the East End of London. He told us how he began caning and kept on until they began to show signs of cracking and then gave them six more for good measure! He reduced us, not to jellies, but to quite a psychologically frightened state.

In the end they only got three strokes of the cane and they went on the picnic, an annual treat at a local château fondly remembered by many of the children.

Some things didn't change: children were still arriving unable to speak English (seven from an intake of seventeen at the start of the 1937 school year) and the roll fluctuated as IWGC men were moved in and out of the Ypres area. None the less, pupils were still travelling in from considerable distances – some from as far away as Harelbeke, nearly forty kilometres from Ypres.

Stephen Grady was thirteen when he started at the Memorial School in the summer term of 1938. His family lived in the small French town of Nieppe, where his father was an IWGC head

gardener in the local cemeteries, so Stephen cycled the forty-kilo-
metre round-trip to the school every day.

This promising new pupil had had a chequered education. After
going to local French schools, he was sent to England in 1937 to stay
with his paternal grandmother in Ramsgate so that he could improve
his English at school there. But his grandmother was already in her
seventies ('she probably didn't want the responsibility of having a
little twit like me around') and money was tight. After two terms he
was brought back to Nieppe and sent to the Memorial School where
lessons were all in English and there were no fees for the children of
Commission employees.

Stephen soon made friends. John Osborne lived in the nearby village of Ploegsteert and their two fathers knew each other well from
work. John would often visit the Grady house for tea. Even then,
John recalls, Stephen stood out from the crowd: 'Stephen was an odd
sort of person, different from the others. He was more mature than
the rest; you knew you could rely on him. He was a bright boy. I've
always admired him: he must have been a very, very astute and brave
young person.' The family's distance from Ypres, their mother's
blindness – and devout Catholicism – and their father's reserve all
meant that the Grady children were outsiders in their own group, yet
Stephen still felt fiercely British. He was a French national, but there
was no doubt about where, as a boy and then as a young man, his
allegiance lay: 'I was hyper-patriotic. I think it was because I was
brought up in France. I felt I was different. I was British. The British
to me were God.'

Stephen's Memorial School photo shows a handsome lad with a
twinkle in his eye. Though he was only at the school for four terms,
he would turn out to be one of its most distinguished former pupils.

Betty Fox, the girl who so much resented doing her teachers' dusting, sums up what many later expressed about their time at the British
Memorial School: 'We did feel special. I still feel proud that we went
to that school. We'd never been to England in our lives, didn't have
a clue what it was like, but we were very proud to be British. Our
fathers were just gardeners, weren't they? But we were privileged to
go to the British School.'

6

Danger

No one knows what will happen in Belgium but where almost 250 women and children are concerned, can we afford to take risks? We know there is distinct danger . . .

Captain Reginald Haworth, Deputy Controller, Ypres,
to IWGC Headquarters, February 1940

SOON AFTER ITS tenth anniversary in May 1939 the Memorial School had a visit from the Imperial War Graves Commission's Education Adviser. He found 'a cheerful atmosphere throughout and the pupils look well and happy'. Life outside the school, though, had been less than happy for some time; in the decade since it opened in 1929, Ypres – and Europe – had become a different and more dangerous place.

As Hitler's Germany grew in confidence and ambition after 1933, nationalist and fascist groups in Flanders started to emerge, exploiting the historic discord between Flemish-speaking (and partly pro-German) West Flanders and French-speaking Wallonia. They were mostly splinter groups from the conservative Belgian Catholic Party and had different agendas; they weren't all overtly fascist, at least not at first. But they were all right-wing and extreme and therefore useful to Hitler in undermining Belgian political unity and stability, a vital prelude to invasion. They were also prime suspects for creating the army of 'fifth columnists' – Nazi infiltrators posing as locals – that spread fear and rumour so effectively among the civilian population in the early days of May 1940.

But for now they held noisy meetings, rallies and marches, wore uniforms of black or brown shirts, openly displayed swastikas and ran youth sections. The British children in Ypres were warned to move away quickly when they came across them in the streets. Despite the legacy of comradeship from 1914–18, the tide seemed to be turning. John Osborne 'could feel a kind of undercurrent of anti-British feeling from about 1936 from the Flemish side'. In 1939 Georgette Hoyles and her IWGC gardener father were at a concert in a hall in Ypres used by a Flemish extremist group; here 'the Belgian audience got up and started singing "Wir sind Deutsch". My father stood up and said we had to leave . . .'

The main movements were the separatist VNV – Vlaams Nationaal Verbond, the Flemish National League – and the fascist Verdinaso, but perhaps the most high-profile group were the so-called Rexists. Elaine Madden was thirteen or fourteen when they came to her grandparents' hotel in Poperinghe.

> Later, in '36, '37, there was this big Rex movement. There was a big meeting in Poperinghe and they used our cinema hall and I remember this Rex man – he was doing all these Sieg Heil movements when he was speaking. He was famous. I know I was quite excited that he was coming – not only to Poperinghe but to my grandparents' hotel and using the cinema. I went to see him because his name was so well known but I don't really remember listening to what he said. My grandparents certainly weren't Rex supporters, my grandfather was a liberal.

The 'famous Rex man' was its charismatic leader, Léon Degrelle. Frustrated with the moderation of Belgian Catholicism, he had founded Christus Rex, a small Catholic publishing house. This soon transmogrified into a political party, 'Les Rexistes', winning a significant number of seats in the 1936 Belgian election. Increasingly pro-Nazi, Degrelle collaborated with the Germans, fought for them on the Eastern Front and was eventually awarded the Iron Cross. Hitler is said to have told him: 'If I had a son, I would have wanted him to be like you.' Escaping a death sentence in Belgium after the war, Degrelle was given sanctuary in Franco's Spain, and died an unrepentant old man in exile.

Other British children remember meetings in Ypres where there was an increasing pro-fascist presence. Sidney Harper recalls:

> In the hall where we had our Christmas parties, there were these big meetings. The gendarmes used to cut the road off top and bottom so no one could get in or out. They were the Blackshirts, old Hitler's lot, in '37, '38. A lot of Belgians in Ypres were pro-German. There was bad feeling between where we lived and Brussels – they were all French-speaking there.

The Menin Gate was a particular focus for tension. Yvonne Lane's family lived directly opposite the Gate on the town side and she remembers seeing 'a crowd of Hitler Youth, about twenty or thirty of them, but I give them their due, they stood to attention and were very respectful'. But others, like Sidney Harper, recall tenser encounters:

> It was quite crowded, and there was a group of about five Germans near me. After the Last Post was sounded they all gave the Hitler salute. There were some Scots with their kilts. They went straight up to them and ordered them out of the Menin Gate. The police got involved and everything.

Bob Simmons had a similar experience.

> My brother and I joined the Belgian Scouts. At the end of every fortnightly meeting the scout troop used to go to the Menin Gate for the sounding of the Last Post. I remember the Scout Jamboree in 1937 and the German Scouts were already appearing in brown shirts and swastikas. And there was a sort of, not a confrontation but a bit of a stand-off, because they were strutting around with an arrogant air, and we didn't like it very much. Only my brother and I were English in the Scout troop and, though the Belgians were equally concerned, I don't think we could have counted on their support if we'd created an international incident . . .

Bob and other children whose families had radios were very much aware of the build-up to war. Those who spoke Flemish could also understand German:

We all listened to Hitler's radio broadcasts with increasing concern . . . and I particularly followed the articles in the *Daily Mirror* by Cassandra. At the Munich crisis when Chamberlain met Hitler about Czechoslovakia, the Belgian army was pretty well wholly mobilised – even the horses were called up for military service. The stations were full of men saying goodbye to their families. Slit trenches were dug at the town's border and manned by machine guns. Important public buildings were sandbagged. So there was a general air that war was inevitable.

Belgium, squeezed between a resurgent Germany and its Great War allies France and Britain, was small and vulnerable. Though the British colony could not have been unaware of the danger, few decided to leave for the UK. Some, like Dorothy Charlton's father, thought it would 'all blow over'. Many had faith in the defensive strength of the Maginot Line and the Albert Canal, or in the idea that the sluices could be opened to flood low-lying Flanders and prevent invasion from the east. Even Robert Rolfe's father Howard, who had warned anyone who would listen that the Germans 'were buying up everything, pigs, horses, everything' in preparation for war, didn't move his large family out of Ypres. It was, after all, where they had built a life from the ruins of war over twenty years, with firm and often familial roots in the community. And for those who had lived through the horrors of 1914–18 – practically every adult in the colony – there must have been shock and disbelief that history could repeat itself within a generation. A strong element of wishful thinking that another war simply wouldn't be allowed to happen was as understandable as it was irrational.

At the same time, the IWGC took a robust line on the men's responsibilities. On 26 September 1938, at the height of the Munich crisis, Head Office issued a circular, 'Policy of the Commission in Case of War', to staff working in its cemeteries in France and Belgium:

> It is the intention of the Commission that the work shall continue with the least possible dislocation and all Gardener-Caretakers will continue to do their duty and to keep their

cemeteries up to the present high standard of maintenance unless actually ordered out of the area owing to its becoming a . . . Military Zone.

Wives and children could be got away 'on Gardener-Caretakers' own initiative', but the men were expected to stay at their posts until the last possible minute – and possibly even beyond that. That so few chose to send their families back to the UK in the months between September 1939 and May 1940 indicates how deeply rooted the colony was in Ypres, but it also demonstrates a widespread confidence that the Commission would act quickly to get them all out if things got really bad. If the community had been privy to what went on behind the scenes at the Commission over those months, that confidence would soon have evaporated.

Boys at the Memorial School, Bob Simmons among them, had their own way of dealing with the threat.

Perhaps this affected our psychological reaction to the world situation and this is when we formed the Tiger Club. We'd read all the books – Biggles and stuff – and we set ourselves up as a sort of Robin Hood gang. We recognised the existence of danger and challenge because we lived with the history of the First World War and our fathers were always going to memorials every year and singing 'God Save the King' and the 'Marseillaise' and all that.

I was eleven years old and we were quite brave . . . We created dangerous situations and then dared ourselves to face them. Things like jumping over canals that were just wide enough to be difficult, but you could slip and hurt yourself. Walking round the outside of the pillars of the Menin Gate – they're thick and they go right to the edge of this balcony with a thirty-foot drop on to concrete. That was quite a frightening thing to do and those of us who actually did it got a lot of kudos from the Tiger Club. And tightrope walking along bars at the end of bridges, climbing over rivers on precarious branches, climbing down the outer walls of the ramparts . . . There were one or two accidents. Each stunt had its merit rating and resulted in promotion and status within the gang. I once stole some bullets from a gun shop, and that made me an Officer of the club. One of our adventures was breaking into the school and starting a fire in the lab . . .

Though the Tiger Club had a shifting membership, its rules were strict and its structure hierarchical: boys' play acting out adult worries.

Bob's father was already involved in hush-hush work in anticipation of another war with Germany. Radio was his passion and his profession and he now spent increasing amounts of time at the British Embassy in Brussels, eventually closing down his radio shop in Ypres and moving the family there. Bob didn't ever find out what he was doing – officially he had a job in the Passport Office – but he put two and two together:

I think he was setting up the transmitters for possible underground communication during the expected war. I had to guess what he was doing. He was taking us to the coast and dumping us on the beach and disappearing for two or three hours . . . and he used to meet people in the house . . . they used to shut the doors and have long discussions. And he kept his amateur radio thing going . . .

The news everyone had dreaded finally came on Sunday 3 September. Many of the British families were at St George's Church for the morning service. Lillian Wilkins remembers them all trooping into the vicarage shortly after midday, crowding round the radio to listen to Prime Minister Chamberlain's declaration of war on Germany.

Betty Parker, then fourteen, was beside herself with worry. Her parents had taken her brother Wally to England at the end of the summer to settle him into his first job, with Crosse & Blackwell, leaving Betty in the care of a neighbour. 'I was terrified in case they couldn't get back. When they did come home, I was so pleased to see them, Dad said, "I haven't had a hug like that for years!"'

A week later, Captain Reginald Haworth of the IWGC in Wimereux, over the border in France, received a telegram instructing him to take up new responsibilities in Ypres without delay. He arrived the following day and moved into Skindles Hotel. This wasn't his first visit. 'Thanks to the Hun, I started the last war in 1915 in Ypres. In the event of another war, I imagine it must have been some millions of chances to one that I should start it in Ypres, but the one chance came off, and I was once more in the same town to start the Hitler war, in September 1939.'

In the tenth, and what was to be the last, report of the Ypres British School in October 1939, Clifford Yorath wrote: 'Since the outbreak of War we have started a new school year and we were surprised to have seventy children keen to restart'; this was only a slight drop from the average roll of ninety during the previous year. After consulting Sir Fabian Ware, Sir William Pulteney had made the decision to keep the school open 'as long as we possibly can'. Belgium was neutral, but the war around them had immediate effects: the French border was closed, preventing some children – Stephen Grady among them – from coming to school. Supplies routed through France were affected and alternative arrangements made via Brussels. But Pulteney was determined to look on the bright side, quoting a letter from Yorath: 'Since the school began the children seem to have been lifted out of their depression'.

Elsewhere in the report, it is very much business as usual, with 'splendid results in Woodwork and Weaving', news of Queen Elizabeth signing up as a new subscriber and the gift of a magnificent oak bookcase by George M. Lawrence of Sheffield. But war preparations were well in hand: at school the children made gas masks and at home fathers prepared cellars. Mothers meanwhile laid in food stocks and fretted: English wives worried about being able to get home and French and Belgian wives worried about having to leave.

The months of 'phoney war' leading up to Christmas gave heart to the optimists and bemused the realists. Some British families who had left Ypres when war was declared decided to come back. There was intense military activity and invasion rumours were rife around Armistice Day. The odd air-raid warning sounded. But these came to nothing and confidence was such that families who went to England for the Christmas holidays all returned in the New Year of 1940. The Christmas party for the colony went ahead as usual and skaters appeared on frozen floodwater along the road to Lille just as they had always done in the cold, wet Ypres winters.

Out of school-time, children like Sidney Harper found new amusements: 'A few of us used to cycle a little way to the French border and there were British soldiers on the bridge and we'd walk across and talk to them. We used to feel pretty important talking to those British soldiers . . .' The soldiers must have been surprised to be approached by local children with such impeccable English. But the Belgians' friendliness couldn't be taken for granted. A group of them crossed a frontier bridge for an off-duty drink and were duly interned. There were other ominous signs: sightings of German planes and stories of dogfights near the French border at Armentières; higher food prices and talk of rationing.

At the Memorial School, headteacher Clifford Yorath was making his own preparations. Yvonne Lane remembers one day in the spring: '. . . he came in and said, "Now I put you all – that's our class – on your best behaviour. I have to go out for a little while with Mrs Yorath." Later we found out that he'd gone to sort his passport out.'

Captain Haworth had been busy over the winter months in the Ypres office of the IWGC, making plans to evacuate the Commission's staff and their families in the event of a worsening situation. The order had come direct from Sir Fabian Ware at the end of September, but this wasn't quite as urgent as it sounded. The plan was 'precautionary' and 'hypothetical', only to be used in the event that the entire civilian population had to be evacuated – a remote and unprecedented possibility. Ypres was considered comparatively safe, to be used as a reception area for refugees from the 'forward' towns in the east close to the German border.

The plan was being led by Haworth's superior, Brigadier Mervyn Prower, head of the Central European District of the IWGC's operations based at Wimereux, along the French coast from Boulogne. Because it was only to be used in the event of a wholesale evacuation of Belgian populations into France, it was dependent on the French reception plan, which itself relied on moving very large numbers of people by train to Normandy and possibly thence further west to Brittany. In October 1939 Prower had met the French officials responsible in an attempt to make special provision for IWGC staff, but the best they could offer was to treat *les évacués britanniques* on equal terms with their own citizens when it came to transport, billets and rations. In a confidential memorandum of the meeting Prower concealed his personal doubts with a brisk pragmatism: 'Academic schemes devised in Offices and working from a map are easily drawn up but their execution (especially with an undisciplined civil population) is often a very different affair and always involves modifications which are very upsetting.'

Indeed, the possibilities for chaos and disaster were manifold. At the end of September Haworth had issued a set of 'Emergency Precautions' in the event of evacuation, instructing people to make an inventory of their household goods, lock up their houses and proceed to 'concentration points' at the school and at Talbot House in Poperinghe, with a blanket, gas mask, hand baggage and food for two days. After Prower's meeting, he drew up a more detailed plan based on the French scheme, assigning roles to various senior IWGC staff – and to the headteacher, Clifford Yorath. But Haworth was troubled. He and Prower didn't get on and now, as real danger threatened, he had little confidence in the French evacuation plan on which they depended, or in Prower's leadership.

Both men had served in the 1914–18 war: Haworth with the 6th Rifle Battalion in the Ypres Salient where he was commissioned as a Captain in 1916; Prower as a young officer with the 8th Canadian Infantry Battalion in the British Expeditionary Force in France where he fought at the Battle of Festubert – a long and bloody engagement with 16,000 casualties. Some weeks after the battle, in July 1915, Prower had written to his aunt:

I am pretty well all right but am scared of my nerves going, as I seem to be getting confoundedly jumpy. I suppose my 'blow up' at Festubert and having been buried by Johnsons five times since, is what is worrying me,

though why I cannot say, as it happens to most people. Still, if I get out
back to England for putting straw in the corner for the crocodile to sleep
on, don't be surprised.

He was obviously worried about his mental state and may already
have been suffering from shell shock: 'Johnsons' were particularly
unpleasant German shells that exploded with dense black smoke. The
Tommies named them after the black American boxer, Jack Johnson,
the world Heavyweight Champion at the time. The following month
Prower wrote to his aunt again, this time from the lunatic asylum at
Bailleul. He hastened to assure her that he hadn't 'been putting straw
in the corner for the crocodile to sleep on' but had walked the six
miles there from his trench to have a bath.

Whatever the original cause of the enmity between the two men,
it came to a head in the autumn of 1939. After a meeting in Wimereux
with Prower on 26 October to discuss the plan, Haworth wrote a
long and impassioned letter to Fabian Ware.

My dear General
I have now had time to give consideration to the scheme of
evacuation as formulated by Prower yesterday. I believe I registered
my disagreement in no uncertain fashion as it requires little
imagination to foresee the dangers, miseries and difficulties inherent in
this scheme . . . I am certain not one gardener will envisage that when
we get them and their families to France they will be handed over to
the French authorities to take pot luck with French and Belgian
refugees.
*   We are demanding that the men should stick to their posts to the*
point of danger. That means their wives and children are in the same
situation. They will say that having carried out their duty to the
Commission they have every reason to expect that the Commission
will have ready a suitable scheme for their evacuation. Prower's scheme
will certainly not strike them as suitable for employees of the
Commission . . . The Prower-Arnott scheme . . . has all the merits of
expediency and enables them to wash their hands of the whole business
. . .

The sensible procedure would be not a wholesale evacuation but a gradual evacuation of women and children, so that they would not be involved in any panic schemes when all arrangements go by the board . . .

These men have worked for the Commission for twenty years and they are now asked to carry on the work till the last minute. They are not asking very much of this Commission to ensure that their wives and children receive reasonable consideration . . .

My view is that if scheme A [the Prower plan] is adopted and goes wrong as it probably will, two people will receive the mud slinging: yourself as head of the Commission and myself as head of Belgium. As for myself, I can clearly see it will be quite useless to tell the men that France made all the arrangements or let us down. They will say: you in Belgium were in charge and led us to believe suitable arrangements had been made.

I need hardly state I am quite unfavourably impressed by the callous attitude of Prower whose interest in the welfare of the employees can be expressed in a nil *return except so far as getting the Wimereux personnel to Montreuil for reasons best known to God and himself . . . I just ask you one question, would Prower be prepared to put his wife and children on the Refugee train which will take two or three days to get to an unknown destination and to be billeted under the conditions of the refugees now in Montreuil?*

And so it went on, ending with a plea that Ware think again and allow special and immediate evacuation arrangements to be made for the women and children in Ypres. The letter was received with consternation. Ware wrote of it to a colleague: 'I find this incoherent in relation to the *facts* . . . Indeed it makes me very anxious. Is Haworth *practically* competent?' In another note he wrote: 'I am really afraid Haworth is losing his head again.'

He sent a handwritten reply, marked SECRET, the following day. Ware was as concerned for the welfare of Commission employees as Haworth, but he had to take the broader view. He was a natural collaborationist and didn't want to work against the French; he also wanted to avoid panic. Any attempt to make independent

arrangements would create 'cross-currents' at a time of mass movements of people and military traffic, annoying the French and unsettling the workforce, perhaps unnecessarily. After the recent evacuation
of large numbers of women and children from London, he doubted,
in any case, that such arrangements would work:

> Even if they suspended the rules against cross-currents in our favour,
> the risk would be enormous – personally, I think, to the point of
> certainty – of our plans collapsing. You probably do not realise, as
> those of us do who were in it, that almost identical regulations
> were made for the evacuation in England from London and other
> centres last month. Long tracts of main road e.g. the Great West
> Road and the Western Avenue were closed to all other than
> evacuation traffic.

Ware's message was unequivocal: 'You must therefore accept the
French scheme <u>without any further discussion</u>, and make the best of
it'. However, in an effort to be helpful, he did append a separate note
headed PERSONAL AND SECRET which suggested Haworth
should use as the basis for briefing gardeners verbally that they might
be advised to get their families away to England sooner rather than
later. He ended the letter with a plea of his own:

> One personal word to you. Do, I beg of you, realise that in this
> very serious hour for our country, all Englishmen, however much
> they may dislike one another personally, must all pull together and
> all private feuds must be sunk. The prejudice shown in your letter
> about Prower's attitude has really disturbed me. If you do get into a
> tight corner in the Belgian evacuation he will be the very first to try
> to help you. This is going to be a war of nerves and any such
> personal friction among ourselves is mere defeatism. I need say no
> more.

Ware then asked his Controller at Headquarters, Lieutenant
Colonel Oswald (who had been Haworth's commanding officer in
the 1914–18 war and the man responsible for getting him a job at the

Commission in 1920), to 'take this up energetically' and 'insist on no further argument from Haworth'. A terse exchange of telegrams followed:

HAWORTH WARGRAVES YPRES
CONFIRM THAT YOU ARE COMPLYING STRICTLY WITH
VICE-CHAIRMAN'S INSTRUCTIONS OF 28 OCTOBER STOP NO
FURTHER DISCUSSIONS PERMITTED STOP POST COPIES
YOUR REVISED SCHEME BELGIUM
OSWALD

INSTRUCTIONS BEING STRICTLY COMPLIED WITH REVISED
SCHEME WILL BE FORWARDED AS SOON AS PREPARED
HAWORTH

Haworth had no option but to obey orders. He buckled down, made lists of the potential evacuees, and issued a revised plan in early November. However, in internal correspondence he continued to point out at every opportunity where the scheme might fall down and concentrated his efforts on producing contingency plans. He was particularly concerned about procuring transport to get the likely 372 evacuees to the railhead at Ebblinghem. He had eight Commission vehicles to call on, but this wasn't nearly enough – he needed coaches as well. He was only too aware that, whatever arrangements might have been made in advance, at a time of crisis coaches – indeed, transport of any kind – would be hard to come by. Nevertheless, he made an application via the British Ambassador in Brussels, to requisition 'three autobuses' for the purpose from Mr P. D. Parminter. John Parminter's Uncle PD was still operating his tourist coach business – now from Ostend – with his buses garaged in Ypres.

With increased tension around Armistice Day, Haworth sent his wife back to England. After that, things calmed somewhat. Ware wrote to him in mid-November:

Things certainly look better at the moment but one never knows when they may change. The strain is very trying and will go on being so –

but that is War. Mind you take a bit of leave whenever you think it
safe to do so. An occasional rest is almost as necessary as sleep.

Later that month, Haworth replied that: 'Things here are quite
calm again. The work is going on steadily and well.' Learning that
the British Consulate in Brussels had arranged their own evacuation
plan for the British colony there to be taken to a Channel port and
then shipped home, he consulted Ware, who agreed that this might
be a good 'second string' to their plans.

Christmas 1939 must have been bleak for Haworth in the all-but
empty Skindles Hotel, despite 'a most excellent Christmas Dinner'.
He returned to the UK for a few days in the New Year, and the
opening weeks of 1940 passed uneventfully enough.

Life for Elaine Madden at her grandparents' hotel in Poperinghe
was becoming increasingly uncomfortable. She was by now sixteen
and only too painfully aware that she was there on sufferance. Her
young aunt Simone was her only friend and confidante among her
extended family. Her father's fortunes had slid further. He was
unemployed and drinking heavily. He had started an affair with his
housekeeper who had left, taking all his money. Larry Madden was
a gambler, an alcoholic, and now a bankrupt. He had tapped the
Duponselles for cash once too often so they paid him off to go to
England. He joined the Army and Elaine lost contact with him
altogether.

After leaving the Memorial School, she was glad to get away to
London in the autumn of 1939 to start at secretarial college. But her
freedom was short-lived. When she came back to Poperinghe for
Christmas, the rows started up again.

Uncle Charles was always quarrelling with my grandmother . . .
Every time I needed something it was the same old quarrel. It
was always about how much money I was costing them. Why
should they pay? If I wanted a college education, I could go out
and work for it.

I think I was full of pride and so mad and so angry all the

time, and I said: 'OK then, I won't go back to England. I'm not going back, so you won't have to pay any more! I'm going to leave here and go out to work!' And one thing I remember my Uncle said, which was the worst thing anyone could say to a young girl of sixteen, was: 'The only job you're capable of doing is becoming a whore. That's the only way. To lie on your back and become a whore!'

Oh, he was unpleasant! I promised that I would go and spit on his grave but unfortunately the bastard was buried next to my mother, so I wasn't able to. But such a horrible thing to say to a child. So I didn't go back to England until I had to.

At the end of January, Haworth made a list of those remaining in the colony and their evacuation preferences: forty-six families wanted to go to France; thirty-seven to the UK; six didn't intend to leave at all; and twenty had no preference. This still represented 288 people who had to be moved in the event of an evacuation. Meanwhile, the plan underwent variations and refinements: it was made clear that only women, children and the sick would be allowed to travel in coaches; able-bodied men were expected to walk or cycle. The Brussels alternative was rejected as impractical – the Commission couldn't run two parallel schemes.

Then, in February, there was a major spanner in the works. The British press reported that there would be no general evacuation of civilians in the event of a German invasion of Belgium: the Minister of Health had told the Belgian Chamber of Representatives that a large-scale evacuation was impossible given that all roads and transport would be reserved for military use. It would therefore be the duty of everyone to remain at home.

Haworth and the Commission now had to face the possibility that if push came to shove they would have to act alone – without official support and probably without transport. Staff were duly warned that, though the Commission would do everything in its power to help them and their families in the event of an invasion, it might come down to every man for himself.

★

Unaware of the fraught preparations being made – and remade – on their behalf, the families of the British colony carried on with their lives at home, at work and at school.

Back in Britain the 27 April 1940 edition of the popular pictorial magazine *Illustrated* carried a six-page feature, 'The Story of Wipers and What It Means to Britain Now'. The byline was that of Ian Hay, the pen name of John Hay Beith. Beith had been a soldier in France in 1915 where he was awarded the Military Cross. He became a successful writer, collaborating with P. G. Wodehouse on stage adaptations of both their work. When he wrote this piece, he also happened to be Director of Public Relations at the War Office.

The feature perfectly combines human interest and wartime propaganda, telling the stories of the British colony and its close ties with Belgium. And in looking back at the successes and sacrifices of the three Battles of Ypres between 1914 and 1918, it invites comparison with the war then gathering momentum: the stalwart British, the bond with Belgium, a joint defence against the forces of destruction and darkness.

The feature's evocative photographs were taken by a successful photojournalist of the time, James Jarche (incidentally, the grandfather of *Poirot* actor David Suchet and his newsreader brother John), who came to Ypres on 7 March to capture dozens of images of the town, the war cemeteries, and the British Memorial School. Only six of these made it into the magazine. Among them are two taken in Charlotte and Priestley Dunn's parents' 'typically British' home: one shows their mother, a Union Jack cushion at her side, reading a newspaper while her husband tunes the radio – presumably to the BBC. Another has them all round the kitchen table drinking tea. Charlotte and Priestley – both now married – appear in the photo with their Belgian spouses.

Thanks to Jarche, there are a number of surviving photographs of the British Memorial School at work, including one of a grave-looking Jimmy Fox playing with wooden bricks in Miss Ryder's infants' class, and a series of charming playground groups of the whole school. Only one of these actually appeared in the magazine, but it shows the essence of the place. It is of the top class at their desks in the Pilgrims' Hall, presided over by Mr Yorath. General Plumer's dress uniform, the signed photographs of the King and Queen, and the large picture of St George and the dragon are all there. In the front row desks are John Gabriel and Bob Simmons, heads down at their studies. It could be any school in England in 1940.

Two weeks after the *Illustrated* article appeared, the British Memorial School would close its doors for the last time and Hay's 'little bit of Britain in Ypres' would be placed in the gravest possible danger.

7

Exodus

It is quite useless to get excited. Remain calm under all circumstances.

Instructions to IWGC staff from Captain Reginald
Haworth, Deputy Controller, Ypres, 18 May 1940

INVASION, WHEN IT came, was swifter and more brutal than anyone expected. From first light on Friday, 10 May 1940, the Luftwaffe started bombing airfields and paratroopers knocked out strategic bridges. Panzer divisions moved in quickly behind them, breaching the Dutch and Belgian frontiers without opposition. It was a highly mobile and mechanised operation, attacking where and when the Allies least expected – the polar opposite of the ponderous trench-bound attrition that marked the Great War. This was to be the start of the Fall of France and, for the British Expeditionary Force, weeks of bitter fighting and terrible losses that culminated in the 'miracle of deliverance' at Dunkirk. In Britain, it was Churchill's first day as Prime Minister. For the British colony in Ypres, it was the beginning of the end.

Reginald Haworth was up early at Skindles Hotel.

Just before 7 a.m. on Friday 10 May I awoke and went along the passage to switch on the radio to hear the early news from the BBC. 'Good morning everybody' came the cheerful tones of the announcer, who at once gave the news of portentous gravity that Holland had been invaded in the early hours, and that this country and Belgium had at once appealed to the Allies for Assistance. So the worst had happened and Belgium, a country that has remained so steadfastly neutral, was now finally involved in the struggle for her existence. What would this soon mean for us all?

Commission gardener Lawrence Dawson also heard the news early.

I got up at the usual time to go to work, i.e. 6 a.m., and heard considerable noise in the street. I went to the door and discovered a line of vehicles drawn up in [the] charge of Belgian troops. Ventured to ask Belgian sergeant cause of trouble. Replied parachute troops had been dropped around Brussels. Belgium invaded, were waiting to move up line. As was my usual habit, went to station to get newspaper and found none available.

Over the next twenty-four hours events quickly gathered pace. Despite the scarcity of hard news and a fog of 'fantastic rumour', much of it spread by suspected fifth columnists, some things were plain to see: French and Belgian troops were on the move, there were now regular air-raid alerts, and refugees had started flooding into Ypres. Haworth noted that on 11 May, among the first refugees:

. . . were many youths on cycles each with a bag of belongings and a blanket, and we understood that they constituted the young class, many of them students, who had been sent back from the forward areas in front of Antwerp and Liège, to prevent them falling into German hands. But they included all classes, young workmen, clerks, and even young girls. As the day advanced they came in increasing numbers, and were later to be seen settling down on straw in the schools and in part of the Cloth Hall. They made a weird picture in the guttering candle-light.

They were followed by a more general exodus from the forward areas. John Gabriel, who lived opposite a large open space, remembers: 'Suddenly we were overwhelmed with refugees. The Plaine d'Amour was just absolutely full of people – they all seemed to have a red blanket. The school closed down and was taken over to feed and house the refugees.'

All those who could, and would, took in refugees, including the British families. Hotels soon filled up and those who couldn't find accommodation slept on pavements, in gardens and in the railway station. John Parminter's mother's Hôtel de la Gare was packed:

Then we had all the refugees from the other side of Belgium. They all thought that the pattern was going to be like the First World War – if you were far enough away, you would be safe – but as it was the lightning war – the Blitzkrieg – the Germans came very quickly. All the refugees were sleeping all over the place – in the cinema, between the seats. We had the hotel full of them. There was quite a bit of bombing, not all-out bombing but the back of a neighbour's house was completely demolished. And then one of the Quislings came round on his motorbike, saying it was wise to leave town because in revenge for the First World War the Germans were going to blow up the town. Lots of people fell for that and left, and the wise ones remained at home. The ones who left came back and found that their houses had been plundered by their neighbours while they were away.

There were worrying stories about German parachutists landing in back gardens with folding motorcycles; of German soldiers handing out poisoned cigarettes and chocolates; of queues miles long and twenty deep at the French border, and of refugee trains being dive-bombed and machine-gunned. With so many unfamiliar people pouring into the area, there was a widespread fear of spies and fifth columnists. The whole point of fifth columnists was that they were indistinguishable from the general population. In fact it was hard to tell if they even existed, but the very possibility spread fear, suspicion and distrust, just as it was meant to. Frightened people were convinced they were everywhere and looked for distinguishing signs. Elizabeth Boucher's mother was so fearful, she wouldn't give anyone refuge: 'She wouldn't let anyone in the house. Granny and Grandpa used to say, "You know when there's a fifth columnist in the house because he has a red blanket on his back." They'd stand up for the Germans, spying on us, you know, and then next minute we'd have a bomb on top of us.'

As well as refugees, columns of French Army lorries came through the town day and night and, in a grim echo of 1914–18, 'a considerable quantity of horse-drawn transport'. After a few days the British arrived. Sidney Harper was there to help out:

I can remember the BEF soldiers coming into Ypres in their convoys. My Dad clobbered me to go down the Menin Road because the English chaps didn't know any Flemish, so he spoke to them and said 'I'll get my son to help you, he speaks Flemish'. So I ended up going on the main road to Ypres, diverting traffic – they wanted the traffic diverted because all the refugees were coming the other way. I was in charge, wasn't I? A young kid of fourteen. I felt very important.

Things were tense in the Fox household as Betty, then nine, recalls:

We had to keep quiet as Father listened to the BBC news on our radio and my mother was often crying. One day I saw a lot of soldiers in lorries all coming along our road, the Chaussée de Bruges, and large groups of soldiers all walking very wearily and as they reached the front of our house they stopped and to my surprise they spoke English. Mother made pots of coffee and tea for them.

By Wednesday 15 May, Haworth was seriously worried. Ypres was under night-time curfew and there was an increasing threat of air raids. The news, such as it was, was bad. The Dutch had surrendered, Luxembourg was overrun and the Germans had breached the main Belgian defensive line at the Albert Canal. Brussels – little more than 100 kilometres away – looked vulnerable and the British colony there had already left. A Belgian Army division had just set up shop in Ypres town hall, a sure sign that it was in retreat. The previous day the Germans had broken through the French border in the Ardennes, and the Channel ports were starting to look vulnerable.

To make matters worse, communication links were either disrupted or commandeered by the military. All Haworth's efforts to contact Prower in Wimereux for permission to execute the evacuation plan had so far failed. In the absence of instructions from above, he acted on his own initiative, issuing 'Orders and Instructions' to staff: 'In view of the present situation, the Deputy Controller suggests that any man whose wife and children are with him should make up his mind <u>at once</u> whether to get his dependants to a place of safety till the situation is clearer.' It was still not an order to evacuate. Men getting their families away would be given up to five days' special leave to do so, but were expected to report back for duty afterwards. Haworth, like his seniors from Sir Fabian Ware downwards, was still anxious to prevent a wholesale rush to safety, leaving the cemeteries unmanned in the path of hostile invaders. Those in outlying areas who were unable to make arrangements themselves could send their families to Ypres, where 'every effort will be made to arrange transport for them'.

After issuing the order on the 15th, Haworth was besieged at his office by men applying for leave and wanting to know what the Commission was doing to arrange transport. The men weren't happy about the order to return to work; understandably, they didn't want to be separated from their families at such a critical time. But Haworth wasn't taking any nonsense. He reported 'noisy criticism of the Commission's arrangement by a sort of Soviet . . . Stifled this by an immediate appointment of a men's Committee. Told them they had been repeatedly warned to get their families away in time.'

It was true, they had been, and as long ago as 1 May 1939. But the decision was a difficult one, particularly for men with Belgian wives. Jack Fox was one of them. Betty, always inquisitive, was listening in:

I do remember that my parents were talking about a letter they'd received and by what I could gather, mothers and children under ten were being sent to England and the men were to stay behind for as long as it was safe . . . I remember hearing my mother saying, 'If we can't go all together, then we'll stay.' The implication of that conversation didn't strike me at the age of nine. I only remember being thankful that we were all going to stay together.

One of the men who had been following the deteriorating situation and had resolved to take up the offer was Lawrence Dawson. He wanted to get his Belgian wife, invalid mother-in-law and twelve-year-old daughter Joyce away to England. He left to escort them to Calais on Thursday the 16th on a fraught journey by train, taxi and on foot. Because of long queues at the border, they could only get as far as Poperinghe on the first night, where they were put up at Talbot House. Despite the surrounding mayhem of a town packed with refugees and the danger of air raids, Dawson couldn't resist a professional appraisal of the 'excellent conditions of gardens and grounds. One could see the caretaker took a pride in his work.'

There were others, too, anxious to leave as soon as possible. John Gabriel's father, through his sideline organising battlefield tours for his old regiment, had transport contacts:

We were in the fortunate position that my Dad knew this taxi driver. I can see him now, a little man dressed in his chauffeur's gear. He was a Greek, and he had this huge Packard taxi and my Dad somehow negotiated with him to take us to Ostend. And in that taxi was my Mum and I, and the three schoolteachers, Mr and Mrs Yorath and Miss Ryder. There was a bit of controversy about that, the fact that they didn't think he should have done that, he should have stayed . . . There was no question that any of the gardeners could leave, which was ridiculous; nothing could be done, the Panzer divisions moved so quick.

The Yoraths' early departure did indeed cause upset, not least to Haworth's carefully laid evacuation plan, but the headmaster was gone and there was nothing Haworth could do about it.

Howard Rolfe still had a wife and five children in Ypres, including one – eight-year-old Doris – with a broken leg in plaster. They needed to be got away. Lillian Wilkins' mother Lily was also desperate to get home to England. She had wanted to go in the autumn when others had left but Harry Wilkins, though nervous about the situation, had a strong sense of duty to the Commission and they had stayed put. But enough was enough. Haworth's 'men's Committee' had managed to procure a small coach. As Lillian remembers, Harry saw their opportunity.

> My father came home at lunchtime in a hurry and he said, 'Lily, you must start packing some cases. There's a coach leaving the school. Come along now, Lily, get the girls in.' And it was then that my mother was frantic and wanted to get back to England as fast as she could and apparently there wasn't even then a complete order to tell the people to go.

The Wilkins packed up hurriedly. Lily abandoned the rabbit she had put in the oven for lunch and Harry let his budgies out of their cage. They left Ypres in the heavily laden coach with the Rolfes – Doris strapped to a kitchen chair – the coach-owner's family and all their belongings, bound for Calais. Lily Wilkins breathed a sigh of relief that they were at last on their way, home to England.

If Ypres was the centre of feverish activity and large movements of people, life in the outlying areas – and in the war cemeteries – went on pretty much as usual. Friday was always burials day at Cement House Cemetery outside Langemark. Here the remains of Great War 'casualties' newly recovered from the battlefields were interred in a simple service conducted by the Revd. Dye from St George's. Cement House received all new casualties, regardless of where they were found, and pupil gardener Danny Quinn was there for the burials on Friday, 17 May 1940, as usual.

Cement House is an austere cemetery of 3,500 graves in wind-scoured farmland on the road to Boezinge. On this day, as Danny prepared fresh graves by the wall abutting the road, a column of British troops came by. 'Oy, mate!' they shouted to him as they passed. 'Are those for us?'

On this day Haworth finally managed to make contact with Prower by sending a motorcycle messenger to Wimereux. Prower and Arnott, his number two, arrived in Ypres that afternoon to plan the evacuation. Haworth wasn't prepared to lose the initiative now. He told them of his plan to ignore the 'impracticable' French rail scheme and evacuate the Commission people by road to Le Havre. They would try to get a crossing to England – or, failing that, go further west into Brittany. But for this he needed transport. The number of evacuees was rising all the time as people who had previously decided to stay changed their minds. Arnott agreed to bring three coaches from Wimereux to the Memorial School for 8 a.m. the next day. By this time roads were blocked to civilian traffic and official passes for the British convoy had to be obtained from the Belgian Divisional Commander. Meanwhile, news from the Channel ports wasn't good: Calais and Boulogne were closed for cross-Channel traffic and Ostend had been paralysed by bombing. Haworth's choice of Le Havre looked to be the right one.

Though the IWGC men didn't know it, a week into the invasion it was already clear that the Germans, with superior numbers, equipment and strategy, were moving frighteningly fast. They had knocked out the Belgian and Dutch air forces, were routing a demoralised French Army and making steady incursions – even through the supposedly impenetrable forests of the Ardennes. Pockets of staunch resistance by the French and the BEF couldn't halt the ineluctable progress of Hitler's war machine. That same day the French Commander-in-Chief, General Gamelin, issued a grim *cri de coeur*:

The fate of our country, that of our Allies, and the destiny of the world hangs upon the issue of the battle now going on . . . All troops who cannot advance must die at their posts rather than abandon the part of the National soil entrusted to them.

Prower and Arnott left in the early evening and Haworth sent two IWGC men out in cars to warn families in Ypres and the outlying areas that if they wanted to leave they should be at the school by 9 a.m. the following day with their blanket, rations and one suitcase each. A second group would gather, as planned, at Talbot House in Poperinghe. Dodging the traffic ban and curfew, they took five hours to complete their mission, leaving anxious families to read Haworth's final written order. Headed EVACUATION, it began:

(1) It is quite useless to get excited. Remain calm under all circumstances.

(2) Every British ex-serviceman attached to the Imperial War Graves Commission is now expected to shew the metal of his pastures . . .

Stiff upper lip and mangled metaphors aside, this was a critical moment for Haworth – the culmination of months of detailed planning, agonising arguments with colleagues and a great deal of last-minute improvisation. If he had been a less practical and upbeat man, one without his habit of making the best of things, forged during four years of trench warfare, Haworth might have indulged in some self-righteous recriminations at this point in the proceedings. Ware and Prower thought he had been crying wolf, losing his head. If they had listened to him, they wouldn't all be in this perilous situation now, with inadequate transport, sclerotic roads, an uncertain escape route and the enemy closing in fast.

Now it was well past the eleventh hour. Haworth was an optimistic soul, but he was also a realist. On the eve of his planned evacuation – the greatest single effort and achievement of his life – he had no idea whether the British colony could be saved.

Saturday 18 May 1940 was a fine sunny day. At nine o'clock in the morning we found large numbers of British families . . . In that schoolyard behind St George's Church there were something not far short of two hundred people, men, women and children, prepared to move off with their bags, blankets, and rations for three days on the road. The oldest among them must have been in the region of sixty-five, and the youngest was two months . . . They were all wearing their best clothes and looking at the party one might have imagined it to be a mixture between a Sunday School treat and an excursion to the seaside.

It was to be anything but.

The babe-in-arms was ten-week-old Dicky Boucher, with his parents, eleven-year-old sister Elizabeth and brother Sam, five. But

Haworth's post-hoc account – written many months later – is incorrect. Elizabeth says they weren't at the school in Ypres, they were in the second party, 'sitting on the floor in the main hallway of Toc House' in Poperinghe, where the Ypres coaches were due to pick them up on their way to the French border.

In all the personal accounts of the evacuation, there will be inaccuracies and misrememberings: the events of the next six days were chaotic and many of those who survived to tell the tale were only children at the time. None has a clear recollection of the whole sequence of events, though all have indelible memories that have haunted them ever since. The formal near-contemporaneous reports of the IWGC senior staff who acted as escort officers – Haworth, Arnott, Grinham and Gill – all vary slightly. Even Haworth's own accounts, written in précis for Sir Fabian Ware immediately after the event and then at more length and leisure in 1941, differ in detail. No account can be precise and comprehensive; a rough time frame to hold the still-vivid memories of those who were there is sufficient to convey the drama and the horror of what all the children describe as a turning point in their lives.

In the Fox household preparations for departure were fraught, but Betty was more worried about her cigarette card collection:

> Everyone was crying, my mother was leaving behind her elderly parents and brothers and sisters. I remember that I had to wear my navy wool winter coat. This had a section in the pocket lining where the stitches were undone and I could feel inside the seams. I hid the whole of my collection of cigarette cards in there, wrapped in an elastic band, hoping that no one would find out. In the excitement, I'd forgotten about the weight of the coat. When the time came for my mother to tell me to put it on I realised she'd discovered and removed my secret cargo. The transition for us so quickly changed everything overnight, from a happy carefree childhood into this enormous turmoil . . .

Margaret Dupres' mother made her own preparations: 'Dear Mum, she put mothballs in the blankets in the beds. Well, I suppose she thought we weren't going to be away very long . . .'

Twins Charlotte and Priestley Dunn were both married by this time. Priestley was a pupil gardener with the IWGC and turned up at the school with his bicycle. Charlotte's husband was in the Belgian Army: 'So [after the invasion] I went home to Mam and Dad. After I'd been there about a week Dad came home and said, "We've all got to leave . . ." I said "I'm not going", and my mother said "If you don't come, I won't go", so we had to go, for Dad's sake. And we thought, well, the next day we'll be in England.'

Minnie and Richard Batchelor, a Commission gardener, and their children Celia (seven), Hedley (nine), and Ernie (fourteen) arrived at the school in a neighbour's horse-drawn farm cart from Vlamertinghe. They nearly hadn't made it. Only days earlier Richard was in an English hospital being treated for a chest condition – a result of the 1914–18 war. Minnie was with him, having left their three youngest children in the care of a neighbour. On news of the invasion, Minnie rushed back to Belgium. Richard, discharging himself from hospital, followed a few days later. Celia's only memory of that first leg of what was to be a long journey is wanting to go back to the house because she had forgotten her favourite handbag.

Once gathered at Ypres the party was divided into three 'companies' and given identifying labels of different colours. Like Priestley Dunn, many of the men had brought their bicycles, First World War models bearing a small plaque: 'Property of the Imperial War Graves Commission'. Lawrence Dawson, now returned from escorting his family to Calais, had with some foresight taken one from the Commission's stores. Five Commission vehicles and three private cars were loaded up with office equipment, files and petrol reserves. These vehicles are described as 'cars' in Haworth's reports, but some children recall being in the back of green IWGC vans that smelled of petrol from carrying motor mowers.

They waited for the coaches from Wimereux. And waited. The morning passed and people broke into their rations for lunch. 'Some . . . began to get a little fidgety at the long delay, and we had to cheer them up as best we could.' There was no means of contacting Arnott or Prower to find out what had happened. Anxiety increased as the afternoon wore on and things were getting desperate when Arnott finally turned up at 4 p.m. with an ancient twenty-seater charabanc and a Peugeot car. His three coaches had been requisitioned by the French Army. The fractious crowd of two hundred at the school were now in a state of near rebellion; they had left their allotted companies and were out on the pavement in a disordered mess with their baggage, all desperate to get on the one available coach. Haworth took control: 'In the most brutal fashion I was capable of I ordered them all back into the school yard with their baggage and to form up in their proper companies, pointing out that not one person would be embarked till this was done.'

There was no alternative but to use the coach and cars in a shuttle service to the French border. The cars were duly unloaded and much of the equipment jettisoned, then loaded again with as many women and children as they could carry. The first convoy of about a hundred people set off in the late afternoon, led by Haworth in his car, bound for Steenvoorde about twenty kilometres away, just over the French border. Georgette Hoyles, who was in one of the vans, remembers stopping at Poperinghe to pick up Mrs Boucher and baby Dicky. The roads were clogged with troops and refugees and they had problems getting through the frontier but finally the forward party was billeted for the night in a Steenvoorde school, while the vehicles returned to Ypres to pick up the remainder.

Passing the station square, packed with refugees waiting for trains, Haworth had a taste of what was to come:

A German bomber suddenly appeared, and in the most horrible and businesslike way zoomed over the railway station. With those great crowds offering an easy target, the worst was feared; there was a moment of breathless suspense, but suddenly from nowhere a British fighter appeared and chased away the bomber. There was a short burst of firing and almost instantly the bomber dived steeply, smoke pouring from it, and it crashed almost vertically into the earth. There was a most tremendous explosion, and a dense pall of black smoke . . . The fighter circled around for a moment or two and then flew away.

In the meantime, the group of thirty or so people at Poperinghe, after a long day's wait, had instructions to start walking to Steenvoorde twelve kilometres away. The men with cycles formed their own company and set off from Ypres in the same direction, led by a man with a small Union Jack fluttering from his handlebars. On the return trip from Ypres, Haworth passed the Poperinghe party: '... cheerfully making their way on foot to the frontier ... They were full of pluck and indeed the courage of all these people, suddenly called on to leave their homes with only the belongings they could carry, and homes, let it be stressed, that were the result of twenty years saving and striving, was beyond praise.'

The remainder of the Ypres group were safely delivered to the Steenvoorde billet by 10 p.m. and some of the cars went back yet again to pick up the walkers from Poperinghe. As the families settled down for the night on a bed of straw alongside a group of French soldiers some of the women were waiting anxiously for the cycling party to arrive. They finally turned up at midnight and 'all slept the sleep of the weary ... after a most harassing day's work'.

Haworth's travails were only just beginning. Up at 5 a.m. the following day – Sunday 19 May – he went with three cars to the frontier to pick up some stragglers who had got stuck there overnight. A trip back to Poperinghe, where more were reported to be waiting, was aborted after he was stuck in a jam on the Belgian side. The roads weren't just packed with refugees. Everyone seemed to be trying to get out of Belgium:

> We passed lines of lorries along the road going back and a number of heavy siege guns which were also being taken back. Belgian soldiers on cycles were pedalling away into France, and one could only conclude as far as the Belgian area was concerned that the situation was as critical as it could possibly be, if not quite hopeless.

His plan for that day was to move the party on to their next staging post at Aire-sur-la-Lys using the coach and cars. The coach, now showing signs of wear and tear, got half of them there by midday, when the driver decided 'to throw up the sponge. He was tired out, his tyres were finished and . . . he wanted to get back to his family.' At this point, with the party split into two groups 26 kilometres apart and transport now reduced to cars, Arnott advised a change of tack. Haworth had always been sceptical of the French rail evacuation scheme, but with insufficient road transport it might now be their only hope. They would bring everyone together at the mid-point – the hamlet of Wallon Cappel – which wasn't far from the railhead at Ebblinghem, from which refugee trains were supposed to be running.

The situation was increasingly serious: escort officer Captain Grinham from the Wimereux office noted serious shortages of fresh food and 'rumours of mechanised German column east of Arras' – less than 50 kilometres away. 'Ought to be armed, but I am unarmed,' he noted. Meanwhile Haworth fought his way through refugees to make arrangements with the French captain in charge of rail evacuation.

> The Captain said he was overwhelmed by refugees beseeching him to give them a passage by train; to such a point he . . . was almost afraid to go along the village street. He was alarmed by the flood of all sorts of aliens getting into France, none of whose papers could be verified, and feared that a mass of enemy agents were finding their way, unchecked, into the country.

But with luck there would be a train for them at Ebblinghem the following day. The disparate groups – at Lys, at Steenvoorde and the cycling party, more than two hundred in all – were brought together at two farms in Wallon Cappel for the night.

For twelve-year-old Margaret Dupres, whose family were devout Catholics, the sleeping arrangements were a novelty: 'On the farm we were all in this great big barn and . . . Mum, Dad and I, we had a bale of straw between us and between the Reverend and Mrs Dye, which was very ecumenical! We slept with the vicar with a bale of straw between us!'

For the younger children it was less amusing. Jimmy Fox, not yet five, was frightened by the bats and the rats and mice scampering about in the hay. Parents did their best to keep spirits up. For Jimmy, this meant being given his favourite toy panda. For older boys like Sidney Harper it was an adventure: 'When we were at the farm, that was the first time I saw some German aircraft. I came out of the barn with my father and there were four German bombers just flying over the top of it. To me it was exciting, seeing the swastikas on the side and everything.'

Arnott and Grinham left the party at this point to return to Boulogne, leaving Haworth, Gill and the Revd. Dye in charge but with even fewer cars than they had before. They settled down for the night, but it was a restless one for Haworth.

Thanks to indigestion or possibly anxiety I slept badly and at 2 a.m. I had the opportunity to calmly review the situation. I decided to verify the Railway Scheme first thing and if it were useless, as I expected it would be, to send an SOS to Prower asking for (A) Transport assistance, (B) Cash for the men. At 2.40 a.m. I drafted an SOS dispatch to be sent if the Rail Scheme proved to be a wash-out.

On the morning of Monday 20 May, after a broken night's sleep at Wallon Cappel, Haworth set off to find out about an evacuation train. At Ebblinghem station he found a train, but every truck was packed to overflowing with refugees and it had been waiting there since the early hours of that morning. The harassed stationmaster had never heard of the evacuation scheme and had no idea when, or even if, there would be another train. Not taking his word for it, Haworth sought out the French Captain he'd spoken to the previous day.

His suspicions were confirmed: the scheme had collapsed in chaos. Haworth was stoic: 'It was better to know the facts rather than to live in a fool's paradise.' He had other problems to contend with. The remaining cars were running short of petrol and he had to keep a constant eye on them to stop them being requisitioned by French or British forces. He and his fellow officers were also suspected of being spies and he'd had to talk himself out of being arrested by the military on more than one occasion. But he did have a bit of luck that morning. He came across an RASC captain looking for billets, so he offered their barns in return for some transport. The Captain agreed to do what he could, but then promptly disappeared.

Rations were now running desperately low. Haworth decided to send those of the cycle party without dependants off ahead, as he had no idea when, or whether, more transport would arrive. They could fend for themselves; the husbands and fathers would continue to rendezvous with the main group at the end of each day. Meanwhile, several people at Wallon Cappel were sick and were treated with beef tea in the absence of anything stronger. The rest were hungry, Elizabeth Boucher and her family among them: 'Some of the women got together with the farmer's wife . . . and they made a drop of soup for us. We'd had nothing to eat. My brother Sam was crying, I was crying, baby Dicky was crying with hunger.'

Sam recalls snatching a piece of bread back from a rat in the barn, they were so desperate, and being bitten by rats as they slept. Minnie Batchelor sent her son Hedley to the farmhouse with a canvas bucket to fetch water:

Some miserable old devil in his eighties sent me into a shed with a rusty old tap . . . I came out with this heavy bucket of water and being only nine, it was hard to carry. Army lorries stopped by the side of the road and I put it down to wave to them but the canvas bucket collapsed and I ended up with no water. I went back to the farm and the owner refused to let me have any more, so I had to go back empty-handed to Mum and she was not at all happy.

Nearby, Haworth and his team had set up an 'embryo mess' at an *estaminet* at the crossroads in Wallon Cappel. From here they witnessed – and from time to time controlled – the miserable tide of traffic:

The procession of refugees continued. Motorcars full of people and children, with voluminous bedding on top, mothers wheeling prams with a couple of children inside, the old farm cart with the grandmother perched on some precarious seat holding a child, wheelbarrows and cyclists without number, all speeding or plodding to the unknown. A grim, desolate despairing pageant of war – French or Belgian troops on foot, in buses, or cycles, Gendarmes pedalling away for dear life, all going back hour after hour, to a destination heaven alone knows where.

Another anxious night passed at Wallon Cappel, to the sound of an air raid on nearby Hazebrouck. That day the ill-fated General Gamelin was dismissed and replaced by General Weygand.

The following morning – Tuesday 21 May – things looked brighter. While Haworth was in Hazebrouck begging petrol from a British Army unit, the RASC Captain turned up in Wallon Cappel with good news: he'd got them two army lorries and was bringing them rations too. By midday two ten-ton trucks had arrived and cases of army rations were being broken open and distributed to the grateful crowd. The children particularly remember being given handfuls of currants. Haworth, back from Hazebrouck, must have been relieved. But then:

> . . . suddenly without any warning of any kind enemy bombers appeared with a mighty roar from the Saint-Omer direction, flying low and bombing the nearby main road and railway track. The crowd lining the bank with their rations in their hands made a rush for the cover of the walls of the farm building, some crawling under farm carts.

Yvonne Lane, fifteen, stood mesmerised beside one of the army drivers as he returned fire at the planes, until she was pulled to safety. Hedley Batchelor was also in danger.

> The German planes were hedge-hopping at the tops of the trees. We were thinking at first that they were our lads, then they opened fire and my brother jumped under one of the British army lorries and mother grabbed me and pushed me up against a wall, shielding me from the firing. Then I recall being pushed on the lorry and gobbling up the currants that the Tommies had given us.

Fifteen-year-old Georgette Hoyles had left her parents to sit by the side of the road with a friend when the planes came over.

. . . they machine-gunned along the road. A British soldier threw me on to the ground and covered my head with his hand and got his thumb shot off from the firing. A bullet had scraped the top of my head, gone through my hair and singed it. My father was screaming as he didn't know where to find me, my mother started screaming . . .

Severely shaken but unhurt, they hastened to load up the trucks and get away without delay. The destination was constantly shifting, according to the latest news from the ports: originally Le Havre, it changed to Dunkirk and now changed yet again to Calais – or at least Guines, just outside, as there were reports that Calais was being bombed. Half the party set off in the trucks and cars.

On the road that ran parallel to the railway line, they dodged craters caused by the raid they had just been caught up in. But then they came across the real target. It was a sight Yvonne Lane will never forget.

The engine was upright rather than horizontal. We were standing up in these army lorries. When the lorry stopped, I pulled this tarpaulin back to see what was happening, and there was . . . all I could see was blood, blood, blood, and I gasped and my mother came to see what I was gasping at. She pulled me away and ordered the others not to look outside. We were really close. If we'd have been there much longer I could have counted the bodies.

It was a refugee train. Had Haworth taken a less sceptical view of the French evacuation scheme, they might have been on it.

With half the party delivered and billeted in Guines, the trucks returned to Wallon Cappel and picked up the rest. Passing Ebblinghem station, Haworth noted extensive damage and another wrecked train. They had only gone about ten kilometres when a dispatch rider delivered an order urgently recalling the BEF lorries to the forward zone. Haworth persuaded them to take them on to Saint-Omer, but just outside they got stuck in a bad traffic jam – and could see Saint-Omer ahead in the throes of an air raid. The lorries, already late, dumped them by the roadside and turned round 'with barely time to thank the officer and his men for the yeoman service they had rendered to us'. There were now up to eighty people, mainly women and children, with all their baggage on a road thronged with refugees and under constant threat of air attack. It was already early evening and their transport was woefully inadequate. Haworth, ever resourceful, had a plan.

He had worked in Saint-Omer and knew the area well; there was a monastery and a convent within striking distance that might take them in. Loading up the cars with as much baggage as they would take, he went to try his luck. With women in the party, they were turned down by the monastery and advised to try the convent. On the way, Haworth enlisted the help of the local mayor: '. . . a typical old farmer of the peasant class . . . He was shaken by the unbelievable catastrophe that seemed to be falling on France, but he was full of courage. He came with me at once to the convent.'

The Abbey of Our Lady at Wisques, then as now, houses a contemplative Benedictine order in an imposing nineteenth-century château surrounded by woods. When Haworth arrived with the mayor on the evening of Tuesday 21 May, it was already quite a busy place. British soldiers had taken over the grounds and refugees were waiting at the door hoping to be admitted.

> When the door was opened the Mayor explained our business and we were admitted to a waiting room . . . the Mother Superior arrived, she was young with a pale intelligent face. She listened to the story and then said 'Yes, we will admit the women and children.' They would have to sleep in the corridors, on the floors, and there was no protection against bombing. We had to chance that.

Meanwhile, the women and children left behind on the road were tired, tearful and vulnerable. Elizabeth Boucher remembers being dumped 'in no-man's-land':

> We were in a small private car driven by one of the IWGC staff members. Mrs Brown and her daughter Mildred, my mother

with baby Dicky, Sam my brother who was five, and myself. He dropped us in the middle of nowhere, and said he had to go. So we were walking along. My poor mother, you should have seen her, the poor soul, she was exhausted. And that's when the Stukas come down and started machine gunning us. I was trying to carry the baby, holding on to Sam for dear life, everyone running and jumping into ditches. People were screaming, including some monks. I've never seen monks so frightened in my life. Then my mother sat down in a ditch and said: 'I'm not going any further. I can't walk, Germans or not!' We were there some time and then out of nowhere a British soldier came along with his tin hat on – I'll never forget that – and Mrs Brown told him the whole story about how we'd tried to escape and he said: 'I'll go and get some help for you.' And he came back with half a dozen others. One took Sam on his shoulders and they more or less carried us to the convent.

By the end of the evening and with much effort on the part of the escort officers, all were reunited at the convent, where Betty Fox remembers:

We slept on a mattress made of hay . . . in a long corridor. There were lots of people, and at the end a whole group of soldiers. To me that was a bit frightening, as it was my first experience of seeing wounded soldiers and their various injuries. Some were suffering shell shock, they were shaking all over, their eyes staring out blankly . . . We were all given a hot drink and some bread and jam.

The men of the party slept in the cars and Haworth and Gill, after 'a meal of biscuits', bedded down in the mayor's barn, where they shared the straw with some French soldiers and a roost of chickens. The Chronicles of the Abbaye Notre-Dame de Wisques for the day recorded:

Refugees are massing on our land. Tonight another thing happened, a colony of English . . . about 80 persons to be put up for the night. We put them in the atrium and the parlour rooms and gave them straw mattresses and armchairs . . . Mother Superior gives her charity to these poor harassed people and blesses them and caresses the small children . . . the English Captain in charge of the expedition expresses boundless gratitude in broken French, and says with great feeling, 'The whole of England will be grateful for what you have done this day for us. I shall never forget the service you have rendered us.'

Haworth was later to repay the Mother Superior's charity in the most practical of ways.

The next day, Wednesday 22 May, Haworth was again up at 5 a.m. and saw the old mayor leading his horses out to pasture: there might be a war on but the work still had to be done.

As I wandered about that quiet farm I really began to have doubts as to whether in the face of increasing difficulties we should ever manage to extricate ourselves and avoid falling into the hands of the invaders. Fortunately there was enough to keep one occupied and from pondering overmuch on the possibilities of the future.

His urgent priority was to secure transport for the convent refugees to Calais. He tried a nearby British Army unit, but they were in the same boat – on the move and short of petrol. After they had all lunched on army rations of beans, bread and meat paste, encouraging news arrived of the forward party in Guines: they were hopeful of getting a boat that day from Calais. There was practically no chance that the Wisques party would get there in time to catch it, but Haworth was determined to try. They loaded up the cars yet again to begin the shuttle service; they were now down to four as Haworth had decided to abandon his at the convent: it was out of petrol and had engine trouble. Haworth, pausing only to accept a small medallion and words of encouragement from the Mother Superior, led the small procession off on to the chaotic main road to Calais, forty kilometres away.

We constantly met British convoys going forward against the tide of refugees. Women held up their children asking for lifts but we could do nothing to help them, loaded as we were. There was a horse down in the road completely exhausted and a Belgian soldier with his arm around its neck was doing his utmost to encourage it to get on its legs. Here and there the road had been heavily bombed leaving farmhouses alongside the road smoking ruins, and demolished cars . . . suggested casualties. The object of the bombers was clearly to get the civilian population on the run.

Those among the seventy-odd people left behind occupied themselves until the cars returned. Elizabeth Boucher was taken into the convent chapel to pray. Nellie Davis wrote a postcard in Flemish to an address in Poperinghe. Never posted, it survives as perhaps the best contemporaneous summary of the exodus up to that point:

We are all sitting here together in a Convent waiting for transport to take us to Calais, where we can catch a boat back to England but we don't know when. We've been having a hard time, sleeping where and when we can in the straw with mice and rats. On Saturday in the late afternoon we left for Steenvoorde and spent the night in the grounds of a school and slept on the straw. From there we left on Sunday to Aire-sur-la-Lys; there we spent a whole day, and in the afternoon we were taken to a farm not far from Hazebrouck and we stayed in a barn on the straw with mice and rats. The Wednesday afternoon we left on the road with English soldiers in their trucks, we were not far from Saint-Omer when we were told to get out of the trucks as the English soldiers were ordered to return to the front. Then German planes arrived above our heads; they shot and dropped bombs not far from us. We had to keep hiding from the German planes that were following us. Then we had to walk on foot for about 10 kilometres and spent the night in the convent. Best wishes to everyone, until later, Love Nellie.

Transport arrived sooner than anyone – including Haworth – expected. Those in charge of the forward party had managed to procure army lorries from Guines to come and get them. Though it seemed as if deliverance was at hand, the worst was yet to come, inching along the packed, crater-pocked roads among burning vehicles and desperate mothers trying to save their children, with swooping, screaming Stukas causing bedlam. Scenes from the journey into Calais still haunt those who were there. Asked to recall their experiences, some broke down, others could barely articulate the horrors they saw. Georgette Hoyles would never forget one tragic scene: 'Nearing Calais we saw . . . a woman picking up a body which had no arms and no legs, she was screaming and indicating that our truck had to stop and shouting in French "Parlez moi, ma fille" to the body she had in her arms, but the child was dead.'

Sam Boucher was five when he saw the burning army truck that is still vivid in his mind: '. . . and the only thing I remember from sixty-eight years ago is this soldier's arm hanging out and all the fat coming down as he was being burnt. We went right past but it didn't sort of register.' His sister Elizabeth's haunting memory is of a woman running with two children in her arms. They had been decapitated.

With the road into the town already a hellish vision of chaos and horror, Calais itself was about to become an inferno. Within little more than forty-eight hours the swastika would be flying from the Hôtel de Ville.

8

Escape

The crew were drunk but they were lovely.
Betty Parker, who escaped on the trawler *Golden Sunbeam*, May 1940, aged fifteen

LAWRENCE DAWSON AND the cycling group had been having their own desperate adventures. They had kept more or less with the main party, travelling separately under pedal power but meeting up in prearranged rendezvous at the end of each day until Tuesday 21 May when Haworth instructed them to make for the coast. They were led by John Watson, an IWGC head gardener with five boys at the Memorial School. On the journey, Dawson travelled with Harry Wilkins. They weren't friends particularly, but they now had a common mission.

They had both escorted their families to the coast ahead of the main party in the hope of getting them away from Calais or Boulogne, a journey that under normal circumstances would take no more than a couple of hours. The Wilkinses – Harry, Lily and their daughters Lillian and Joyce – had a slow but relatively straightforward journey on the coach with the Rolfe family. The Dawsons – twelve-year-old Joyce, her parents and invalid grandmother – had a more difficult time, finally arriving in Calais late at night after a ten-hour train journey, more than twenty-eight hours after they had left Ypres. Dawson's detailed account, written soon afterwards, describes the events of the next few days, which would change their lives for ever. In Calais, Dawson managed to find rooms for the night:

Enemy had dropped bombs on a row of houses just opposite hotel and made a nice mess. Wife remarked, 'They have dropped bombs here' and I tried to console her by saying the demolition contractors were in . . . did not get much sleep owing to air-raid warnings. There was not a window left intact in the place, all having been boarded up – some hotel.

First thing the next morning, Friday 17 May, he went to find out about a boat but was told by the military Transport Officer in charge that the port had been shut to commercial traffic for the past week. Ferries were still leaving from Le Havre but rail and road links had all been destroyed. Undeterred, Dawson went to the British Consul for advice and there met Harry Wilkins and Howard Rolfe doing the same thing. The Consul rang through to the Wimereux IWGC office and the men were advised to report there. After trouble finding transport, the three families finally arrived in Wimereux in the early evening. Captain Grinham found them billets and the following morning, Saturday 18 May, they met Brigadier Prower.

Prower, who had been to Ypres the previous afternoon to discuss the evacuation with Haworth, was still not prepared to allow the men to leave with their families. He offered to take the women and children to his house at Montreuil from where, he said, he would arrange to get them away to England. The men could either stay in France and attach themselves to a work group in Etaples, or return to Ypres. Howard Rolfe decided to stay (though he managed to get away with his family a few days later on a hospital ship, the SS *St Julien*, with 150 IWGC evacuees from France). Offered this Hobson's choice, Wilkins and Dawson elected to go back to Ypres and joined Major Arnott on the charabanc just departing for the Memorial School. At the Belgian border the Chief Customs Officer asked them to convey a party of French soldiers to Ypres where – in a bizarre and pointless re-enactment of the 1914–18 war – they were to dig trenches at Hill 60.

Back where they started in Ypres, the two men joined Haworth's evacuation party, having left their families under the protection of Brigadier Prower. Dawson's account does not record what he thought of Prower at the time, probably because it was written for a member of his staff, Captain Grinham. And he didn't know then quite how badly the arrangement would turn out. But given the seriousness of the situation, it must have been distressing for them to be parted from their families and turned back to Ypres, only to be evacuated all over again. So it's likely that he and Wilkins had now found a new common enemy, and it wasn't Hitler.

Three days later, on 21 May, they were pedalling together on their way to Le Havre, having become separated from the rest of the cycle group after a couple of men had punctures. Five kilometres outside Hesdin Dawson recalls that they met chaos and confusion:

> Gendarme said Germans in Hesdin . . . arrived next village, again cut off. Managed to find another by-road. Road choked with refugees. Winded [sic] in and out of traffic on foot. Spoke to Frenchman to ask position, told me we were surrounded, case of everyone for himself. Said Boulogne was occupied. Asked another Frenchman if this were true, said 'No' . . .

Both men were now very anxious to get to their families at Montreuil.

> Spoke to French sentry to ask it if were possible to make for Montreuil. Informed me Montreuil was being shelled, possibly occupied. Proceeded to Boulogne most of the way on foot, due to roads being jammed . . . heard machine-gun and rifle-fire in the distance, thought all was up. Pushed on, on foot, impossible to ride cycles . . . Met two English women who said they had walked from Brussels. Asked if they could attach themselves to us. Replied 'Sorry, wife and family waiting at Wimereux, must get there to-night'. Started to cry, saying 'It means an internment camp for us' . . .

Reaching the Commission office in Wimereux by nightfall, they found it had been evacuated. They approached four British soldiers to ask if they could use a telephone and were promptly arrested as spies. As soon as the RASC Commanding Officer realised who they were, he agreed to ring through to Prower, returning with the advice that all families had been evacuated and to get themselves to England as soon as possible. They spent that night in an army billet with British troops, who 'gave us what food they had, with tea'.

At 5 a.m. the next day, 22 May, with blazing oil tankers off the coast shooting flames five hundred feet high, they hitched a ride into Boulogne where they saw British soldiers with fixed bayonets guarding the entrance to the Maritime Station. No one was being allowed through without a special visa. They spent some time getting the necessary passes and joined the crush of refugees at the station. 'Saw two battalions Welsh Guards, tank and armoured column pass through. Spoke to sergeant in charge anti-aircraft gun at bridge. Gave us 2 large "Players" each. Advised us to wait, thought warship would be coming in to take troops away.'

By this time, the German 'sickle stroke' strategy had severely disrupted Allied supply lines and was pushing the BEF back up against the Channel ports, as it was designed to do. The British response was confused and the chain of command dysfunctional at this point. Efforts to evacuate so-called 'useless mouths' (injured troops, noncombatants and, perhaps, British refugees) had begun from the Channel ports the previous day, but the War Office was still undecided about whether to pull its troops out. Dawson's sergeant obviously believed evacuation to be imminent but Churchill had other ideas. A spirited BEF defence at Arras on the afternoon of the 21st had prevented the 10th Panzer Division from capturing Dunkirk and may have convinced the new Prime Minister that Calais and the other ports – and their British defenders – might have to be sacrificed to keep Dunkirk open.

Boulogne was certainly in a bad way on the 22nd when Dawson and Wilkins were waiting with hundreds of others for news of a sailing. By the end of the afternoon they had managed to make contact with the rest of their cycle party, who had thought they'd been captured. Then:

7 p.m. up dashed rider who said, 'Jerry on outskirts of town, little hopes of holding him back'. Order given to all troops to fall-in, civilians dashing to underground shelter. While there

Watson arrested as spy by British sergeant. Five minutes later sergeant returned . . . all IWGC members . . . were taken in front of British Major KRRC [King's Royal Rifle Corps] who said he would not allow us to remain in station. On leaving station, German artillery opened fire on town. Decided to find shelter, which we eventually found in side street . . . falling flat on our stomachs on hearing the hiss of a shell.

Split again from their group and in the company of a few other IWGC men, the two men were finally directed to a shelter by an air-raid warden and spent the night in 'a damp cellar with water streaming down the walls. Pitiful to see old women and mothers with children in their arms sitting on small kegs.' At 4.30 a.m. there was a lull in the bombardment and the men decided to try and get back to the Maritime Station. 'Streets strewn with broken glass and debris. Spoke to Private in West Yorks, wearing Mons ribbon. Said "Bit of all right, ain't it, chum, got a wife and ten kids at home" . . . Returned to Maritime Station entrance – barricaded.'

They talked their way through the barricade and Dawson left Wilkins in a shelter while he went to find the rest of their party. Despite the intense bombardment, he dodged in and out of shelters looking for his colleagues. He didn't find them and was worried about Wilkins, so he made his way back to the station shelter. Wilkins was gone.

Then his luck ran out:

Shelter crowded but managed to squeeze in near stair entrance. Remained there some time, when suddenly a shell burst over stair entrance. The explosion was deafening and I found my left hand hanging and left knee badly grazed. Lay bleeding some time, felt getting weaker. Asked soldier to help me . . . applied tourniquet at wrist and gave me tots of rum . . . French first-aid nurse came along, took off her cap and tore it into bandages to dress wounds of an airman (left foot shot away) and self . . . Taken up on platform and placed flat on back under Red Cross train drawn up at station . . . finally fetched by RAMC [Royal

Army Medical Corps] stretcher bearers and placed in dressing station. Stayed there for hours with other wounded men, one naval officer was dead.

At 3 p.m. Dawson was taken aboard the destroyer HMS *Vimy* and placed beneath the gun turrets. 'Deafened by roar of guns. Was given plenty of cigarettes and rum by troops on board. Heard shrapnel of German shells striking armoured plating of ship, thought every moment boat would get direct hit beneath waterline . . .'

But they arrived unscathed in Dover at about 4 p.m., 'the fastest crossing I've ever made'. He was taken straight to hospital and operated on at 11.30 p.m., 'after having all my clothes cut off me'. The effects of the anaesthetic began to wear off about 4 a.m. and he woke to the sounds of 'terrific bombardment at sea'. It was 24 May: Boulogne was about to fall to the Germans and the bombardment he could hear was the destruction of Calais.

At about the same time another IWGC cyclist, Danny Quinn from Poelkapelle, was still crossing the Channel. He was on a destroyer with other Commission evacuees – all part of Haworth's original group that set off from Ypres on Saturday 18 May. Eighteen-year-old Danny, a pupil gardener and former Memorial School pupil, was one of about twenty men without dependants who had left Wallon Cappel on their bikes on Tuesday the 21st. They had been making for Abbeville on their way to Le Havre when they heard that the town was already in German hands, so they diverted to Boulogne, arriving on the 22nd. The port was already under heavy bombardment and artillery fire and they found themselves uncomfortably close to street-fighting; Danny got a shrapnel wound in the arm. Then, in the late evening of Thursday the 23rd, a group of them left the cover of a deserted building and made a run for it to the Maritime Station by the dockside.

Crawling across the cobblestones with their suitcases over their heads to protect them from shrapnel and machine-gun fire, they got to the quay to find two destroyers waiting to load wounded troops. These were the *Vimiera* and the *Whitshed*, recently arrived with the

20th Guards Brigade, which Danny recalls seeing disembark. In the early hours of the following morning, as stretcher cases and wounded were taken up ramps to the ships, rope ladders rolled down for the able-bodied. Danny was nearly home and dry. 'I remember going up the rope ladder and the bloke in front of me wore clogs. And as he climbed up there – I was the next man to go up – then, poufff! – machine-gun fire. He got caught, he fell, and I went up quick. The Germans were just outside the docks with their machine-guns . . .'

What had become of Haworth's group? The forward party who had left Wallon Cappel by car and army lorry on Tuesday 21 May were billeted that night in a school in Guines, just outside Calais. The enemy was closing in and they had been instructed by a British officer to offer no resistance if the Germans came, but to wave something white and surrender immediately. Georgette Hoyles was there:

> We . . . had to remain very quiet as the Germans were suspected to be in the area and Rev. Dye had to stand guard. We had arrived earlier, but the men and husbands [on bikes] arrived about 4 a.m. The wives and children were all very worried. Rev. Dye kept saying during the night: 'Who goes there?'

When they arrived in a Calais already under fire, most of the party were able to get away on trawlers requisitioned for minesweeping. Georgette, fifteen at the time, remembers:

> We had to walk planks to get out to the fishing trawlers on the quayside. The three trawlers were all positioned side by side so we had to step from one boat over to the next. Ours was the *Golden Sunbeam* and it had a machine gun on the top deck and the crew were firing at floating mines and I got soaking wet because I was standing on the top deck. Most of the sailors were pretty drunk.

One of the sailors brought her a duffel coat because she'd got so wet. When they arrived in Folkestone, he 'grabbed the hood off and kissed me on the mouth. It had never happened to me before, and I was very taken aback.' Betty Parker also remembers the crew being drunk, '. . . but they were lovely. I was put in the hold but I said "I'm sorry, but I can't stay down there", so they let me up on deck'.

The Batchelor family, part of the same group, lost all their luggage. In the chaos of boarding, their father Richard got separated from them and left it unattended while he went to look for them. By the time he went back, it had been thrown on to the quay to make room for more evacuees. He didn't dare risk leaving the boat to retrieve it. Among their belongings, they lost a tin containing family papers and Richard's precious trophy from the British Legion flower show. (Three months later a British officer turned up where they were living in north London. He had served in the final hours of the defence of Calais and was one of the few to escape alive; he had found their tin of papers on the quay and brought it back with him, but the trophy was lost for ever.)

The party from the Wisques convent eventually arrived in Calais the day the *Golden Sunbeam* left. Haworth reached the Guines billet that afternoon to find it deserted; he had to assume they had got away safely. He and Gill fought their way on into Calais and finally reached the quay, where they saw the SS *City of Christchurch* laboriously unloading its cargo of carefully mothballed armoured vehicles in between air raids. The Naval Transport Officer told them that most of the forward party had left but there was the chance of a ship if they could get everyone to the quayside by nine the following morning. In the meantime Haworth had no idea where the Wisques contingent, being delivered by lorry, had got to.

Search parties were sent out. They, and some people who hadn't been able to get away on the trawlers, about a hundred in all, were rounded up and billeted in a disused lace factory for the night. Here, in the early hours of the morning the main cycle party, Jack Fox among them, were reunited with their families for the last time: they wouldn't be separated again. Weary and hungry, Haworth and Gill went out at about 11 p.m. in search of food. After the earlier bombing, it was eerily quiet: 'Silence brooded over this stricken town . . . Silence everywhere except for an occasional horrible groan from some sleeper further up the street suffering from shell-shock or nightmare, which made one's flesh creep.' They found nothing on the deserted streets and, well after midnight, they parked Gill's car outside the town hall and dined on their remaining rations: a tin of sardines, some sweet biscuits and half a bottle of water. They didn't get much sleep; it was their fifth night since leaving Ypres.

Up at four thirty on the morning of Thursday the 23rd and after a rough shave at a standpipe, Haworth and Gill started planning how to get their flock to the quay for 9 a.m. By soon after 6 a.m. they had transported all the baggage and over the next two hours had shuttled the whole party to the Maritime Station, air raids going on all around them. The *City of Christchurch* was still in the process of disgorging its cargo, but this was the ship they pinned their hopes on. By now the whole area was swarming with restless refugees and the quay itself was under the control of armed military police. Haworth ran up against 'a red-faced little Rifle Major who apparently hated the sight of civilians. He shot me off the quay with two seamen with anti-quated rifles to ensure I did not lose my way.' Miraculously, they met up with Grinham and a party of IWGC evacuees from the northern France area, together with sundry stray cyclists.

They were in the final stages of their journey, but bombing had turned the port area into an assault course. Jimmy Fox, four, was terrified and the memory of the obstacles they had to overcome is still with him: 'The sluice gates from the inner harbour to the quayside were destroyed. Holding my mother's hand I had to walk across planks over a large expanse of deep, dirty water as smoke billowed from nearby buildings.'

Betty Fox remembers the air raids as they tried to get to the quay:

No sooner had the sirens started, than there was gunfire from what seemed like every angle and people were scurrying about everywhere. The gunfire got louder and the next thing I knew we were scrambling underneath goods wagons, fitting ourselves beneath them any way we could to shelter from the raid, my parents and their three children all under eleven. After the all-clear we could see all sorts of small boats out beyond the shoreline and soldiers wading in up to their waists, scrambling into these boats.

Finally came the order to proceed to the embarkation point, a long glass-covered corridor – just in time for another air raid. Haworth remained stoic:

> Our party could do nothing except get as near the floor as pos-
> sible and await events. It looked as though we were in for a grim
> business when our fighters suddenly appeared and gave battle to
> the Hun Bombers . . . [they] brought down five Germans, and
> one of our fighters crashed. To sit there with nothing but a glass
> roof over them was rather nerve-trying . . . but they nobly stood
> the test . . . Then, oh joy! We were told to get the party on
> board.

Betty remembers the order to embark:

> 'Just leave everything, come as you are. Don't try and carry
> anything,' we were told. Then we found out why. We had to
> walk across a plank to the boat from the harbour wall with the
> water below. All manner of people were being helped across
> the planks, mostly wounded soldiers, some on stretchers, no
> ropes or rails to hold on to, just a slippery wet railway sleeper.
> It was nightmarish. I remember looking at my parents and
> seeing my mother shaking her head. We were all very tired.
> Dad encouraged us by saying, 'Come on, we've got this far.'
> That was all we needed. The next thing I remember we were
> in a little dark cabin . . . I was given a drink and a big square
> hard biscuit.

In the rush to board, some other families – like Elizabeth Boucher's – lost precious belongings, burned or jettisoned among the bombed chaos on the quay: 'My mother had all our papers including our pass-port, her marriage book, my Dad's medals – they were all in the suitcase.' Haworth too boarded without his luggage; having managed with great effort to get everyone's sparse belongings as far as the quay, only some of it made it on to the *City of Christchurch*. Never mind: his people were safe.

Once the ship was packed to capacity, and beyond, with refugees and wounded men (including the RAF fighter pilot shot down earlier), it embarked for Dover in the early afternoon, negotiating air attacks, mines, debris, and a mass of other craft as it inched its way across the Channel. Grimy and exhausted, Jimmy Fox and the other young children fell asleep on benches, bunks and tables in the officers' cabins, while older children watched from the deck with their fathers as spiky black mines bobbed perilously close. The *City of Christchurch*, diverted from the heavily mined Kent coast, finally docked at Southampton almost twenty-four hours later.

It was now Friday 24 May, exactly two weeks after the invasion. By this time the Germans, in the words of Sir Fabian Ware, '. . . had overrun, or were immediately threatening, practically all the British graves of 1914–21 in France and Belgium'. In Britain on this day the BBC, at Ware's request, twice broadcast an emergency message to any remaining gardeners in France to gather at the IWGC's temporary HQ at Fougères in Brittany, to where Brigadier Prower had decamped.

In Calais the 10th Panzer Division, backed by heavy artillery, had by now surrounded the town and captured its main defensive position at Fort Nieulay. British strategy was still confused. In the early hours, the War Office ordered the evacuation of Calais 'in principle' and two more vessels, *Christchurch*'s sister ship the *City of Canterbury*, and the *Kohistan*, left the harbour full of troops and equipment under heavy shellfire. They were the last. By the end of the day, Churchill had countermanded the evacuation order and told Brigadier Claude Nicholson, the man charged with the town's defence, that he must fight on.

All concerned knew it was a hopeless cause but Nicholson stood fast, twice refusing to surrender. Three thousand British and one thousand French troops held out till the bitter end on 26 May. Those who weren't killed were taken prisoner; Nicholson himself died in captivity three years later. The old town of Calais, like Ypres by the end of 1918, was destroyed. Many hundreds of lives were lost. It was a heroic sacrifice soon forgotten in the battle for Britain that was to follow. But without it, Churchill believed, the mass evacuation of the BEF from Dunkirk over the following ten days would not have been possible. In the 'miracle of deliverance' that followed, the *Golden*

Sunbeam – manned no doubt by its drunken crew – went on to make four Dunkirk runs, saving a total of 397 people.

The British evacuees from Ypres, together with IWGC staff and their families from northern France, were very lucky to get away. But there was more to it than luck. A couple of weeks later, Sir Fabian Ware gave credit where it was due in a secret report to Commission members: 'Captain Haworth's courage and resourcefulness during a six days' journey, in every circumstance of danger, difficulty and disappointment, deserve the highest praise. Altogether he evacuated approximately 250 men, women and children.' The report concluded:

> We found ourselves looking on at an inferno of indescribable confusion, terror-stricken refugees, bombed and machine-gunned, obstructing all ordered movement . . . in these conditions all carefully laid plans having been dislocated, the Commission's officials whom I have mentioned doggedly devoted themselves, hour by hour, to those for whom they were responsible; and to us, as we look back, it seems marvellous that they succeeded in mercifully extricating so many of our staff and their families and bringing them back to safety in England.

Ware was so proud of the evacuation efforts of his officials (with one exception), and the dedication of his gardeners to their cemeteries, that on 13 June he sent the report to the Minister of Information, Duff Cooper, suggesting that it might be put into the public domain in some form. He was rebuffed with a brutal reminder – probably not for the first time in his IWGC career – that the country's priority was the living not the dead:

> . . . I doubt that the present would be an appropriate moment to issue it to the Press. The country is so deeply concerned about the fate of those who are actually engaged in fighting that the public are hardly in the mood to take sufficient interest in a matter of this sort and might be critical if much prominence were given to it . . .

★

The evacuation, tremendous achievement though it was, was incomplete; not everyone had got away. Ware reported that out of 527 staff in France and Belgium, 207 were unaccounted for. Lawrence Dawson – minus his left hand – and Harry Wilkins had both escaped and expected to find their families waiting for them in England. After all, they had left them under the protection of Brigadier Prower and were told they had been evacuated. But they had been misinformed.

In Dawson's handwritten draft of his evacuation experiences, made for Captain Grinham soon after the event, the final paragraph is crossed out. It reads: 'In conclusion, I am still living in hopes of seeing my dear wife and daughter again, although it should be noted I have heard nothing since May 18th.' Instead he writes: 'Let us all be of good cheer and hope for better days.' He was to hear nothing from his wife and daughter Joyce, twelve, until June 1941 and wouldn't see them for another four years.

Before her memory failed, Joyce, now over eighty, wrote about what happened to them once they had got to Wimereux on Saturday 18 May:

> My father reported to the Head Office of the War Graves Commission. We did not know when the next boat would be. Brigadier Prower in charge told my father and Mr Wilkins, who was also trying to get his family on a boat, to return to Ypres and that he would take us to his country mansion outside Boulogne at Montreuil and get us on the next boat leaving Boulogne.

Joyce, her mother and grandmother, and Lily Wilkins and her two daughters, Lillian and Joyce, were duly taken to Montreuil and installed in the servants' quarters. A few days later, in the late afternoon of Monday the 20th, a Red Cross ambulance drew up at the house and into it got Prower's wife and daughter together, according to Lillian, with 'loads and loads of luggage'. Prower arrived in his chauffeur-driven Delage to see them off and then left, explaining to Mrs Wilkins that he would return the following day. Lillian watched them go:

And that was the last we saw of them . . . he said au revoir and off he went. But he never came back. And then the Germans were bombing and the British were being blown up and there we were, stuck there. Mother said: 'See if you can find a baker's or some shop open'. . . So I was in the square trying to find where I could get what my mother wanted and all of a sudden all these German tanks were in the square. Then they started bombing . . .

As Joyce Dawson recalls:

The shops were closed and we were left with nothing to eat except some potatoes in the garden. The following day the German soldiers came to Montreuil and camped on the meadow across the road. They were going to people's houses and taking over any spare rooms. They were looking through our windows and were a rough-looking lot. My mother then said to Mrs Wilkins, 'It won't be long before they break in, so it would be better if we go looking for some well-behaved soldiers and offer them accommodation.'

They found some young Austrian soldiers who moved in and helped them milk a cow and shoot a calf for food. Joyce says the two women buried all Brigadier Prower's uniforms in the garden to avoid reprisals. They managed to survive in the house like this for five weeks. Mrs Dawson 'more or less took charge': she was Belgian and spoke good French and poor Lily Wilkins was in a state of nervous exhaustion, 'out of her mind with worry'. Given that they couldn't get away to England, the next best thing was to try and get home. They managed to find a car and someone to drive them, and arrived back in Ypres towards the end of June.

Ypres was now occupied. On 1 June Hitler swept triumphantly through the town that the Germans had failed to capture during 1914–18. On his way to the German military cemetery at Langemark to pay homage to his fallen comrades from the Great War, he stopped to inspect the damage around the Menin Gate.

On their return, the Dawsons were aghast to find an 'Occupied' sign on their front door – but it had been put there by neighbours to prevent the Germans taking over the house as a billet. The Wilkins weren't so lucky: they found squatters in their home in the Chaussée de Bruges. The two families were safely back in Ypres, but their troubles were far from over.

> The last thing I remember is going into the garden and picking some radishes and boiling some hard-boiled eggs for the journey. I gave my roller skates to the chap opposite. I knew I wouldn't be back. It was an adventure I had to sort out for myself, because my father couldn't. It made me grow up.

John Osborne was sixteen and lived with his IWGC gardener father and Belgian mother in Ploegsteert, not far from Stephen Grady in Nieppe. It's not clear why the Osbornes didn't join the main evacuation party. Some of the men in the outlying areas didn't get to hear about it until it was too late; others perhaps decided not to leave. John believes it was because of a failure of nerve on his father's part:

> When things were going wrong in Belgium in 1940, he was lost. No go at all; he couldn't organise anything. Things seemed to move a bit too quickly for him. He left everything to me and my mother. He was still thinking in 1914–18 terms – one step forward, one step back. But I could see it was different this time. For a start the British troops were very orderly marching into Belgium but as they were retreating it was a shambles . . .

So John organised their evacuation. He and his father cycled while his mother travelled in a car driven by another gardener, Wally Powell, with their luggage. They left some days after Haworth's party and travelling conditions were very difficult. After many trials they found their way to Calais but having got as far as boarding a destroyer they were almost immediately turfed off without explanation. John has lost all track of dates and times but the Germans were on the outskirts of Calais and the city was full of evacuating troops, so it must have been on or after 24 May.

Desperate, they went along the coast to Boulogne, which was

being heavily shelled. There they finally got on a hospital ship ('full of very badly wounded – many were left on the quay to die') bound for Southampton and safety. They managed to escape, but the experience destroyed John's relationship with his father: 'I never got on with him, not from the war on. He wasn't the strong man that I wanted to look up to. From then on, I lost faith in him.'

Not all the men of the British colony worked for the IWGC, so many other families had to make their own evacuation arrangements. At the time of the invasion, Bob Simmons's father was working for the British Embassy in Brussels, but Bob was still at the Memorial School in Ypres and boarding with his Belgian grandparents. In the week before Haworth's party left, they managed to miss the Embassy evacuation and decided to try and catch them up in his father's Oldsmobile:

> When we got to Lille there was an air raid in progress and all traffic was supposed to stop but we carried on and we soon picked up a police escort. We spotted a British Army staff car and stopped and my father went to talk to the officer inside. The French police came over and asked what my father wanted. When told that he wanted to know where their HQ was, they marched him off . . . the Belgian number plates didn't help. They thought all Belgians were spies.

Bob faced a dilemma at this point. He had learned to drive the Oldsmobile when he was thirteen by sitting on his father's lap and then progressing to sitting on the edge of the driver's seat. In these circumstances, he might have to put this newly acquired skill to use.

> I'm sitting in the car. I'd read all the Biggles and Bulldog Drummond books and now I thought, what's going to happen next? Maybe I have to make a decision. I knew how to drive and the options were to wait or try to get back to Ypres or drive to the coast. But after about an hour my father came back, red in the face and puffing his cigar, saying: 'Blinking idiots! But at least now I know the Embassy people are in Lille!'

After a few more scrapes, they dumped the Oldsmobile and commandeered a French Army bus for the Embassy party. They were surprised to find they had picked up an escort of two French motorcycle outriders with machine guns ('I felt very important!'). The French had assumed that the British Ambassador was on board. He wasn't but it got them to the coast that much quicker. They managed to get away on one of the last passenger services to leave Le Havre and arrived safely at Southampton. Their ferry, the SS *Normannia*, was sunk by enemy action little more than a week later at Dunkirk.

John Parminter's father – brother of P. D. Parminter, the coach and tour operator – had died in 1937 when John was six. Now he lived with his Belgian mother and grandparents at the Hôtel de la Gare in Ypres. After the invasion, he and his mother tried to get into France 'but the border was closed, so we came back home again'. A little later they made another attempt to leave by car with a family of refugees from Antwerp. After being on the road for some time, they arrived in Bruges to find a 'glorious parade' of occupying Germans in the streets.

They parted from their Antwerp friends and went on alone, hitching lifts where they could and ending up with former neighbours in Ghent. By this time Belgium had capitulated and the Germans were in evidence everywhere; it looked as if they were trapped in an occupied country. John's mother got a lift back to Ypres with a fruit merchant and found little damage to the hotel's fabric, apart from a broken window and a broken sign, but it had been looted '. . . by the people next door. We had a whole group of British people over to lunch one day after the war and Mother went to borrow some cutlery and they presented two sets of cutlery that were recognisable. They were definitely ours because they'd been bought for the hotel . . . but we couldn't prove it and had to give them back.'

After more than a fortnight on the road, they were both back in Ypres where they started, and 'normality was resumed'. But it was a strange kind of normality.

Elaine Madden celebrated her seventeenth birthday three days before the invasion. She had been living with her Belgian grandparents at their hotel in Poperinghe since her mother's death. She had left the Memorial School in July 1939 and no longer had any connection with the IWGC, so she wasn't invited to join the evacuation party and wasn't even aware that there was one. In the last week of May the Germans were close to Poperinghe.

It was my grandfather who said I had to try and get away, as I had a British identity card – it was yellow with a red bar across it, stating that I was British. He said, 'You risk much more than we do because if they catch you and know that you're British, they'll put you in a camp or in a prison and God knows what'll happen to you. They'll probably rape you – I know what soldiers are like.' So he gave me a little money and said, 'Get out, try and get to England whichever way you can.'

Her nineteen-year-old aunt, Simone, begged to be able to go with her, so the two girls started out on a dangerous adventure of their own. At the end of August 1940, Elaine wrote a detailed account in a letter to her Memorial School chum, Rene Fletcher.

My dear old Rene,

 . . .I dare say old pal you would like to know about our adventure so here goes . . . Well darling we had a pretty rough time. Poperinghe hadn't been bombed for a fortnight after the war started, but it was crowded with refugees from Limburg and Brussels and do you know there were thousands of people wandering about the streets and at night sleeping on the pavements. You couldn't get any food and they were simply starving and going mad. It lasted for a fortnight and then on the Friday we were bombed for the first time and a lot of damage was done, our glass roofs and windows came tumbling down but nobody was wounded in our house. About 250 people were killed and 300 wounded in that first raid. Simone and I went out shortly afterwards and it was horrible, women and children lying in the streets, we saw a head lying in the gutter and legs and arms lying about. No matter how hard I try to get it out of my mind I always see that horrible

picture before my eyes. I've seen enough bodies for the rest of my life . . .

After that first raid, the rest of the extended Duponselle family locked up the hotel and left. Elaine and Simone moved into the cellar.

Believe me we stayed in that darned cellar five days and I can tell you it isn't fun sleeping in a damp cellar; those beggars didn't even give us time to go and have something to eat, they came and bombed us practically every five minutes. Talk about slimming eh!

Just before dawn on the morning of Wednesday 29 May – the day the Germans took Ypres – the girls decided to make a break for it. Dragging their bags behind them, they started walking towards the coast. After about eight miles they stopped, exhausted, in a barn to rest.

We'd been in this smelly thing called a barn for a few minutes when 27 German planes came over and what was still left of Pops they put to sleep. Some people who had been able to escape told us that there was no need to go home as it had been wiped off the landscape. There we were stranded, homeless. We tried to drown our misery by sleeping but they didn't give us much time to. About an hour or so later we saw some German tanks stationed in a field nearby. You've never seen two girls hurry away as fast as we did.

They started walking again, and after some miles had the most extraordinary piece of luck:

. . . we met some English soldiers on lorries. They were throwing chocolate to the people who were passing. When Simone and I passed they shouted 'Do you want some chocolate?' and I yelled back 'No, but you can give us a lift'.

The Tommies – the last in a convoy of the 2nd Battalion, The Dorset Regiment on their way to Dunkirk – were bemused to find an

English girl on the road and asked her to prove her identity. Elaine showed her card with the red bar across it and told them her story. The sergeant, a Great War veteran with a daughter her age, conferred with his colleagues. Yes, they would take her, but not Simone because she was Belgian. Elaine was adamant: Simone was not only her aunt, she was her dear friend. She couldn't leave her there alone; in fact she wouldn't leave without her. The soldiers relented and the two girls clambered up into the lorry.

Off we went, heading for I don't know where, anyway it was better than walking. We'd done about 20 miles in our Rolls Royce when we had to leave it behind and march . . . the roads had been badly shelled and a car couldn't possibly pass. It was simply pouring with rain and there wasn't a house to be seen, so as our soldier friends wouldn't leave us behind we marched with them.

They made slow progress on foot and by using abandoned vehicles found along the way, avoiding the crossfire as they went. Bridges had been destroyed and sluice gates opened, flooding fields so that they often found themselves 'marching in knee-deep water'. To cross one river the soldiers pushed abandoned lorries into the water and they 'just walked over them'. Worse, at some points they had to walk between – and over – dead bodies. Further on, they were all picked up by another retreating BEF lorry and arrived in Dunkirk at nightfall and as German bombers and artillery were pulverising the town.

Oh God, when we got to Dunkirk about eleven at night the whole place was on fire. I've never seen anything like it, even in films it wasn't as terrible as it was there. What a mess we were in, we had to find the docks and nobody knew the way. The more we rode, the deeper we got in the flames. Do you know that was the first time on the whole journey I thought my last moment had come. The Tommies apparently thought the same as I did, because they were swearing and yelling to the driver to get out of the town.

A shell fell between them and the lorry travelling behind them and it ran straight into the shell hole. They were in the middle of a battlefield. Then, more by luck than judgement, they came to the docks where thousands of BEF troops were massing for evacuation. It was dark apart from the light of the raging fires, but the girls were still conspicuously unmilitary. To get on to the pier and have a chance of escaping with the men, they needed to look the part. Their chivalrous protectors – whom Elaine and Simone knew only as Knocker, Smudger and Gary – lent them 'greatcoats, tin hats, gas masks, everything except the trousers'. They were already wearing women's army boots ('because it was the great fashion in those days to have boots, as it is now') and the greatcoats reached almost to their ankles. With their hair tucked into their helmets and their 'three saviours' forming a close guard around them, they made for the pier.

One incident Elaine didn't relate in her letter to Rene shows how far the lads were prepared to go to protect them. When they got to the pier, they were challenged by French military police:

One of them must have seen our legs because we weren't wearing trousers and they wanted to see . . . They said: 'You've got two civilians' and the three around us were saying: 'Non, non, non'. There was a shot . . . I don't know if he was killed . . . And then it was: 'Come on! Go, go, go!'

Once on the pier, they waited for the best part of a day and a night with thousands of others 'like sardines, one standing next to the other and not being able to move and not being able to sleep' as fires burned and bombs dropped around them and into the harbour, drenching the waiting troops. Then came the real test of their disguise:

Eventually it was: 'Come on, our turn next!' What I recall is that there must have been quite a lot of ships and boats in the harbour because I could see some small boats – kind of fishing boats and I thought, Good God! Are we going to cross the Channel in these small boats? We'll never make it! I think it was a Dutch trawler. We had to go down a rope ladder from the pier so I went down first and somebody at the bottom of the rope said: 'Well, well, well! Ladies' legs!' in a sarcastic tone and then he looked up at Simone, who was coming down, and said: 'More ladies' legs! Now what is this?' Then he pulled us aside . . .

The British officer gave them a brief interrogation and then put them in the captain's cabin ('we can't have you with all the men'). They never saw Knocker, Smudger and Gary, to whom they owed so much, again.

Once they were safely in England and staying with Elaine's aunt in Streatham, the press seized on their story: 'THEY JOINED B.E.F. – SHAPELY ANKLES GAVE GIRLS AWAY' ran one headline, with a warming photo of the girls sitting together in a deckchair. Now, though, life began to take a different turn. After the excitement of her escape Elaine ends her letter to Rene conventionally enough:

> I've talked enough about myself now what about you and the family. Are you married yet? Or are you still hairdressing? I am for the present looking for a job and I hope the next time I write to you I'll be able to tell you I've found one. Well I'll leave you for the present.
>> Lots of love
>> Elaine

She did find a job, though it wasn't quite what she was expecting.

On 4 June 1940 Churchill delivered his most famous speech of the war to the House of Commons. In a rhetorical overview of the Fall of France, he acknowledged the sacrifice made at Calais and the 'colossal military disaster' that ended with Dunkirk. The evacuation of so much of the BEF had been miraculous, but 'wars are not won by evacuations'. The stirring call to 'fight on the beaches' marked the start of the most dangerous stage of the war for Britain, but also its most profound psychological turning point.

The following day Sir William Pulteney received a letter from Windsor Castle. He had written to King George VI who, with Queen Elizabeth, subscribed to the Memorial School, to report its forced closure with the evacuation of the British colony. An aide acknowledged the cancellation of their subscriptions and conveyed the King's personal message:

The King considers that [the evacuation] reflects the highest credit on those responsible . . . The King realises of course what the feelings must be of all those who have worked for so many years for the School with such success. His Majesty attaches great value to the work which the School has undertaken in educating so many children, and training them to become good citizens of this country.

No doubt Pulteney was touched by this acknowledgement of his efforts as its co-founder and staunchest supporter, but the circumstances were poignant. The Memorial School had been open for little more than a decade. Now Ypres was in enemy hands, the school was shut and its children scattered. Who knew if it was even still standing?

On 10 June Lawrence Dawson was transferred to the Radcliffe Infirmary, Oxford, where he found himself in the company of several wounded British and French soldiers.

One British soldier, serving with the REs [Royal Engineers], told me he went through Ypres and was the party responsible for the blowing up of the bridge in front of the Menin Gate. He said the monument was badly damaged by shellfire . . . the houses were badly damaged and the British Church and School were practically down to the ground.

9

Occupation

They weren't all barbarians.

Nenette van Bost, a schoolgirl during the German
occupation of Ypres, 1940–44

We suffered a bit in prison: we were knocked about, I lost eight kilos.

Stephen Grady, sixteen, arrested for sabotage, 1941

IN FACT, DESPITE alarming reports of destruction, Ypres was relatively unscathed. The shrapnel damage to the Menin Gate – due mainly to the efforts of the British sappers who blew up the bridge in front of it – looked worse than it actually was. In rue d'Elverdinghe the British church and school were still standing, though a retaining wall had been demolished and items of value or national significance had been removed for safe keeping by local people. Nenette van Bost's father took down St George's many regimental flags:

> Dad was a great patriot and when the Germans were about to arrive he went to the English church and moved all the banners and he never told anybody. I do remember those banners in a big bag in the bottom of a wardrobe in our house and mother grumbling about it but not knowing what it was.

But if Ypres itself had survived, its people were having to adjust to a different kind of life under an occupying power. There was a 9 p.m. curfew, businesses closed or were requisitioned, and German lessons were introduced in schools. Food was in short supply, soldiers were billeted on everyone with a spare room, and those with British nationality – by birth or through marriage – had to report weekly to the Kommandantur, risking arrest and internment at any time.

Nenette van Bost's future husband, John Parminter, was British. He was ten when the Germans arrived in Ypres. When their escape attempt failed soon after the invasion and John and his widowed Belgian mother returned to Ypres, Mrs Parminter was summoned three times before the German authorities, 'but she managed to talk her way out of it . . . she was quite somebody'. Business was poor at the Hôtel de la Gare and her 'guests' were mainly German soldiers, John recalled.

> We had very few customers . . . the odd commercial salesman coming for one, two nights. We never had any trouble with the Germans billeted with us. I think they knew they weren't welcome. They never stayed for drinks in the café; they just passed through to go to their bedrooms. But the Flemish Gestapo were a very different proposition . . . they were terrible, they were shot after the war for collaboration. We had two of them [in the hotel] fighting amongst themselves. Mother had to get the German Kommandant to come and separate them and get rid of them. The room was full of blood.

The occupying forces were mainly older Wehrmacht conscripts, many of whom had fought in the 1914–18 war. They were glad of this relatively comfortable posting. Ypres, cold and damp as its winters were, was still preferable to the Eastern Front. They were well behaved, had their own drinking places and brothels, and didn't trouble the locals unless confronted with bare-faced resistance or rank insubordination. Nenette recalls that her family's hotel was also full of soldiers:

> They came in through the side entrance and went immediately upstairs and we only had one who would occasionally knock on the door, come in and say 'Heil Hitler' . . . and as virtually everybody in those days did, we had a big map on the wall on

which we used to follow the Allies' movements with pins. And he saw this map on the wall and he just tore it down. That was the only time though.

Nenette, nine at the start of the occupation, preferred the 'nice big fat one':

He asked Mother if he could come in and sit down and she said yes and he asked her if I could sit on his lap. And Mum said yes and I remember feeling uneasy about sitting on his lap and then he started to cry. He said: 'Do you know, I have a daughter that age? I haven't seen her for many years.' So you see, they weren't all barbarians, they had feelings as well.

Human empathy was one thing but collaboration was another. Though there was a pro-German element among the Flemish in Ypres, the majority – especially those with family or business connections to the British – were punctilious in their dealings with the occupiers and avoided anything that might be construed as helping them in their odious task.

That didn't extend to buying on the black market. As food in this once-rich farming community became scarce, people who could afford to used it to supplement their subsistence rations. As a child, Nenette remembers eating carrots and sugar beets – grown for animal feed – raw from the fields; she also recalls hiding black-market butter from the inspectors in her brother's plus fours on a hot summer day and seeing the melting fat run down his legs. The Germans had taken over her father's small printing business and there was no real income from the hotel; the family of five children and a grandfather had a good meal once a week with an aunt and the rest of the time they made do. When Nenette needed a new dress, she made one from the dining-room curtains. 'Yes, I know what it is, being hungry and being cold because at one time Mother put all the mattresses from the bedrooms into what used to be the salon and we slept there just to be warm . . . We got along as best we could.' Sometimes they found small treats – a chocolate, sweets or a couple of slices of bread – left in the glove box on the hall stand by the soldiers billeted on them. To offer such gifts in person would have landed both parties in trouble.

John remembers an easier time: travel restrictions meant that those with money spent it on meals and drinks in his mother's hotel, but he knows of others who 'had to stay in bed because they were so hungry'. Later on in the occupation, during the school holidays, Nenette heard that the Germans were giving food to children in a château being used as a military rest centre just outside the town. She and her friend deliberated whether to go. It would mean not telling their parents, as it amounted to collaboration and would be forbidden. Hunger won over principle and the threat of punishment.

> So off we went to the little château. I'll never forget it, there were big grounds and when we walked in there was this big, big hall, and there was this large table decked with food: sardines, hard-boiled eggs, bananas, oranges (which I didn't even know existed), bread, cheese – all the food you can imagine. And we, as hungry children, ate and ate and ate . . . I remember eating sardines and hard-boiled eggs as if there were no tomorrow.

Afterwards they went swimming and played boisterous games organised by the soldiers. They had 'an absolutely wonderful' time until that evening when a number of children in the town, including Nenette, became ill. The doctor diagnosed severe indigestion. Parents were nonplussed: indigestion when food was so hard to come by? Eventually the truth came out. The Germans were accused of trying to poison the children, when the most they could be blamed for was trying to win young hearts and minds.

John's mother was finding it difficult to knuckle down to German rule. Within weeks of the occupation she was fined 200 francs for serving drinks after curfew and she was a regular visitor to the Kommandantur, speaking for those who had been hauled up for some minor infringement or insubordination. Her refusal to be ordered about by the Germans eventually got her into serious trouble. John was thirteen when he returned to the hotel to find his mother outside, being manhandled by a member of the Luftwaffe Feldgendarmerie – a military policeman – brandishing a pistol. He had been in a nearby café looking for the owner, a notorious local smuggler, and had held the customers more or less hostage. One of them was John's sister, but she had managed to get out through the back and had come home in hysterics, unable to explain what was going on. Mrs Parminter decided to go and find out for herself. Once in the café she was told she couldn't leave. She refused, saying she had left her hotel unattended. Ignoring warnings, she left, pursued by the furious policeman.

After a tussle, she got away, grabbed John and slammed the door of the hotel in the policeman's face. But he fired through the glass, and a dum-dum bullet lodged in her breast, just missing her heart.

I was screaming and shouting in Flemish 'You've hit my mother!' There she was with all these little milky veins hanging there through her dress. The cook went to the Feld Kommandantur just across the road and they came to fetch him away . . . and my mother was taken to hospital. Strangely enough she was home again that night after the bullet had been removed! The thing had exploded . . . she kept a patch of her dress with all the little burn marks – and the bullet!

She also kept the bill – 275 francs – for the operation. The Kommandant later visited the hotel to apologise and assure her that the policeman would be punished. He seemed to John at the time 'a very nice man'. Much to Mrs Parminter's discomfort, he would make a point of coming in to her hotel bar for a drink. On the surface, order and decorum were strictly maintained but – whether the Kommandant was aware of it or not – disobedience and resistance were going on under his nose. And his feet.

The doctor who removed Mrs Parminter's bullet was also known to attend to injured British airmen who had been shot down and were being hidden in lofts and cellars in the town, assisted by local people. The original cellars under the rebuilt shops and cafés in the market square around the Cloth Hall were all interconnected, so it wasn't difficult to hide people and move them around, even in the very heart of the town. John remembers his mother telling him of an airman hidden in the Regina Hotel in the square: 'They had Germans billeted there. It was only after the war that she told me she'd been to see an airman there. Apparently the Germans and the airman met on the stairwell occasionally – unbelievable – sort of openly!'

A judicious blind eye was turned to more orthodox aspects of Ypres life. Sounding the Last Post at the Menin Gate was officially suspended during the years of occupation, but Nenette said that it did happen occasionally if one of the fire brigade volunteers was free and felt so inclined. 'I can still see it so very vividly. He would come on his bike with his bugle on a piece of string in his pocket, put his bike against the wall of the café and just blow the Last Post . . . and I've seen the odd German soldier standing to attention.'

John and Nenette remember German brass bands playing 'lovely music', soldiers enjoying the trench humour of Bruce Bairnsfather's cartoons on the walls of the Hôtel de la Gare, and local children plied with lemonade and biscuits happily playing jacks with the occupying forces outside their train carriage billets. But neither can they forget the pathetic sight of starving slave workers brought in to do heavy manual labour:

> One summer evening there was this big steamroller coming along the road towards us with just one soldier with a pistol and this poor little foreigner driving this thing. There was a shop next door to us and my mother bought a bar of chocolate on the black market and they gave her another one and I went to take it, saying 'Kann ich das abgeben?', and I gave these two bars of chocolate to this poor man. I wonder if he ever survived?

The Parminters' mixed experience of occupation – hardship (harder for some than for others) and petty regulation under a regime that treated the Flemish population humanely – wasn't unique, nor was it shared by everyone.

When Lily Wilkins and Blanche Dawson returned to Ypres in late June 1940 after their misadventures with Brigadier Prower, life was difficult. Without their husbands, they had no income. Lily was the more vulnerable because she was British-born; Blanche was Belgian and had already proved resilient in a tricky situation. But Lily soon learned. After turfing out squatters from their house in the Chaussée de Bruges, they settled in to their austere new life on Lily's small savings and the produce from Harry Wilkins' allotment. Lillian was sixteen and would have left the Memorial School that summer term anyway. Her sister Joyce, eleven, like Joyce Dawson, went to the Ecole Moyenne in Ypres where they had to adapt quickly to lessons in Dutch and German. They were both bright girls; they worked hard and made rapid progress.

After a comfortable life on Harry's Commission salary, the Wilkins women now found themselves on the breadline and had to accept charity. Joyce was sent to Dunn's teashop at the end of the day to collect unsold buns, and Lillian was given an equally humiliating task:

> Mother didn't have much money and there wasn't any way of getting any. She said to me, 'The nuns in the rue de Lille have opened up a soup kitchen and I want you to go down and take a jug with you and ask for some soup because my little bit of money isn't going to last and every little bit is going to help.' And I said, 'No! I'm not going to the nuns to ask for soup. I can't tell them a sob story. Send Joyce!' She said, 'I want you to do it. You must understand, we have to eat and you're entitled to it. Tell them your father's gone and we're stuck.'

Lillian went, but by a circuitous route: 'I didn't go through the town, I used to walk all the way round the ramparts to the Lille Gate, run down to the convent and ask for the soup. I was dead scared that someone would see me asking for food. And Mother used to wonder why it took me so long!'

There were other distasteful tasks. Lily bought a consignment of potatoes on the black market and the girls had to go down into the cellar every week to pick out the shoots to keep them edible; they sifted sacks of coal dust for usable lumps and went gleaning for wheat at harvest time to make flour. Good Belgian neighbours helped them out: they were given offcuts from a timber yard for fuel, invited for Sunday dinner, and given rabbits for the pot.

For almost a year Lily and Blanche heard nothing from their husbands; it wasn't until the beginning of 1941 that Harry Wilkins and Lawrence Dawson even knew their wives were safe and well in Ypres. Both men had made frantic efforts on their return to England to discover what had happened. On 8 June 1940, while Dawson was still recovering in hospital from his hand injury, Wilkins wired Prower at Fougères in Brittany asking where his wife and family were. Two days later, he went to IWGC's London office to tell the sorry story of how he had left them in Prower's care and to enlist the Commission's help in finding out where they were now. Fabian Ware took a personal interest in the Wilkins and Dawson cases, sending his own wire to Prower on 6 June:

> TO MEET UNINFORMED CRITICISM WRITE ME FULL FACTS
> REGARDING IMPOSSIBILITY YOUR RETURN FROM ABBEVILLE
> TO MONTREUIL AND WIMEREUX ON MAY 20TH.

Prower's five-page handwritten reply about the 'most unfortunate affair' blamed impassable roads, unexpected enemy incursions (contrary to official information) and the general fog of war for his inability to return to pick up the two families as promised. He admitted:

> *I am afraid the above makes poor reading and gives no satisfaction to the two gardeners concerned. I can only hope that the three women and the three children who were left in one of the . . . most comfortable houses in Montreuil will be allowed to remain there . . .*

Correspondence between the two men continued over the summer of 1940, with Ware encouraging Prower to make his own enquiries about the families. 'I want to keep in touch with this matter,' he wrote at the end of July. There was no official reprimand and the Commission did not accept responsibility for what had happened, but it is clear from internal correspondence that Prower's actions – in abandoning the two families and his Wimereux office to decamp to Brittany and then failing to control a near-riot when he evacuated the last party of gardeners and their families from Bordeaux in late June – raised eyebrows at IWGC headquarters and damaged his reputation. His fate was sealed. In a letter to a friend in Ypres, written in September 1941, Dawson reported brusquely but with feeling: 'Prower dismissed – shall never forget.'

In an electronic world it is difficult to appreciate how painfully slow written communications were between the UK and occupied countries during the war. Letters could be exchanged with occupied Belgium via the International Red Cross – but these weren't letters in any normal sense. They were brief messages of no more than twenty-five words and could be sent only once a month. They were subject to strict censorship and took several months to reach their intended recipients, having passed through many hands and inter-mediary countries (and no doubt resting for long periods in various in trays) on the way. Replies – also of no more than twenty-five words – could be handwritten on the reverse of the special Red Cross pro forma and would endure the same excruciating journey in reverse. As a result, no sensible exchange was possible and communi-cations were reduced to the 'All well here' variety. Nevertheless, as the only means available of staying in touch with loved ones, they were precious: anxiously awaited, received with joy and often kept for decades afterwards.

News that the Wilkins and Dawson women were now in Ypres filtered back to England only slowly. Ware wrote to Prower on 17 January 1941 that he 'had just heard' that the Wilkins were reported safe 'on the 4th October last'. The following month he had similar news of the Dawsons. In November 1940 one of Dawson's IWGC gardener colleagues, Albert Jones, wrote to him from a German internment camp: 'Am pleased to inform you that your Wife and Daughter are both quite well and have returned to Ypres and are hoping for news of you.' Dawson obviously hadn't received this by the start of the following year, when he wrote to Captain Arnott to see if he could throw any light on the matter. Arnott could provide only 'cold comfort'; he'd had to leave his own wife and two children behind in France. Confirmation must have arrived by 24 January as this is the date of Lawrence Dawson's first Red Cross letter to his wife Blanche at their home in rue d'Elverdinghe. It reads:

WILKINS AND SELF SAFE AND WELL AT HOME. HOW ARE
GRANDMA AND JOYCE? LOVE TO YOU ALL. HUBBY.

Joyce's handwritten, precisely 25-word reply is dated 6 June:

> *Daddy Darling,*
> *Mummy, Grandma, I safe. Is Auntiebee or Uncle Leslie with you?*
> *Owing to cost of living, staying at Auntie Godlieve's.*
> *Many kisses, Joyce*

Despite the skeletal nature of these missives, many are immensely
touching. They speak of the anxiety of waiting ('No news since
26.8.43' – written in February 1944), the mundanely domestic ('Joyce
dear, Is Chinese tea-service safe?') and the agony of being parted
('Longing for you,' Blanche often wrote). Joyce too missed her
father, though she seemed to be coping heroically without him:

> *Daddy Dear,*
> *I miss my little Daddy for homework. Never mind, doing best at*
> *everything.*
> *Your ever loving little daughter,*
> *Joyce*

Some 'indiscretions' in Lawrence Dawson's letters were picked up
by the Chiswick and Brentford branch of the Citizens Advice Bureau
who had the job of pre-vetting letters before they went to the Censor
(no wonder it all took such a long time). 'END APPEARS TO BE
IN SIGHT' and 'SING A & M HYMN 135' were both rejected as
being useful to the enemy or likely to be interpreted as code – which
the latter was, albeit entirely innocently: number 135 in *Hymns
Ancient and Modern* is the Easter anthem 'The strife is o'er, the battle
done'.

The Wilkins and Dawson women had endured much strife by the
time this was written in 1944. The event Lily Wilkins and her
daughters most dreaded came soon enough, in March 1941.

We had no warning but we knew it was going to happen. There
was a banging on the door at four o'clock in the morning. Bang,
bang! Kick, kick! It was a Gestapo chap, an interpreter and two

or three soldiers. They marched in for Mother. 'Zehn Minuten! Zehn Minuten!' She had ten minutes to pack her bag. She was calm then. Before she went she said, 'Now you work hard, Joyce. Work hard for me and do what Lillian tells you to.' And then she was gone.

Soon after that they came for Blanche and Joyce Dawson.

The Wilkins girls were now alone and under virtual house arrest. The Germans had removed the telephone, radios and bicycles. Lily's money soon ran out and the allotment was bare. Eventually a small allowance came through via the Red Cross in Geneva but it was hardly enough to cover rent and food. 'We used to have one loaf of bread a week. But we could get butter beans – pounds and pounds of dried butter beans. We used to have a dish of butter beans and one Christmas we had a baked potato and that was all.' But they had very good neighbours who looked out for them. While Joyce was studying hard at school, Lillian would do housework in the mornings and spend afternoons with her next-door neighbour, Mrs Reinhaert.

She taught me to crochet and all kinds of things. We had an understanding that if ever I was in any trouble – because the soldiers were lodged all the way up and down our road – I had only to knock on the wall and she would come running because she could speak a bit of German.

When German officers arrived one day to billet three soldiers in their attic, Lillian put the arrangement to the test. In marched Mrs Reinhaert and argued with the officers. In the end she signed a form ('there was always a form'), and took in two soldiers herself so that the girls wouldn't have to have them.

Gradually, as people got to hear about their plight, more help came to hand. The bank manager delivered a surreptitious weekly food parcel from a local benefactress under cover of curfew. The Baron de Vinck and his wife invited the girls to stay with their family at their château at nearby Zillebeke. Lillian had to go to the Kommandantur to ask for permission for two short visits. She remembers a picnic in the grounds and boating on the lake with one of the older sons: 'We were very, very well treated and if they had some visitors, we were all introduced. Very, very nice.' How different from their reception at the Prower house, she might have added, where they were put in the servants' quarters.

The Wilkins girls were also about to have an offer of help from an unexpected source.

There was a knock at the door and there stood Stephen Grady with his bicycle. I said, 'Hello, Stephen, what are you doing here?' I knew him from school of course, but I didn't know how he knew about us or where we were. 'Are you going to ask me in?' he said, so I said, 'No, I'm sorry but there's Germans to the right of me and there's Germans to the left of me, the whole road is swarming with Germans! I'm sorry, I'm too scared to ask you in.' He tried to persuade me, saying he'd cycled all the way from Nieppe, over the border. He wouldn't tell me what he wanted, and I wouldn't let him in, so he said bye-bye, and so did I. And do you know, for years and years, that's preyed on my mind. Why hadn't I asked him in? What was I afraid of?

Lillian didn't discover the truth about Stephen's aborted mission for another sixty years. The sisters struggled on in Ypres until the autumn of 1943 when they, too, had a visit from the Gestapo:

Bang, bang! Kick, kick! On the door at midnight and I knew perfectly well what it was all about, so once again I knocked on the wall and Mrs Reinhaert came in. 'What's the meaning of this?' she said. 'We're taking the two English girls,' they said.

Stephen Grady had tried to escape from Nieppe with two neighbours – his friend Marcel Lombard and his father from the farm next door – on 24 May. They had cycled to Calais, where they found 'absolute pandemonium', and were on the road to Dunkirk when French troops barred their way. The two boys wanted to carry on but the older man 'got the wind up' so they returned to Nieppe, just in time for Stephen's fifteenth birthday and the arrival of German troops:

The Germans arrived on my birthday, May 30th. I remember being in the house and seeing two side-cars arrive from the direction of Belgium with German soldiers. The following day, a nearby farmhouse was occupied by German infantry. They must have been walking a long way; their feet were in a terrible condition. It was very hot in May, and obviously they had had a very difficult time. The French and British troops left very quickly in the last days of May, and the British were ordered to drop everything: all their equipment except their rifles, light packs and light uniforms. All the rest was left behind . . . the area where we lived from Armentières to the French coast was absolutely littered with everything you could imagine: horses, trucks, equipment, ammunition, guns – you name it, there it was – armchairs, accordions . . .

Stephen Grady senior hadn't considered escaping: he wasn't prepared to leave Berthe, his blind wife, behind and he was still waiting for instructions from the Commission, instructions that never came. So the Grady family were together in Nieppe for the whole of the occupation. His father was issued with false papers by the mayor and effectively hidden from the Germans for four years, dodging between cellars and safe houses whenever danger threatened.

But at the beginning, those few days between the BEF's retreat and the Germans' arrival were bizarre and chaotic. Stephen recalls:

We got back to Nieppe and there was a British three-tonner with two British soldiers and two French tarts. Full of booze – they'd raided a brewery or something. It was parked in a field not far from us next to Pont-d'Achelles cemetery, so I went in there and they said: 'Hello, mate!', and I said: 'I speak English.' 'Listen, mate, can you get some beer for us? If you can get some beer, we'll swap you for anything we've got. We've got champagne, anything you want.' So I got a case of beer from a nearby pub and they gave me a case of champagne and a case of Cinzano. I handed most of it to my parents and stashed the rest away. A couple of days later we tried it all and got absolutely blotto, the two of us. The Stukas were bombing everywhere and everybody was in the cellar. We were right in the middle of a field getting blotto and they thought we were lost, gone or shot.

Stephen and his friend Marcel also made the most of what they found abandoned on the roads by the retreating troops:

The stuff was incredible . . . most of it abandoned by the French. So we collected arms. We had about ten rifles of different kinds, grenades, and the French equivalent of a Bren gun . . . We took all this stuff and buried it in a Bren gun box on the farm. We didn't quite know why, but we were fascinated at that age by all this weaponry, and we thought the arms would be required later on . . .

By early June the first dispiriting columns of prisoners came through on the road from Dunkirk, each column headed by the British.

The Germans were escorting, and were quite ruthless. I saw a French soldier shot when he couldn't walk any further. They just shot him and left him there. It was very hot. People were putting buckets of water along the route and the Germans were coming along and kicking the buckets over.

After a couple of weeks, everything seemed to go quiet. There was little evidence of German troops, except on the Dunkirk–Lille road, and the public infrastructure had collapsed: there were no buses, schools or police. Then a few British stragglers who'd managed to evade capture started to appear:

I came across two British soldiers in civilian clothes and managed to put them up in one of the tool sheds at the war cemetery. They stayed there for about a week and my parents allowed me to go and feed them and then they disappeared, saying that they wanted to walk towards the coast. I never saw them again. There were two or three others left around Nieppe. One, a Gordon Highlander named Grassick, stayed with a woman. He was eventually caught; the woman was sent to Germany and never came back.

Over the autumn and into the winter of 1941, the Germans took a stronger grip of the country areas and started rounding up anyone they could find with British nationality. The mayor of Nieppe, Jules Houcke, offered to protect Stephen's father 'until the British return' – an inspiring act of faith in the dark days of winter 1940. But with his father in hiding and unable to work, the family had no income. Houcke saved them all from starvation by employing Stephen to tend the three British war cemeteries within the commune – and the village square. His small wage, paid by the *mairie*, kept the family afloat throughout the occupation.

Stephen had his first taste of amateur sabotage in the early days of occupation by removing a German 'Go Slow' sign and chucking it in a pond. He graduated to putting sugar in German petrol tanks and a year later he and Marcel embarked on a more ambitious project. Watching one of the frequent air battles over Nieppe in the early summer of 1941, they saw a Messerschmitt shot down a few miles away just over the Belgian border. By the time they got there on their bikes, the plane was swarming with soldiers and onlookers, so they decided to go back early the next morning for souvenirs.

> There was nobody there, so we investigated and got into the cockpit. I started unscrewing all sorts of bits, for souvenirs, and having done that, as there was still nobody around and I'd taken some tools with me, I started smashing the dials in the cockpit. Having done that, we wrote on the side of the plane: 'Vivent les aviateurs Anglais qui ont abattu ce sale Boche' [Long live the English airmen who brought down this filthy Bosch]. Then we thought we'd try and take the black cross off the wing and started knocking off rivets, but there were hundreds, and while we were doing this we saw a German recovery lorry and a staff car arrive at the end of the track. No sooner had we got on our bikes and started pedalling off than another staff car appeared, and two Germans arrested us.

At the Kommandantur at Armentières they were 'received by a very irate German officer who beat us about and was extremely annoyed at what had been written on the side of the plane'. From there they were sent to the Feldgendarmerie at Lille where they were left in a cell with two others for forty-eight hours without food. Their fellow prisoners were a woman accused of ripping down a German poster and a boy supposed to have spat on a German flag; they were all ill-treated and the woman was kicked in the stomach.

After interrogation, Stephen and Marcel were sent to the military prison at Loos-Lille. 'It was already full of people who were there for anti-German activities – four or five people in cells built for one. Conditions were already terrible. We were told that we were going to be sent to Germany, to special labour camps. We were told that we were going to be shot, all sorts of things.' In fact, after three unpleasant months, they were released. Two factors probably secured their unexpected deliverance: Mayor Houcke interceded on their behalf – they were only boys, after all; and a bureaucratic glitch meant that because the arrest had taken place in Belgium, they should never have been taken to a French jail but to a tribunal in Brussels.

Whatever happened, we were miraculously released. We suffered a bit in prison; we were knocked about; I was sixteen and lost eight kilos. Food was extremely scarce, but we were very lucky and we got away with it. We were interrogated by the GFP [Geheime Feldpolizei – plain clothes military police]; if it had been the Gestapo the consequences would have been much worse. We would certainly have been sent to Germany, because at the time people were being punished with five or ten years in prison for nothing. Whereas we were being accused of sabotage, a crime that carried the death sentence.

The experience marked a turning point. Some time after his release in September 1941, Stephen and his parents had a visit from Jules Houcke. Houcke, his brother and a local headmaster were starting up a resistance cell and Stephen's services – particularly his English – were needed. Still only sixteen but fired with unquestioning patriotism and impelled to avenge the brutality he had already witnessed during the occupation, Stephen was more than ready to oblige.

10

Detention: the Men's Story

Five years of life have passed away,
That nothing on earth can ever repay.
Lost to all that shared with me,
Five years of hell in Germany.

Jean Scott, British internee arrested July 1940, liberated
April 1945

O F THE 207 War Graves Commission men unaccounted for by
the first week of June 1940, one or two, like Stephen Grady's
father, had gone into hiding. Others, realising that they had literally
missed the boat and had no other options, carried on regardless. They
received no wages and, by the end of June, had no management
supervision. All senior IWGC staff had by this time made their way
back to the UK: Brigadier Prower, in charge of the northern France
area, had left Bordeaux for England with a small party of gardeners
and their families on 20 June.

The men left behind knew their duty and continued working in
their cemeteries, some of which had suffered badly in the BEF retreat
to the coast. Albert Roberts, a head gardener based in Arras, forty
kilometres from Ypres in France, told the Commission later:

The German Wehrmacht never interfered with me; that was not
their business. I kept steadily working as though nothing had
happened up to the day of my arrest . . . I immediately visited
all the cemeteries and memorials under my care. A great deal of
damage had been done in the Gorre British and Indian Cemetery.

Our troops had held position in the cemetery, dug trenches in many parts. I set about trying to clear debris and was later able to scythe the grass and clear things up in general. The surrounding wall was blown up over nearly its whole length, a large portion of headstones were smashed to pieces, the tool house had a direct hit. . . .

Over the following weeks Roberts gathered up a number of British and German dead and buried them where they had fallen, putting any identifying papers in inverted bottles on their graves. He expected to be arrested at any time but half-hoped that 'the authorities would consider we people to be politically immune'. No such luck. By the end of September 1940 he and the remaining gardeners still at work in France and Belgium would be rounded up to start an indefinite period of internment in camps far away from their homes.

Thanks to the heroic efforts of Haworth and his escort officers – and the bravery of individual escapees – a large contingent from Ypres had managed to get away to England. Even so, fifteen IWGC men, some with their families, were left behind to face arrest and internment.

Fred Fisher was a stalwart of the Ypres British community, a staunch Legion man and a regular fixture at pre-war Christmas parties and events. He came from a family of soldiers and fought with the Hampshire Regiment at Mons in 1914, where a shell blew part of his face away, a disfigurement he bore for the rest of his life. After the war he came back to Belgium to work for the IWGC, where he met and married a French nurse. Their five children all went to the Memorial School. When Haworth's party evacuated on 18 May, Fred stayed behind. His wife had gone to France for a family funeral and was stranded there after the border closed. He wouldn't leave without her. In July 1940, as the Germans were flushing out British citizens in Ypres, they knew where to come and find Fred. A short time before, he had fallen in his cellar and broken his arm. German soldiers heard his shouts for help and came to his rescue. They came back later to arrest him, together with his fifteen-year-old son Harry.

Former Memorial School pupil Arthur Jones had left his father, Albert, living alone in Ypres at the start of the year. Though his English parents were still married, they had lived apart since the death of their youngest child in 1936:

> My little brother of ten months died in Ypres and Mother left for England to get over the tragedy but never returned . . . Because of the dangerous situation my father had sent me back to England in January 1940. I was fifteen then and had already finished school. Having left him in Ypres, I heard nothing of him for two years. Apparently he'd cycled to Calais, but got caught up in the bombing of the roads and had his bike stolen, so that when he got to the port the last boat had left. So he walked back to Ypres. By July he was having to start selling things off to get money for food. Then one day a German officer and two soldiers banged on his door and took him away to a prison camp.

It was bitter bad luck for Albert Jones. He had already been a German prisoner of war – in the Somme in 1917 – and was now about to go through it all again.

The lives of Scottish brothers William and James MacDonald diverged after the 1914–18 war. William joined the IWGC in Belgium, married a local girl and had two boys, one of whom – André – went to the Memorial School. James went into service with the Royal Household: as King George VI's valet, he was the first to discover the monarch dead in his bed at Sandringham on a February morning in 1952. William and fifteen-year-old André were among those to be arrested, with Fred and Harry Fisher, in Ypres that first summer of the German occupation.

Internment camps were used by both sides to incarcerate enemy aliens. Women as well as men were interned; even children ended up in the camps, though those under eighteen and over sixty weren't supposed to be there. Unlike military prisoners of war, the treatment of civilian internees was not regulated by the Geneva Convention. However, the International Committee of the Red Cross (ICRC) made agreements with the Axis powers to extend the protection offered by the Convention to those in civilian camps. Its intervention on their behalf, particularly in the form of food parcels, saved the lives and the sanity of many prisoners of war.

In retrospect, internment camps (Internierungslager, or Ilag for short) represent the acceptable face of German war prisons, but only by comparison with the atrocious extremes of Auschwitz, Belsen and the rest, whose full horror was revealed only towards the end of the war. The Ilags were far from death camps – though people certainly died untimely deaths in them – and wartime internees have understandably attracted less attention and sympathy than the victims of Nazi extermination and concentration camps. Here there was no semblance of humanity, much less compliance with Geneva Convention standards. Nevertheless, enduring enforced separation from work, home and family in harsh conditions for four or five years in an internment camp was intolerable enough.

No testimony survives from the Ypres IWGC men about their internment, and their families say they chose to say little about it after the war. But living side by side with them were prisoners who recorded their experiences in detail and often very soon after repatriation. Some of these reports were made by interned gardeners from other IWGC areas in the form of debriefings for the Commission, which did its best from the relative safety of its Buckinghamshire headquarters to stay in touch with employees who had been left behind. As ever taking the optimistic view, it had hoped initially to keep the work going in occupied France and Belgium. As late as August 1940 it had secured agreement with the Trading with the Enemy Department of Britain's wartime administration to pay any remaining gardeners at work the equivalent of £10 a month through the (then neutral) US Embassy in Brussels. Sadly, this proved unnecessary as there were soon none left to pay. By March 1942 the Commission had confirmation of 159 of its staff in internment, with thirty-six at liberty and eleven dead or unaccounted for.

Bernard Parsons, an IWGC stonemason arrested with other British men in Le Touquet in late July 1940, recognised many of his fellow prisoners on the coach taking them away, but there was one he didn't know: 'Wedged away in a corner of the coach, looking as if he hadn't enough room, was a man who had the appearance of being "some-one in the church", but I learned later when having a chat and a glass of Stiedam with him, that he was P. G. Wodehouse, who writes the funny stuff.'

Wodehouse wrote – and broadcast – 'funny stuff' about his intern-ment experience and suffered opprobrium in Britain for the rest of his life as a result. Though he shared many of the privations of camp life with his fellow internees, he was able to carry on writing and he seemed genuinely to enjoy the company of people he wouldn't otherwise have met with on equal terms. Most importantly, after less than a year of incarceration he was reunited with his wife and trans-ferred to more comfortable quarters at Berlin's Adlon Hotel. His reflections, entertaining and revealing as they are, perhaps say more about Wodehouse than about the life of an ordinary British internee.

Diaries, reports and memoirs are supplemented by a surprising number of photographs taken in the camps, some of which feature the Ypres men. From all this evidence emerges a vivid picture of the trials and meagre comforts of camp life, its loyalties, hierarchies and petty rivalries, the elaborate efforts to keep boredom and despair at bay – and the attempts to escape.

For the British men captured in France and Belgium in the summer and early autumn of 1940, the internment experience was remarkably uniform, as they were kept together as a homogenous group for much of the time. All those who lived above the line of the Somme came within the jurisdiction of the German Kommandantur in Brussels; those who lived below it were the responsibility of the German High Command in Paris. This demarcation determined which prisons they were sent to. The British in Belgium and north-ern France formed part of a large group of about a thousand internees whose experience in captivity followed much the same pattern over the course of the next four or so years. The Fishers, the MacDonalds and Albert Jones, together with nine other IWGC men from Ypres, were all part of this group.

After arrest, they passed through a number of transit prisons before reaching what was to be their settled place of internment. Wodehouse,

Parsons and the Le Touquet contingent first went to Loos prison outside Lille – where Stephen Grady was to spend three months exactly a year later. After a few nights here they joined eight hundred other British internees on the tortuous journey by cattle truck to Liège, about 130 kilometres away. Nineteen-year-old Jean Scott and his father Arthur were part of the Le Touquet party: Jean's diary records his feelings on that journey:

> After thirty-six hours in the cattle wagons the door was opened for the first time to give us some fresh air. It was stinking very badly in the wagons. For ten minutes we were on the banks of the River Meuse breathing some nice and good fresh air, then the doors closed and we were once again on the move. Everyone was working in the fields in Belgium, like they did before the war started, happy as birds . . . and here was I enclosed in this wagon. There was nothing to eat and nothing to drink.

When they finally got to Liège, the prisoners were marched through the town to the former barracks, keeping their spirits up by singing 'Tipperary' and other 1914–18 songs.

> I shan't forget seeing a woman looking out of her window and I heard her say 'What are they singing for?' On the other side of the road a lot of people were drinking and smoking beneath the trees in the warm summer weather. I was terribly thirsty, the men had lots of fruit, yet I couldn't get any because if a civilian tried to give us detainees something, the Jerries were there with their bayonets.

For the next six days in the squalid barracks at Liège, they lived on black bread and cabbage soup and had to stand around for endless roll-call parades. During this time Harry Fisher, at fifteen too young to be interned, was liberated and sent back to Ypres with a Red Cross convoy – for the time being anyway. The rest were soon off again, back in the cattle trucks destined for they knew not where or what.

> At about 11 a.m. everyone was closed inside the wagons. We remained there for a few hours. When we left Liège the train was going very slow and stopping every few miles. On the way

Belgian people threw us apples and pears, but it was very difficult catching them between the iron bars and barbed wire which surrounded our cattle trucks.

When they arrived at Huy, little more than twenty kilometres away, they were ordered out, 'counted at least ten times', and put on the march again with their blankets and luggage on their backs. From afar, Jean could see a bleak Napoleonic fortress perched high above the Meuse, overlooking the town. He bet his comrades that it would be their destination and indeed it was. The ascent to Huy Citadel was up a vertiginous zigzag path. 'We had an awful job to reach the top of this new prison. I saw some men who couldn't walk at all, and they were collapsing on the ground but the Jerries with their bayonets forced them to walk.'

Finally, about eight hundred men were 'squeezed like sardines' into the inner courtyard of the Citadel. Their new quarters were worse than at Loos or Liège: damp and dirty, there were no mattresses for the first weeks of their stay and they slept on the bare floor – 'it was hard as ice'. Food was scant and of poor quality: the Germans, Jean learned, were selling the sausages, potatoes and flour allocated for the detainees on the black market. For the first week they had no bread, only biscuits and thin soup. Those with Belgian relatives could have food parcels brought in, and the prison authorities allowed one man to go into the town every day with prisoners' orders, but even if they had the money – the exchange rate for those with only French francs was punitive – little was available in the shops. Alfred Goddard, another of the Le Touquet party, remembers how extra provisions were shared out among those who could afford them: 'Sometimes there would be for instance a quarter of an apple, two candies, two ounces of cheese, three and a half cigarettes . . . however we were in dire need of these little extras, soap was very scarce and the price made it untouchable which made it very difficult for the washing of our clothes.'

Lack of soap and proper washing facilities – they had only a 'cold water douche' in the mornings – meant that lice and contagious skin diseases soon took hold. In one of his broadcasts from Berlin, Wodehouse spoke of his relief when, on reaching their permanent camp, he realised that a particularly unfortunate character whom they'd dubbed Scabies was no longer with them.

Comforts were few in this initial period of fear, uncertainty and homesickness. Alfred Goddard took solace in something he had managed to bring with him:

> I had a nice piece of tobacco which my dear wife had put into my bag before I left and I thought of it many times, and of her, as I indulged in a pipe smoke in the courtyard in the brilliant sunshine or the cool of the evening with hundreds of swallows swooping around the Citadel towers. The world was theirs as we watched them in their freedom to fly away where they wished, while we were here locked up.

For Jean Scott and his father there was nothing but subsistence rations and whatever they could buy or scrounge from other inmates. 'One day I bought a piece of cheese and one onion, that was all I had for my supper that evening and I was very glad to have it. On another day I had half a pot of jam which I ate with a spoon because I had nothing else . . . after six weeks of that life everybody was half dead. I was in a terrible state, as dry as a bone.'

Though it was late summer, their eyrie was exposed and dust swirled around them constantly. Not all the men had blankets; Wodehouse wrote in his diary of bitterly cold blanket-less nights. There was little light relief as the weeks went on. The Le Touquet group – Wodehouse, the Scotts and Goddard among them – were all in the same 'cell', a bare room housing more than twenty men. Jean remembers Wodehouse, then barely fifty-nine, as 'stocky, looking rather like an old man, slightly bent over'. He was in awe of the writer and 'because of our age difference I could not easily go up to have conversation with him'.

While they were there 'a German General' accompanied by two guards came to their cell to take Wodehouse to lunch in Huy. Jean gathered that they'd been at Dulwich College, the public school, together. They spoke in French (which the internees but not the guards would have understood) and left at ten in the morning, returning at five in the afternoon with a suitcase full of provisions including cigars, cigarettes, biscuits and chocolate to share with them all, which 'made a difference to the atmosphere for us in that room'. Wodehouse never explained to his room-mates who the General was or how he knew him. He did, though, make other efforts on behalf of the internees. The men had had no contact with their families since their arrest and this was adding to their distress. Wodehouse wrote a letter to the Red Cross in Brussels appealing for their right to communicate with them, a letter that got no further than the Gestapo officer in charge of the camp, who tore it up in front of him.

The harsh regime – wake-up call at 5 a.m., final roll-call at 8 p.m., lights-out at 9 p.m., with nothing much but cleaning latrines and more roll-calls in between – was relieved by games of Housey-Housey (Bingo), Crown and Anchor, and Pitch and Toss, all simple games of chance in which the sentries would occasionally 'nip in if the Officer wasn't watching and put a franc on here or there'. There was excitement a couple of weeks after their arrival when a young Belgian-British boy of sixteen managed to force his way through one of the narrow slit windows of the Citadel, drop forty feet by rope into the stinging nettles below, and escape under the noses of the guards. The regime was immediately tightened and every scrap of rope, string and clothes-line was confiscated. 'Atmosphere like Dotheboys Hall after escape of Smike' noted Wodehouse in his diary. But, as far as the internees knew, the boy was never recaptured.

On 24 August fifteen-year-old André MacDonald, like Harry Fisher, was freed and returned to Ypres. Two weeks later the detainees were all assembled in the inner courtyard. The majority were told to collect three days' rations – a loaf and half a sausage. The rest were told they were 'unfit' and were being sent home, seeming to confirm rumours that they would be making the journey to their next destination on foot. But at 8 p.m. that evening they were marched off to the railway station. Jean Scott recalls:

An army of soldiers came to collect us and I was very happy to leave our 'Starvation Hotel'. I said to myself they could put me

anywhere they liked, it would not be worse than here at Huy
. . . The Germans had enough soldiers and machine guns to form
an attack, with cars and motorcycles escorting both sides of us
and also in the rear.

The internees were told that if they tried to accept anything from
townspeople on the way, or if they attempted to escape, they would
be shot. Goddard says their miserable column was followed by a small
crowd of crying women and children – the families of some of their
number – all contact between them strictly forbidden. At the station
the men were packed, eight to a compartment, into a passenger train
and then, late at night: '. . . we steamed out of this dreary place where
we had spent many long days and weeks with still no news of our
loved ones and for a destination unknown.'

During three days of hunger and discomfort in the train, there was
no reliable information on that destination – the guards told them
only that they were going 'to the salt mines' – nor how long the
journey would be. Finally they reached their new home, Tost in the
bleak open countryside of Upper Silesia, now the Polish town of
Toszek. They were about to begin a rather different internment
experience.

Ilag VIII at Tost offered purpose-built accommodation for over a
thousand residents and at least had the benefit of properly equipped
modern buildings, with central heating, dormitories, a dining hall,
hospital, theatre and recreation facilities. But there were bars on
every window; it had been a lunatic asylum.

The internees – not just at Tost but at other former asylums
throughout Greater Germany – must have wondered where the
inmates had gone in order to vacate these secure, well-equipped
premises. In fact, from January 1940 they were being systematically
exterminated, by gas in mass killings, by lethal injection with sco-
polamine and morphine, or by deliberate starvation. 'Mentally
defective' children were killed in special premises and this particularly
demanding work attracted salary supplements for those who did it. A
number of mental institutions with these killing facilities were kept

on for the purpose of eliminating such *Untermenschen* from the Third Reich. Alongside the mentally ill, the insane and those with intellectual disabilities, Polish and Russian prisoners of war and slave labourers – all sound in mind but too starved and weakened to work – were being similarly disposed of. Though some managed to escape death, their fate was pitiful, as Jean Scott discovered later on in his internment:

> I'd found out from a village farm outside the camp where I sometimes had to do work, that the other workers had been inmates of the Tost Psychiatric Institute and had survived the 'euthanasia' programme the Nazis practised on mentally retarded persons. These people came to the camp to collect the garbage, but there was little that remained to eat apart from bones. They were so famished, they flocked on to the rubbish bins stuffing . . . their mouths.

It was as well that the new residents weren't aware of their captors' barbarous policies towards other human beings at the outset of their internment. But even before the local rumours started, there was something about the place . . .

William Duncan arrived at Tost in February 1941, when the group from France and Belgium had already been there some months. He had been arrested in Denmark, where he was the local representative of the Cunard White Star shipping line. He had spent some time in another camp with detainees from the German-occupied Channel Islands before they were all transferred to Tost. Duncan took an immediate dislike to it: 'The whole atmosphere of the camp was wrong and there was something decidedly disagreeable about the building which made one feel that it would be a good place to get away from at any price.'

In fact, he got away sooner than he expected. Days after arriving, he was diagnosed with renal colic and was immediately sent to a military hospital a three-hour train journey away. By the time he got back, still weak, two months later, the camp had become so overcrowded that arrangements were already in hand to set up an annexe at Kreuzberg, about 100 kilometres away, where several hundred men from Tost were transferred between 1941 and 1943. Here, as Camp Captain (senior spokesman and representative of prisoners' interests), he was part of a regime that he later claimed ran 'the best camp we had known in Germany'. In the meantime, and for those who remained at Tost, conditions were, to say the least, mixed.

Ilag VIII Tost consisted of a four-storey red-brick accommodation block housing over a thousand prisoners in large dormitories off long corridors. Each floor had five dormitories of up to ninety bunks, with a washroom and four toilets for approximately three hundred people (no toilet paper and long queues). Across a small park was a building housing the dining hall and infirmary. Another building, known as 'the White House', was used for religious services and recreation. Here, in a former padded cell, prisoner 796, Pelham Wodehouse, worked on a new novel and his diary.

On arrival, prisoners were deloused, showered and relieved of money and personal possessions such as lighters and penknives, to be returned at the end of their detention. Younger men were housed on the upper floors; the elderly and disabled on the ground floor. Jean Scott, who started out on the fourth floor, asked to be moved to be with his father in a ground-floor dormitory they shared with other fathers – mainly 1914–18 veterans – and sons.

A Red Cross inspection of December 1940 reported a total of 1,135 British detainees, the majority of whom were living in, or visiting, the occupied countries at the time of their arrest. Despite agreements on age-limits, the youngest was thirteen and the oldest seventy-one. Among Tost's facilities, the Red Cross delegation noted a canteen where prisoners could exchange their *Lagergeld* (camp currency) for a limited range of goods that soon ran out altogether. 'Food is short', noted the report, 'but they can buy beer and limonade'.

One reason for the overcrowding by the early months of 1941 was the arrival of two hundred seamen, the crew of the SS *Orama*, a troopship sunk off the Norwegian coast in June 1940, who had been moved from a naval POW camp near Bremen. Their reception by the other inmates was mixed: for some, the seamen livened things up

(Wodehouse thought they would cheer anyone up); for others, they were a raucous crowd who didn't fit in and upset the dynamic of a place already established in its routines and relationships. Getting on with people was critical in such a closed institution. Class, race and cultural distinctions were, if anything, more acute than in peacetime though some internees, like Wodehouse, found the unaccustomed social mix invigorating. He wrote to a friend in 1942:

> I really do think that there is nothing on earth to compare with the Englishman in the cloth cap and muffler. I had friends at Tost in every imaginable walk of life, from Calais dock touts upwards, and there wasn't one I didn't like. The War Graves Commission gardeners are the salt of the earth.

Some of those friendships survived long beyond his nine-month internment at Tost. Wodehouse was still corresponding with Bert Haskins, his IWGC gardener room-mate, from his home in the United States twenty years later.

Minority groups must have had a more difficult time than most. The 1940 Red Cross report noted the presence of five 'blacks', adding, in the unconscious racism of the time (also evident in many contemporary references to Jews, Poles and Czechs), 'but [they] have their own table in the dining area'. Homosexuality – then a criminal offence in Britain – was a fact of life. Relationships were usually conducted with discretion but outré behaviour was punished. Jean Scott recalled:

> On the fifth floor of our building [used as extra accommodation after the arrival of the *Orama* men] there was a bathtub in the corridor and the men who couldn't be bothered to go downstairs to the toilets urinated in the tub . . . One day a person from the fifth floor and his mate were hauled by the others and dumped into the urine-filled tub. Perhaps they'd been caught in bed together. With such a large number of men there were obviously certain liaisons taking place – but nothing was obvious. I personally saw some who slept together: in my room a Swiss and another were in the same bed together during the daytime,

when I happened to return to the room. I was perhaps too young to understand . . . I didn't know such things happened.

A young internee from Ypres, Edwin Tester, who was twenty when he arrived at Tost with the main group in September 1940, recalled seeing a Catholic priest and a young boy 'behaving like a courting couple, night after night in the corridors until 10 p.m. when everyone had to be in bed'.

But inmates had better things to do than persecute minorities. Their main preoccupations were food and filling the long hours between reveille at 6 a.m. and lights-out at 9.15 p.m. The basic diet of boiled swede, fish soup and ersatz coffee was hardly enough to keep body and soul together. Detainees were allowed Polish cigarettes but these weren't popular; in the early days Edwin Tester remembers men selling their wedding rings for a packet of Players.

From February 1941 the arrival, distribution and consumption of Red Cross parcels soon occupied many hours, raising spirits and health standards at a stroke. Each internee was entitled to a weekly five-kilo parcel containing tea, cocoa, non-perishable foods and soap. Clothing and cigarettes came separately, though supplies of the latter were never enough to satisfy heavy smokers who had to rely on barter or the generosity of others. Parcels arrived by train in sealed trucks and were unloaded by internees under guard and hauled back to camp on wooden carts. In the camp's parcel room everything was recorded and the contents searched. Once the parcels were distributed, items were swapped, bartered, used to bribe guards, and finally enjoyed at leisure in the dormitories.

Clothing was a problem, especially during the Silesian winters when a two-foot blanket of snow often covered the ground for months on end. As the war went on, coal was in short supply and the heating woefully inadequate. The 1942–3 diary of an IWGC gardener from Arras, Alfred Wells, is dominated by the cold:

12 Jan. Freezing cold it is minus 15 degrees. 13 Jan. Even colder it is now minus 20 degrees. 21 Jan. It is minus 22 and I am going to a lecture on Africa. 27 Jan. It has now gone down to minus

28 centigrade. 4 February. It is so cold that I ran 30 times around the Parc inside the camp. 6 Feb. Now have a gall-bladder problem and the very cold weather does not help.

Some internees were provided with British battledress from stocks captured by the Germans. Others had to make do with what little they had brought with them when they left their homes in high summer, supplemented by what the Red Cross could provide. Edwin Tester befriended an old seaman who made some needles and knitted him a thick sweater by unravelling the wool from two worn ones. He was still wearing it long after the war ended.

With their basic needs more or less satisfactorily met, the men had to find ways of passing the time. There was work to do in the camp, but much else to occupy them if they chose to join in. The main organ of communication was the camp newspaper, the *Tost Times and Advertiser*, produced by internees twice a month. This 'bright little sheet', as Wodehouse called it, carried official news, details of events, clubs and activities, small ads ('Let Mr Farrell cut your hair or set your razor as it *can* be done. Room 207'; 'Exchange left foot white canvas rubber shoe size 9 for right foot same size'), gossip and gripes, and a spoof agony column. Wodehouse contributed a 'Bingo' story in three instalments. An early editorial set out how internees were expected to fill their day:

> The essential duties of the Camp must come first. The place has to be kept clean, food prepared and various other work has to be done. All this is for our own comfort. These 'fatigues' must come first. Self-improvement should follow, and sports can always fill in the rest of the time.

Apart from fatigues, there was paid work on offer. Men could volunteer to join a work camp 100 kilometres away at Jedlitze where they drained swampland in exchange for the equivalent of a local wage and a regular supply of beer. The Camp Captain of the eighty-eight Tost men living there temporarily in the summer of 1941 managed to make it sound positively wholesome in his report for the *Tost Times*: 'The boys, after a day's manual labour, come home brown as a nigger through working in the open air, to enjoy, first, a swim in our own little lake and then a sound meal.'

There were other jobs that internees undertook, paid or unpaid, on a voluntary basis. This work had to be of a 'non-military character' to be acceptable to the British government, but it was still controversial. Those who chose to do it were accused by some of 'rowing with the Germans' – collaboration – and at least one gardener was the subject of an IWGC investigation following allegations made by fellow internees after the war. Nevertheless, some three hundred British men at Tost were engaged in paid work at this time.

There were less contentious options for filling the day. Alfred Wells mentions going to a lecture on Africa, perhaps to take his mind off the cold. These talks, 'designed to entertain as well as instruct', were held every morning in the dining hall and were among the first activities to be organised by prisoners. They were fortunate to have among their number a Dutch university professor, several language teachers and a ready-made ensemble of professional musicians, including the classical harmonica player Tommy Reilly, arrested at the Leipzig Conservatoire where he had been studying.

'We were not so much internees as a student body,' said Wodehouse, who recalled classes in modern European languages, French and English literature, shorthand and first aid. The 'eleven o'clock talks' weren't just conducted by professional educators. Everyone willing to share his specialism had a go, including Wodehouse himself who, the *Tost Times* reported, 'delighted everybody by just being Wodehouse'. Head gardener Albert Roberts joined in and found this a welcome diversion in the early stages of his internment, as he reported in his debriefing to the IWGC:

After the first few months of distress and mental agony, those of us who could, decided to give talks and lectures on subjects in which we were conversant. I gave four talks on the work of the Imperial War Graves Commission, which were eagerly listened to, and several others on Horticulture during the period of 1941.

This led to greater things:

> I became a teacher in Horticulture on the camp teaching staff
> and classes were organised, two in the mornings and two in the
> evenings. They were enthusiastically attended over a period of
> three years. Many of our [IWGC] men attended. Botany and
> practical and scientific Horticulture were taught throughout. In
> 1942 I entered myself for the HD [Royal Horticultural Society
> Higher Diploma], and obtained it. In 1943 seven other detainees
> entered.

The benefits of Roberts' horticultural classes weren't just educational;
they were later to be the cover for a most audacious escape attempt.

Sports were well provided for with a playing field and cricket,
rugby and soccer teams. Prisoners made an eighteen-hole miniature
golf course in the compound and there were escorted walks in the
surrounding countryside. An extensive library, art and handicraft stu-
dios were equipped with gifts from the Red Cross and the YMCA.
There was a camp orchestra and an active theatre group. Productions
ranged from contemporary classics to more earthy entertainments
featuring a large number of men dressed – convincingly or otherwise
– as women, causing Jean Scott to wonder whether they could all be
homosexuals. 'Camp was really great fun,' wrote Wodehouse without a hint of sarcasm, '. . . life was one long round of cricket, lectures,
entertainments and Red Cross parcels.'

Undoubtedly for many it was a time of comradeship and discovery. Circumstances compelled men to draw on their inner resources
and make the best of things. But none of the other surviving accounts
paints anything like as sunny a picture. Bernard Parsons, the IWGC
stonemason from Etaples, later described another side of camp life in
a letter (defending himself from accusations of collaboration) to the
Commission:

> *In an internment camp there is a mixture of every nationality & social
> grade, massed together in a very confined space; in daily and hourly
> contact with one another & unable to escape each other. Discussions and
> quarrels over trifles are rife. It gets many people down, gives them*

warped minds & a scandalous & bitter outlook. Mud-slinging becomes the order of the day, particularly at those who are active & try to do things in the Camp. Suspicions & jealousies arise faster than feelings of gratitude & consequently, people who kept their morale high by work soon became the object of hatred & suspicion to the inactive element who had nothing to do all day but brew their Red Cross tea & spread poisonous scandal.

Wodehouse left Tost in June 1941 after a last game of cricket among men he had grown to 'love like brothers'. He had to endure only one winter, only one Christmas away from friends and family. For the internees left behind, this first year at Tost was just the overture to several more acts in a long and gruelling confinement.

In the same month, a sombre *Tost Times* editorial exhorted its readers to prepare for the long haul, to 'pull our weight together', and not let petty differences undermine morale. It ended:

Those in authority over us are watching, and their opinion of us will be their opinion of the English people. We judge them in the same way. Whilst here, we represent the whole British nation. Let us take a big pride in this and act accordingly. The war is outside this Camp – not in.

In 1942 Harry Fisher and André MacDonald were rearrested in Ypres. Still barely seventeen, they ended up joining their fathers at Tost where conditions were getting more oppressive. Prisoners had to stand to attention and remove their hats whenever an officer passed. Loudspeakers everywhere pumped out German music, Lord Haw-Haw, and 'news' in English. Letters to and from home were censored, rationed to two a month, and languished for weeks in transit. Men became sick and died; others went mad or succumbed to despair and took their own lives. The Red Cross reported six deaths in 1941. The following year there were twenty-one.

Life got even harder with the winter of 1942–3 and Germany's defeat by the Red Army and the cold at Stalingrad. Coal supplies were cut by half – dormitories were rarely above freezing – and staffing the camps became increasingly difficult as manpower drained away. Recruitment for the Eastern Front went on even among internees. William Duncan claimed to detect a marked pro-German 'column' among internees at Tost from the start. Certainly the presence of informers was suspected by Jean Scott, who witnessed people being spirited away:

> There were several people who disappeared, even in our room. There was no explanation. At Tost and Kreuzberg the Germans had their own 'recruiting officers' to try and convince detainees to switch sides . . . to increase their ranks and replace casualties with sympathisers. It was well known that they wanted to recruit men for the Eastern Front. 'We'll give you a uniform and you'll not be in the front line' was their promise. It's possible that those who disappeared joined up. I know there were people who switched sides.

As 1943 wore on, many of the British detainees – the Scotts and Edwin Tester among them – were transferred to the annexe at Kreuzberg, another former asylum, where conditions were a little more congenial. Camp Captain William Duncan took pride in his relationship with the camp authorities and the facilities he was able to negotiate for his men. A working party renovated the local football pitch and swimming pool in return for use by internees. There were regular filmshows and even visits to the town cinema – at 8.30 a.m. and under guard – for Hollywood favourites such as *Shall We Dance?* and *Bringing Up Baby*.

Internees' own entertainment efforts were no less ambitious, with a production of the 1923 classic *The Ghost Train*, complete with sound effects of a steam train rushing through a station using a municipal garden roller and cylinders of compressed air. As Duncan noted, attention to detail was paramount in every production:

> We were fortunate in having with us a first-class ladies' hairdresser with professional experience of wig-making and make-up. The appearance of the 'ladies' was a matter of great importance, hair, eyelashes and make-up requiring hours of

preparation on the day, but with the assistance of a generous supply of paint and powder provided by the British Red Cross and the YMCA the final effects obtained were almost 100% perfect.

At first the 'girls' frocks' were made out of coloured paper but later fashioned by professional dress designers and tailors out of old clothes, achieving 'almost incredible' results. Edwin Tester, a lad with delicate features and previous experience of amateur dramatics, appeared in female form in a number of Kreuzberg productions. He also featured in a 'Bank Holiday festival' with sports, stalls and sideshows, a fancy-dress parade (one man dressed as a Red Cross parcel) and an English tea garden: 'The tea being served', Duncan wrote, 'by the fair hands of our own "ladies", beautifully gowned in the most gorgeous summer creations with large picture hats, all perfectly cut out of coloured paper.'

All this flamboyance contrasted sharply with the harshness of everyday living conditions. Just as at Tost, winter temperatures indoors at Kreuzberg were often well below freezing. As a Red Cross report of 1942 noted, the ancient steam heating system was 'absolutely insufficient' and hot water was available only on one and a half days out of seven. The clothing situation was 'bad' and basic rations were inedible, as the normally upbeat Duncan confirmed:

The meat ration . . . was horse flesh which often included the head and always a big percentage of bone. [After Stalingrad] we received sacks of dried swedes and peas brought back from Russia. The dried swedes were a very rough, coarse mixture containing bits of wood and straw and when cooked became a greyish, brown mass with a most unpleasant odour. The dried peas were also of little use to us as the majority contained a small black beetle which came out of the pea after it had been immersed overnight in water.

Without their Red Cross parcels, internees would have had a very lean time of it. They knew they were better fed than their guards or the Germans living around them: chocolate and other items soon found their way out of the camp and into the hands of local children.

Apart from the theatricals, there were other distractions. An unknown IWGC gardener led a motley team of amateurs to create a kitchen garden that supplied produce throughout the summer and cultivated magnificent flowerbeds:

> . . . with that immaculate finished touch that only a professional gardener can give. These beds were the showpiece of the camp . . . and gave a real joy to many. To stand and contemplate those flowers . . . in the pleasant warmth of the early sunshine, seemed to . . . give one a renewed sense of well-being and confidence for the future in spite of the barbed wire.

Meanwhile, by the autumn of 1943 Tost had become untenable. Renewed overcrowding due to an influx of American prisoners, deteriorating physical conditions, poor morale and the threat from an advancing Red Army led to a decision to close the camp to internees. Those who hadn't gone to Kreuzberg – the Ypres men Fred and Harry Fisher, William and André MacDonald and Albert Jones, and the Arras IWGC gardener Albert Roberts among them – were moved to Giromagny, a former French army barracks near Belfort, close to the Swiss border. Before long, the evacuation of Kreuzberg started too. Jean and Arthur Scott began the long train journey to Giromagny, leaving William Duncan, Edwin Tester and several hundred others behind.

With the dawn of 1944 and the glimmerings of an Allied victory, the 980 British and American internees now at Giromagny grew restless. Conditions, though no better, at least offered more scope for disobedience. They were now in France: instead of a cowed local population they had Resistance activists and people who were prepared to take risks for them. The rubbish collector enlisted the help of a disaffected guard and smuggled food and alcohol in and messages out in bins of horse manure. The wine merchant left the camp one day with an internee hidden among his beer crates. The electrician helped seventeen more escape and the priest with Resistance connections lent prisoners spiritual and practical support. Both were arrested and sent to Dachau, but survived.

There were opportunities too to get out of the camp, for example to the dentist. While his wife entertained the guard with food and drink, the dentist passed the patient parts for the camp's illicit radio and took messages for onward transmission. Significantly, for the first time since their confinement, men from France were allowed visits from their families. Jean Scott recalls it taking three or four months to get approval, and even then the visit was anything but relaxed:

> My mother and sister were allowed to visit us. There was a spe-cial room . . . we were allowed to only see them for an hour. There were two German guards standing in the room. In the middle of the table was a vase; one of the other inmates said, 'Be careful. I've a feeling there's a microphone hidden somewhere.'

Nevertheless, it was a chance to see loved ones for the first time in years and hand over precious items from Red Cross parcels to fam-ilies often in much greater need.

There had been attempts to escape from both Tost and Kreuzberg, but Giromagny was a hive of escape activity. Arras head gardener Albert Roberts had kept up his horticulture classes from Tost and there was soon an enthusiastic team – including Fred Fisher and the MacDonalds – building an ambitious 36-metre-long rock garden on a bank in the camp grounds. As Roberts explained to the camp authorities, it kept the prisoners interested and also gave them physical exercise.

> I had written to a big French nursery (which knew me well), asking them to send us plants for the rock garden. My card got through the German Censor and in due course I received an immense collection of small rock plants. The German Commander did not refuse delivery but I was severely repri-manded for having corresponded with French nationals.

If the Kommandant had realised the real purpose of the rockery, Roberts might have got more than a reprimand.

The 'Camp Committee' having decided to dig a tunnel 9 yards long from the wood-chopping building under the barbed wire fence to an outlet in a sunken road, the soil had to be conveniently disposed of. Bucketfuls at a time were discreetly brought out and emptied on the bank . . .

While the IWGC men built up their rock garden, the tunnel team led by Tom Sarginson, a structural engineer from Calais, were constructing a sophisticated escape route supported by log beams from the woodshed and lit using cable smuggled in by Sarginson's wife during family visits. Rocks and spoil were transported to the rock garden in empty Red Cross cartons. The stonemason Bernard Parsons broke up larger rocks and used them to line camp paths, prompting compliments from the Kommandant for keeping the place looking so neat and tidy. Tunnelling could only be done for an hour every afternoon and it was months before the tunnel was ready.

Some men had already escaped to the Swiss border and the camp was on high alert when, one wet night, Jean Scott had a visit from his friend Eric Moore:

I was asleep, it was midnight. He put his hand on my shoulder and said, 'Get up and come with me, we're escaping.' I said, 'The weather's terrible, are you crazy?' I said I wasn't coming, the risk of reprisals to my father was too great. 'Go, you get away,' I encouraged him.

Moore made it as far as Spain, where he was arrested and brought back to solitary confinement in Giromagny. Here he befriended his German guard and they eventually escaped to Switzerland together.

The tunnellers were soon betrayed by an informer but the rock garden survived to feature in an exhibition of camp arts and crafts in July 1944. The souvenir programme acknowledged all the materials – from a piano to 296 ping-pong balls – which the YMCA had provided so far that year to 'help us pass our time more pleasantly and profitably'. A concert featured the specially composed *Rondo Brillante for Mouth-Organ and Orchestra* by Tommy Reilly. The British internees, after long years in captivity, were determined to go out with a flourish.

They had good reason for optimism. The British were back on French soil following the June D-Day landings and Paris would soon be liberated. The war was far from over but prisoner exchanges via neutral countries – operated throughout the war – were now gathering momentum. The Fishers and Albert Jones got to England on an exchange later that summer, among a hundred IWGC men from France and Belgium. William Duncan was repatriated from Kreuzberg at the same time. The MacDonalds, the Scotts and Edwin Tester weren't so lucky. They were moved on to other camps and suffered extreme hardship before being liberated by Allied troops in the final months of the war in Europe.

In a welcome letter to the first returning IWGC men, Fabian Ware wrote:

> *You have been often in our thoughts during the past four years and I think you know that you have had our keen sympathy in the severe trials you have so patiently and courageously borne, and that we are proud of the way in which you have maintained an unbroken spirit. But I will not dwell on the past. You will from now onwards wish to look forward to the happier years which, as we all trust and believe, lie surely ahead. I pray that the kindly atmosphere of familiar things and, in many cases, reunion with those dear to you will soon restore your health and strength.*

But for the men from the tight pre-war community in Ypres, things would never be the same again.

I I

Detention: the Women's Story

*It is a glorious morning, the sun is shining so beautifully. It really
is a sin to be shut up here in this place, and at Whitsun time too.
If we were all together, we should all be out somewhere. Still, we
must hope & pray for those days to come again & very soon Dear.*
Lily Wilkins to her daughter Lillian, written from
Internierungslager Liebenau, June 1941

FOR MUCH OF the war the Wilkins family was split asunder.
IWGC head gardener Harry Wilkins had escaped to England,
Lillian and her younger sister Joyce were scratching a living alone in
Ypres, and their mother Lily was far away in an internment camp in
southern Germany. The men's experience of internment was testing
enough; for women like Lily Wilkins and the others interned with
her, separation from their families was hardest to bear.

The dozens of letters Lillian received from her mother during that
time – every scrap of space filled with tiny looped writing – are chatty
and practical: about money and how the girls are managing, instructions not to black the stove as it will make the kitchen mat dirty, to
keep up with their French and piano practice, and to be sure to pass
on her thanks to the neighbours for helping them to survive. But the
pain of separation often punctures the determined optimism. When
Lillian passes on the news that her bright little sister has started to
think about a career, her mother replies:

So Joyce would like to be a nurse. Well I am afraid I could not
bear to part from her after the parting I am going through now.

When I am gone, then she can please herself, but while I am alive I would much rather she stayed near her Mother. I suppose I sound selfish but it's only a Mother's love & feelings for her children, as perhaps one day you will yourself understand.

Lily had been at Liebenau internment camp for only eight months when she wrote this. She was to endure the best part of three more years in captivity before the Wilkins family was finally reunited.

The Dawsons were more fortunate. At least Blanche Dawson managed to stay together with her daughter Joyce when she was separated from her husband in the chaos of the Ypres evacuation. Blanche was Belgian, so their internment experience was rather different from Lily Wilkins'. Joyce was thirteen when she and her mother were arrested in January 1941. They were disgusted that a Belgian policeman turned up to arrest them and indignant when a neighbour made a bid for their home: 'You wouldn't believe it but this woman came over to my mother and said: "I don't suppose you'll be coming back. I'd like your house – who did you rent it from?"'

After spending a night in the orphanage in Ypres, they were put on a train with other detainees to Arlon, not far from Luxembourg. Here they were taken to the Jesuit monastery of St Francis Xavier, a vast building with the older monks still in residence, the younger ones having fled to avoid being sent to German labour camps. It was now a detention centre, but the regime was relaxed. Joyce doesn't remember guards or barbed wire and she was allowed to attend a local fee-paying school run by nuns. Here her previous good progress at the Ecole Moyenne in Ypres came to a halt: 'I was considered the poor refugee and was given one exercise book for all the subjects and had to write in it with a pencil because when it was full up I had to rub everything out and start again.'

Joyce never knew why, but after a year at Arlon she and her mother were released. They went back to Ypres, where they were obliged to report monthly to the Kommandantur. But they struck lucky. The officer in charge – perhaps the same man who was so solicitous to Simone Parminter after she had been shot outside her hotel – took an uncharacteristically kindly view: 'He said to my mother: "Leave that child at home. She is English by birth and when she gets to sixteen will be taken prisoner of war. I don't want to see her again and I am not registering her on my books. Out of sight, out of mind.'"

Years later, Joyce contrasted his compassion with the behaviour of Brigadier Prower who had, as she saw it, abandoned them in Montreuil in May 1940. She went back to the Ecole Moyenne and caught up with her schoolwork. Within two years she was top of the class. Blanche and Joyce were finally reunited with Lawrence Dawson after Ypres was liberated in September 1944.

Like Tost and so many of the internment camps, Liebenau was a former mental asylum. Unlike Tost, its situation near the Swiss lakes was idyllic. Internee Anitha Feuerheerd later recalled:

> The dining room . . . was very large [with] long windows that looked out on to a most beautiful landscape. Being very near the border, we could see the mountains of Switzerland in the distance and indeed on a clear day, Lake Constance, shimmering in the sunlight. Surrounding us were farmlands and woods.

The nuns who had run the asylum now looked after internees. Anitha, who was arrested in Holland, was one of the first women to arrive in January 1941. Despite her 'foreign-sounding' name, her father was third-generation British and had fought at Gallipoli. Her mother was Swedish. Though she had been brought up in Germany and still had many relatives there, she thought of herself as 'a true British national'. Nevertheless, she had to defend herself from vicious rumours and accusations:

> [One of the women] confronted me with a nasty remark about my nationality and if there was one thing I could not stand it was to have my patriotism doubted. I flew at her and gave her a slap, upon which she grabbed my hair. A nice brawl would have developed had not one of the women on my floor come to the rescue and helped to restore the peace. It all sounds like a storm in a teacup now, but at the time it seemed so very important.

Anitha's memoir of her four-year internment, written in remarkable detail shortly before her death in 1985, is the fullest surviving account of life in Liebenau during this period and puts Lily Wilkins' letters in context. Soon after she arrived, Anitha learned the history of the place.

> We'd landed up in a lunatic asylum. The nuns who were now to look after us had been terribly upset when their former charges, for whom they had so lovingly cared, had been gassed: victims of the Nazi regime. Soon after these traumatic events they had heard the rumour that English internees were to come and be boarded with them. The nuns had prayed for hours that this would happen, as it would mean they would not be thrown out of their convent. They were therefore as kind as they possibly could be to us during our stay there, being careful at the same time not to arouse the suspicions of the police who guarded us.

Their guards, though armed, were local civilian policemen, 'recruited from around the villages and certainly not very Nazi. They were ordinary family men, who . . . behaved correctly and were decent chaps.' However, they had regular visits from a young Gestapo chief, 'a most odious character . . . with such a stony, ice-cold face and look of arrogance as if the whole world belonged to him'. He was only in his early twenties, but she saw how he terrified the guards.

Lily arrived some months after Anitha, in April 1941, with other women from France and Belgium. They found Liebenau unexpectedly comfortable after conditions in their transit camps. The women slept in rooms of between four and twelve beds. They had feather duvets, bedside cabinets and wardrobes – very different from the men's camps where dormitories were so cramped and rudimentary there was nowhere even to pin family photographs.

They were housed in three buildings: 'the Schloss', Clara House and Joseph House. There was also 'a pretty chapel' and a wash-house. Heating – initially at least – was 'simply luxurious' and they were able to have a bath once a week for a few pfennigs. The nuns did the cooking, with the women helping to prepare vegetables. The convent had been self-sufficient before the war but internees were not entitled to share in the bounty, which went elsewhere. Lily complained that 'there is no nourishment in the food we get here, it's all very starchy'. Despite the rich farmland around them, fresh milk or an egg were unaccustomed delights.

The arrival of the first Red Cross parcels made all the difference and Lily's letters are full of references to their contents. In June 1941, for example, she got a surprise parcel from the Canadian Red Cross:

> . . . such a lovely one, there was 1lb of butter in it, chocolate, cheese, jam, salmon, sardines, tea and a little sugar, tinned beef, so you can imagine how pleased I was, oh by the way, also a large packet of biscuits you can eat with cheese Dear, also dried apples & prunes. We have to sign a card to say we have received it & send it back. I signed mine with tons of thanks & best wishes to everybody in Canada.

Lily worried constantly about her girls going hungry and sent many items on to them in Ypres ('I am trying to send you another parcel of yum–yum after Xmas Dear'). She also made them clothes. As a trained dressmaker, she worked in the camp sewing room between 9.30 a.m. and 4 p.m., where she was also able to do 'private work'. The American Red Cross sent woollen cloth to make dressing gowns and the women sometimes received material from friends and family:

> A lady on the floor above me has given me some lovely flowered silk to make you some pyjamas. I didn't know how to thank her but I have bought her a pretty ash tray in return for her kindness. If you send me your measurements I will make them here for you. Would you like nighties or pyjamas?

In the same letter of December 1941, Lily says she will be very busy the following day:

> I am making a dressing gown for a lady who is leaving here on Saturday for Palestine, they are Jews of course. My turn will soon come I am thinking & sincerely hope so. I am longing to sit around the table again with you both & Dad. I guess you are too Dear, what

a day that will be to be sure when we meet Dear Dad again. The dressmaking helps pass away the time.

Prisoner exchanges had been going on sporadically since early in the war and at this point it was still Nazi policy to use captive Jews as bargaining chips for prisoners held by the Allies. Lily mentions a number of British Jews held at Liebenau who were released on exchange. So she was confident that her time would come. But those first weeks and months were among the hardest. She didn't receive her first letter from Lillian and Joyce until the end of May, three months after she had left them in Ypres; and it was weeks later that she heard from Harry, whom she hadn't seen for more than a year. She confided in Lillian:

> *I feel much more miserable than lonely, as there are 75 here on this floor with me & some are a jolly lot at times . . . I feel more sad at night in my bed & my prayers upset me. I long for some news of your Dear Dad, it's that also which makes me sad & lonely, but perhaps one day I shall hear something from him.*

Some of the women had their children with them – enough in number to justify a small school run by young teachers among the internees. Although all the children had British or American nationality they came from a variety of countries and spoke many different languages. Anitha was amazed at how quickly they picked these up, so that 'they could all understand each other in no time at all'.

After the first unsettling months, Lily got used to the routine and made the most of the small comforts that communal living allowed. 'I have had my hair washed & curled today by one of the young girls here, the new fashion done high in the front. I am looking very smart for Sunday & my summer frock on too. I went to Church this morning, it is only a short service but very nice.'

The women, like the men, made their own diversions. There were Easter and Christmas celebrations, whist drives and summer shows (Liebenau too had its share of professional performers: one, a singer, had been briefly married to Cary Grant). Lily made costumes and appeared in sketches. There was even a fancy-dress ball, to which Anitha went as Haile Selassie:

I wore a white sheet, folded so as to make trousers and a white jacket. My face was darkened and I had on a sort of turban. Hair was taken from a mattress to provide me with a beard, stuck on with glue. I carried an old-fashioned open umbrella which I found in the attic. I looked a real sight!

National holidays were a good excuse to raise spirits with special celebrations. For Queen Wilhelmina's birthday on 31 August 1941, Anitha and her Dutch fellow internees created a menu entirely from their Red Cross supplies:

> *Soup à la Reine*
> *Saumon ou Pilchard à la Crois Rouge*
> *Viande froid avec Salade Russe*
> *Bisquits avec Fromage Hollondaise*
> *Salade de fruits des Allies*
> *The Imperial and British Cake*

So life went on. With Lily in Joseph House was a group of women captured after their merchant vessel, the *Zam Zam*, was torpedoed. On the return voyage in captivity, one woman's husband was shot dead by a panicky German sailor. When she got to Liebenau the young widow discovered that she was pregnant. Baby Francis was born in December 1941 and christened in the chapel in a service arranged by Colonel Mary Booth, granddaughter of the founder of the Salvation Army, with singing by the newly formed choir. Francis was fussed over by the women and became a mascot of hope: Lily sent her girls a photograph of him, aged ten months, holding on to the perimeter fence.

Anitha was one of very few women in Liebenau who had a camera. It is likely that she used her Kodak Box Brownie to take the photo of Baby Francis – and others of internees, their shows and even their guards – that Lillian still has from her mother's time there. Anitha became something of an unofficial camp photographer. She recalled 'dozens and dozens' of copies being ordered of her photos of their production of *Snow White*: 'It is quite astonishing to contemplate today, that in those war years it was possible to get films and also to have them developed and copied. We were lucky.' Or perhaps nobody thought women capable of using cameras for anything other than jolly, domestic scenes. Indeed, the photos Lily sent to her family are all jolly and domestic; even the group of guards have put their guns away and are smiling benignly for the camera. Anything more realistic wouldn't have got past the Censor.

But their menfolk in camps were denied cameras. The photographs that did emerge were carefully controlled, staged to convince the outside world that internees were being well treated and having rather a good time. Hence the large proportion of photos of plays and festivities, and none at all showing guards, fences or barbed wire. Some camp authorities were also careful to ensure that no photographs were taken of homogeneous groups, for example, people from the same town or workplace. This explains why it is rare to find a photo containing more than one IWGC man; they were usually shown as part of larger mixed groups.

Outwardly, at least, life in Liebenau was bearable enough for the first year. Things began to change from the spring of 1942. After America came into the war there was an influx of new internees and overcrowding for the first time. The families of high-ranking Nazi officials started to arrive, fleeing from Allied bombing of German cities. The installation of a loudspeaker in the dining room treated internees to a diet of propaganda with every meal. Occasional visits to nearby shops and walks in the countryside stopped. The 1942 summer show was the last. The mood of the Nazi authorities had definitely chilled.

Using the excuse of bad treatment of German women internees in South Africa ('of all places!') the young Gestapo officer announced one day that the women would have to be punished. Every night for months, eighty women were picked at random to take their bedding and sleep in the crypt under the chapel. Though Anitha makes light of this as 'no great inconvenience', the many nights Lily spent in the cold and damp made her ill and depressed, and she was finally exempted from the punishment on medical grounds.

In the winter of 1942–3, with the war on the Eastern Front going badly for the Germans, the camp was heated for only a few hours a

Above right: Evacuation leader Captain Reginald Haworth (*right with glasses*) with two of his escort officers, Captain Greensill (*left*) and Captain Gill (*next to Haworth*)

Below: Fleeing refugees throng the roads after the German invasion of the Low Countries in May 1940

Abandoned vehicles and belongings litter the bombed Gare Maritime on the Calais quays in this German propaganda photograph taken shortly after the departure of the evacuees 23 May 1940

The writer P. G. Wodehouse (with glasses) was imprisoned with IWGC gardeners and other British men at a civil internment camp, Ilag VIII Tost, in what is now Poland. He was released to more comfortable quarters in Berlin in June 1941; the gardeners had to wait another three years before they were freed

keep spirits up, internees put on elaborate plays and entertainments – often featuring
...ies'. In Kreuzburg, an annexe of Tost, this 1943 Whitsun Bank Holiday fancy-dress
...ade shows Edwin Tester (with parasol) and an inmate dressed as a Red Cross parcel –
... prisoners' lifeline

...ernees at Giromagny camp in 1944 constructed a showpiece rock garden under the
...ervision of IWGC gardeners – cover for an escape tunnel. Front row centre is escape
...aniser, Tom Sarginson. To the right of him are IWGC gardeners William MacDonald and
...d Fisher (*extreme right*)

Top: Women detainees, like the men, made their own entertainments. Here, Lily Wilkins (with top hat) takes part in a show at Liebenau camp, southern Germany, *c.*1942

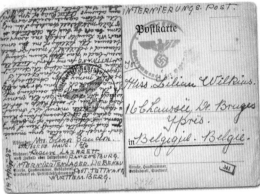

Middle: Internees were allowed to send only two single-page letters and three cards each month, all of which were censored. Nevertheless, they were a vital link with home

Below: Lily and Harry Wilkins are finally reunited at London Victoria Station in June 1944 after Lily has spent more than three years interned in Germany

Above left: Elaine Madden (*right*) as a little Devil, *c.*1929

Above right: Elaine in the uniform of the First Aid Nursing Yeomanry (FANY), military cover for women Special Operations Executive (SOE) agents

Right: Elaine's false papers showing her cover identity, Helene Meus

Above left: Stephen Grady, British Memorial School pupil, at fourteen

Above right: Stephen's drawings of his street (his parents' house is second from the right) and the Lombards' farm next door, made in 1941 when he was sixteen and in Loos-Lille prison, northern France, for daubing a pro-British slogan on a Messerschmitt

Left: Stephen Grady's parents married in 1917. They were typical of the mixed marriages produced by the 1914–18 war: his father was a British ex-serviceman employed after the war as a gardener by the Imperial War Graves Commission; his mother was a Frenchwoman from Armentières

ght: Stephen (*left*) and Conrad Kersch, the
AAF airman he hid from the Germans.
rsch refused to escape and joined
phen's Resistance unit. Stephen wears
tish battledress left behind after the BEF's
reat from Dunkirk

ow: German 88mm guns sabotaged
Stephen's Resistance unit, Nieppe,
5 September 1944

Buglers of Ypres's fire service perform the Last Post at the Menin Gate in 1930. With the exception of the German Occupation, 1940–4, this short but moving ceremony has taken place every evening since July 1928 as a mark of respect and remembrance for the war dea

In May 2001, for the first time in over sixty years, former pupils of the British Memorial School return to their old playground and are welcomed by Ieper's burgomaster, Luc Dehaene. Jimmy Fox, who traced and reunited them, is seated front row second from left

day. At Christmas, Anitha and her friends sat in their coats in their attic room, making the most of a Red Cross Christmas cake and a welcome gift of wine:

> We enjoyed it all and forgot for a little while what a terrible state the world was really in. It is extraordinary how one's life can become so self-centred, but of course for relief from worries plaguing us about relatives and loved ones outside, it was important to at least feel safe and homely with our friends. So although the attic was icy, we felt an inner glow.

Several of the new arrivals were British or American Jews and rumours about pogroms and the existence of Nazi extermination camps were soon circulating. Two women from Poland received news that family members had probably suffered terrible deaths. The letters were censored so they couldn't be absolutely certain of this, but with the arrival of a new batch of American internees in January 1943:

> . . . they confirmed that it was true about the massacre of their Jewish communities. Of course these frightful revelations affected everyone in the camp; in the beginning we could hardly believe these stories, but when we heard them repeated again and again, we had to accept them as fact.

Lily must have heard the rumours too, but she never shared what she knew with her daughters. Lillian recalls:

> We never used to discuss Belsen and Auschwitz and all those camps. We didn't know about them till after the war. My mother thought it was hell on earth in Liebenau! She always called it a concentration camp. And so do I. If you've got hundreds of women all together in one place against their will, that's a concentration, isn't it?

With exchanges of Jews and others still happening from time to time, Lily continued to hold out hope that she would be next to be released. Then, in January 1943, came a new possibility. She wrote to Lillian: 'The Head Captain has told me that I shall either be sent home, or you will go with me on the next transport, it's either one or the other, so of course I am waiting patiently for news to come through. Please don't get too excited, but be prepared.' She gave Lillian instructions to put all but essential furniture in store and make arrangements with the landlady so that they could move out at short notice if necessary.

Never fully reconciled to living in Belgium, Lily was relieved to learn from Harry that they wouldn't be going back: 'Dad said in his letter, he has made up his mind to stay in England after the war. He hopes to keep his job & the locality is very nice & open where he is living & he likes it very much, so we will sell up and buy a new home in England.'

A note to Joyce in the same letter is more revealing: 'Your Dad is longing to be with us again & and he will not be coming back to Belgium to work again, so guess we will all say good-bye to Ypres for good, thank goodness, what do you say?'

As 1943 wore on, Lily expected the girls to join her at any moment so that they could be repatriated together. She even stopped sending parcels in case they weren't there to receive them. But she still had months to wait.

After their arrest in the late summer of 1943, the Wilkins girls were sent to a detention centre in a former boarding school in Dongelberg on the Belgian–German border, where they had to sleep in the stables. They had been there a few weeks when Lillian took the initiative:

Well, I went to the camp Kommandant and I said, why was it, if our mother is in Liebenau, that my sister and I couldn't join her there? And eventually we did. It took four soldiers to take Joyce and I down to Liebenau. In Brussels we were waiting for a train in a canteen full of Germans and Joyce said to me, 'I want to go to the toilet.' I said, 'Well, I'm very sorry, Joyce, but I can't do anything about that.' Sitting next to us was a group of German officers and one of them got up and asked us, in perfect English, what the matter was and why were we there with the soldiers. I explained and he told our guards to take us to the toilets. I might tell you they made us keep the doors open, but anyway . . . I did say to this officer, 'How come you speak such beautiful English?' and he said, 'I was at Oxford for three years.'

Their journey south took days, passing through the bombed-out shell of Cologne on the way and spending their nights in transit in police cells. They hadn't seen their mother for more than two years, but Lillian doesn't remember an emotional reunion when they finally got to Liebenau. 'She was waiting, yes, but we could only just say hello and then we were bundled into the washing place to have a shower and someone to look us over.' They were put in Lily's room with seven other women. Lillian was stunned by the scenery, so different from what they knew in Flanders: 'Oh, the scenery was out of this world! You could see the Swiss mountains and where the sun shone they were pure silver. Absolutely gorgeous it was!' But the camp food was terrible: 'You'd have a plate of water with a few pea shucks in it. And ersatz stuff. There were Red Cross parcels, otherwise we would have starved, but if the Germans were nasty with you about something that had happened – if there was bad [war] news – then you wouldn't get a parcel.'

After they had been there some weeks they were told that they would be on the next transport. All three of them would be repatriated on an exchange scheme.

I can remember the morning that we got packed and off. You know how it is when you watch French people going to have their heads chopped off in those tumbrel things? One of those came up to the barbed wire fence to collect us. We went to the railway station and got on a train. Mother was on the train, we thought we were leaving together. And then they pushed Mother off the train and said, 'No, you're not going. Just the girls.' And she was taken back to the camp.

Lillian and Joyce, now alone with their German guards, were escorted across Europe to neutral Portugal, where on arrival in Lisbon they were greeted by the British Ambassador and treated royally while they waited for transport to take them to England. After some weeks of enjoying themselves in Lisbon, they flew home on a converted Lancaster via Shannon Airport, where Lillian remembers them enjoying a slap-up breakfast, finally touching down at an airstrip in Dorset.

> When we got to Poole we spent all day being interrogated about everything. How we'd lived. What we'd said. What they'd said. How long Mother had . . . everything! And then they put us on a train to Victoria Station and when we got there, there were all these photographers, dignitaries, my father . . . all there! I think he was very upset, because poor Mother was still in Germany. We were having a lovely time in Lisbon and there was poor Mother . . . I felt dreadful! I said to Joyce not so long ago, 'Why did we leave Mother? Why didn't we demand to go back to the camp with her?'

Lillian still doesn't know the answer. 'I don't know why. It's the same as when I didn't ask Stephen Grady in after he'd cycled all that way to try and help us. There must be a reason, mustn't there? I suppose I did what I thought was right at the time.'

After such a devastating end to her hopes, Lily had a physical and mental breakdown with the 'nervous strain aggravated by this new separation'. She had to endure six more months in Liebenau before she was approved for repatriation on medical grounds. After a journey of several weeks, she arrived at Victoria Station in June 1944 where Harry was waiting to meet her. Their four-year separation was finally over.

Anitha Feuerheerd left Liebenau the following month and joined other liberated internees on the Red Cross ship *Drottningholm* en route for Liverpool. On the voyage she got friendly with a group of IWGC men – the first contingent from Giromagny to be repatriated – and one of the gardeners, 'such a jolly chap', found her a deckchair and brought her bedding up to the deck every night as she found it impossible to sleep in her tiny cabin below the waterline. In the evenings their Welfare Officer escorts gave them lectures on what to expect when they reached England.

They were in for a shock. The long years away had made them completely unprepared for the war-weary Britain they were now coming 'home' to. Life was difficult; cities had been ravaged by bombing; everything was rationed; they'd have to do war work. It would be tough. Some homecoming.

These lectures . . . made us feel terribly anxious. After all, we had been interned for a pretty long time. In those years, all decision-making had been taken from us . . . Soon now we would have to use our own initiative once more and build a new life for ourselves in the outside world. There were many who had never lived in England, such as the members of the War Graves Commission, and they were quite disturbed by the lectures. I don't believe these young people who told us about wartime England realised how depressing they were.

They were free at last, but the long fight against Hitler wasn't over yet.

12

Hitting Back

When I got back to England I felt, 'I've got to hit back.' Hitler had chased us out of Poelkapelle and I thought, 'Right, I'll join up and chase him back!'

Danny Quinn, IWGC pupil gardener
evacuated in May 1940, aged nineteen

IF THOSE RETURNING from the camps in 1944 found Britain an alien, dangerous and challenging place, their more fortunate comrades who had escaped four years earlier knew exactly how they felt. The evacuees from Ypres were bewildered by their reception. They had arrived fraught, dirty and dishevelled, many without belongings or papers, after their wearying week-long exodus living rough by night and facing Stuka fire on the road. Now that they had finally landed in the mother country, they didn't expect to be greeted with suspicion and hostility. It started as soon as they docked. Margaret Dupres, who was in the first party to arrive at Southampton, remembers being interrogated by Customs officials:

> We were all there in this warehouse place and they said: 'Have you got anything to declare?' So Dad, who was quite a quiet type really, turned round to these officers and said, 'Do you realise what these people have been through? They've all left their homes, many have left their families!'

They faced interrogation by police and the security services and those who had lost their papers in the chaos at Calais now had to convince British officials that they weren't illegal immigrants, spies or fifth columnists. Pupil gardener George Sutherland, part of the cycle party, had been separated from his father, Walter. He had destroyed his papers in France in case he was caught and on arrival in England was suspected of being a spy. The Boucher family, whose suitcase containing all their family papers had been destroyed on the quay, were marched off the *City of Christchurch* by soldiers with fixed bayonets. There was little immediate understanding of what they had gone through.

These fiercely patriotic families were in a double bind: they were treated not as British evacuees, as they had expected, but as foreign refugees. When the Fox family arrived in London from Southampton, they were put up initially at the Union Jack Club, a servicemen's hostel in Waterloo. It was there that nine-year-old Betty realised she was a stranger in her own country: 'It was my first experience of seeing English houses and streets and the other children in the streets were staring at us . . . we had suddenly become a curiosity: "Belgian refugees".' However, as British passport holders, they didn't qualify for the refugee aid that Belgian nationals received, and had to rely on Salvation Army handouts and the kindness of strangers.

Betty Parker, who was fifteen when her family arrived, remembers a very difficult first few months:

My Dad went up to Brixton and met some Belgian people we were on the boat with. They'd been rehoused and furnished. And we had nothing. It was very hard going for Mum and Dad. Dad got a job as a grave digger in Morden cemetery for a few months, and I got a job making up boxes of Christmas cards.

The evacuees stayed with relatives or friends if they could, but some knew no one they could impose on. Louise Francis, then twenty, was separated from her parents:

We had nowhere to go. We were split up, to go where people were taking refugees in. Mum and Dad and my younger brother were billeted in Romford with very nice people and I went quite a few miles away in Kenton. Eventually we rented a house and people were so kind. We had no furniture, nothing, and we had furniture given to us, we had beds, the lot.

The Commission helped place men in jobs with council parks departments, or on farms and country estates, but some had to take what work they could get. Many found jobs in reserved (essential) occupations, working at night as fire-watchers and Air Raid Precaution (ARP) wardens. Some families stayed in and around London. The Fox family settled in the north London suburb of Burnt Oak, where Jack Fox got a job delivering precision tools to factories on his motorbike. Grateful for the help they had received when they first arrived, the family joined the local corps of the Salvation Army; Jimmy signed the 'Young People's War' pledge and his sister Jacqueline learned to play the euphonium – the start of a lifetime's love of music.

The young evacuees settled into new schools. Though their accents marked them out, the children were welcomed – as Belgian refugees – and the older ones were surprised to find themselves ahead of their peers academically. Settling in was made all the more difficult in London and other cities targeted by the Luftwaffe: they were out of the frying pan but just in time for the Blitz. Some children were evacuated all over again – this time, to their distress, without their parents. Robert Rolfe, the youngest of nine until his baby brother came along in 1941, stayed with his mother and was taken aback to discover that he had older siblings when they were finally brought home after an unhappy time in Weston-super-Mare.

What once had been a tight-knit community was now scattered throughout the United Kingdom. George Sutherland and his father were reunited at last in their native Glasgow five weeks after they landed. Margaret Dupres and her parents went back to Plymouth where her father worked in the docks and did ARP duties at night, a dangerous job as German bombers pulverised the port during March and April 1941. The Boucher family returned to their native Cornwall where young Sam quickly earned the nickname 'Beljink' from his schoolmates, a name that stuck for the next fifty years. Their father worked among the rubble of Plymouth, cleaning up Blitz victims for burial.

Betty Parker's father eventually found employment as head gardener at Springfield House near High Wycombe, and the family moved into a lodge on the estate. Springfield was no ordinary country house; it was the home of Bomber Command and Charlie Parker found Air Chief Marshal Sir Arthur 'Bomber' Harris a sympathetic and supportive employer. Parker tended the grounds and kitchen gardens and looked after the family's pony and trap. Betty still has photos of the Harris family at home at Springfield and a glowing reference written by Harris for her father.

After the initial shock of discovering that they weren't as British as they thought they were, the families buckled down and joined in the war effort. As soon as she was eighteen Betty Parker trained as a radar operator with the ATS – the women's branch of the Army, the Auxiliary Territorial Service. She was part of the first female team to be based at a rocket site at Hackney Wick where, on twenty-four-hour shifts, she tracked enemy planes and sent information on to the plotting room. She hated confined spaces, which was a problem when the V-1 rockets ('doodlebugs') came over:

> If we were off-duty we had to get under our beds, and I couldn't do that, so I used to stand in the doorway. We had a V-1 that went round and round our site; one of our Bofors guns shot one down once but there was such a loss of life that they were told not to shoot them down any more – 'just let them fall'.

It was dangerous, but she will always remember: 'That feeling of togetherness which you don't get now, all together, looking after each other. We all just took a chance. You never think it's going to happen to you, do you?'

Louise Francis wanted to join the WRNS (Women's Royal Naval Service) but they were full, so she went into the WAAF (Women's Auxiliary Air Force). After training as a wireless operator she lived on a base 'somewhere in central England' with naval personnel, American servicemen and high-ranking civilians. Her 'hush-hush' job with the RAF's Y Service was to intercept coded enemy communications. She wasn't involved in decoding – places like Bletchley Park did that – but it was still highly sensitive work. She loved it, but when her parents were both diagnosed with terminal cancer and died within four days of each other, leaving her ten-year-old brother, she had a terrible choice to make.

My friends said, 'Oh, you can't, you mustn't, give up your life, you must carry on what you're doing, he'll have to go into an orphanage or a home or something.' And that's where the French in me surfaced: 'I can't do that. He's my brother. I've got to look after him.' So I left the WAAF and went back to Kenton. It was a dreadful time, we had the doodlebugs and everything, but we managed.

Newly married Charlotte Dunn had to leave her soldier husband behind when she left Belgium. Now she found herself doing night shifts working on Hurricane engines in a north London factory. 'I loved my job, loved it. There was me and an American girl and we were the first women in that factory. The men booed us at first, but as they got called up, more women came in and I was very happy there.'

Even returning internees were expected to do their bit. It wasn't long after her repatriation that the War Office caught up with Lillian Wilkins:

'We understand you aren't doing any war work – and you should be.' So I said, 'I've been doing an awful lot of war work – in Belgium and then in Germany – holding up the flag.' They let me go on that occasion but they were back a few months later and said I had to go on the buses, into munitions, or go nursing. I said, 'Well, I can't see myself on a bus and I'm definitely not going into munitions but I will go nursing.' And that's what I did.

As a result of that wartime call-up, Lillian spent the rest of her working life in the Health Service.

Rene Fletcher, the Memorial School Britannia and May Queen who left Ypres with her family before the war, now ran a hairdresser's in Sussex with her sister Pam. She never understood why, but they managed to avoid being called up. This was a disappointment for Rene: 'I would have liked to do my bit in the war. Of course everyone of my generation who I meet now, they all did something during the war. What did I do? I cut people's hair.' With a German invasion imminent, she did take rifle-shooting lessons with the Home Guard, but could never manage to hit the target, 'so that was a waste of time'. To rub it in, her two friends from the Memorial School were about to embark on the most exciting kind of war work. One day she met Dorothy Charlton, now in WAAF uniform, and asked after their mutual friend, Elaine Madden:

> I met Dorothy up in London and she said that she and Elaine were going to join the secret service but to keep quiet about it, not say anything. And I thought, well, that's a silly thing to tell me! From that time onwards I never heard from Dorothy or Elaine again and all I could presume was that they'd joined the secret service and the Gestapo had got them.

For the boys, it was an exciting time. The leading light of the Tiger Club, Bob Simmons, was now fourteen. He and his radio ham father had got away just before the main evacuation party and the family now rented a house in Selsey on the Sussex coast, not far from RAF Tangmere and the Fleet Air Arm base at Thorney Island:

> We had a front row seat for the Battle of Britain! My mother and I would go to a neighbour's shelter, but often I used to try and stay with my father to hear this exciting battle going on – 'Bandits at 10,000 feet!' and 'Follow me, Blue!' – on the radio speakers.

They also watched the battle in the air.

> About three o'clock, the sky was aroar, full of hundreds of planes. Ten minutes later they were overhead, then they went for Tangmere or Thorney Island a few miles away. Then the Spits started getting in amongst them and the machine guns started rattling away. And then some of the planes started crashing. It was very exciting! And we used to stand by with screwdrivers and cutters and tin openers and when a plane crashed not too far away we would get on our bikes and get to the plane before the Home Guard and try and get swastikas off the tails and Perspex from the windows.

Selsey wasn't the safest place to be in the late summer of 1940. A Spitfire came down near their house and blew up as Bob approached on his bike. Fields were dotted with obstacles and wires to prevent airborne landings and the beaches were covered in concrete blocks, barbed wire and hidden mines 'so that every so often a doggie would walk into one and disappear in a puff of smoke'. And they had regular visits from hit-and-run raiders:

> The first day of Spitfire Week – a lovely day – a single Heinkel 111 appeared from nowhere, flew down the centre of the village, dropped a stick of bombs right across it and disappeared. My father, sister and I walked round to inspect the damage a bit later on and when we were standing in the front gate of a house with a big crater in the garden, there was a blinding explosion. The air was filled with black smoke and my father shouted, 'Get down! Get down!' and I looked up and saw hundreds of bits of debris hurtling up into the air and, as the smoke cleared, paused in mid-air for what seemed like ages and then started to rain down on us as we all crouched down, covering our heads as best we could . . . That night Lord Haw-Haw mentioned it on his broadcast.

By 1941, Bob's father was working for the BBC in London and got him a job as an 'Unestablished Youth in Training' at £1 7s 6d a week – slightly more than the minimum wage today. He was still only sixteen when he started work in the London Control Room at Broadcasting House, manning continuity for the Home and Forces radio services, and living in a BBC hostel in Grosvenor Square. In the studio he would sit next to Alvar Liddell or John Snagge as they read the news, and make sure listeners heard the sound that told the world London was still standing, Blitz or no Blitz:

> Big Ben was transmitted live every night before the nine o'clock news without a single exception for the whole duration of the war. We had microphones in Big Ben, permanently tied to the fourth channel of our mixer. You could often hear the sound of fire engines, bombs whistling down, the sound of explosions

and guns, in between the bongs. We would listen on pre-fade by pressing a button to hear how the air raids were going and whether we'd get a quiet walk home that night or whether Oxford Street would be full of hoses and fire engines.

Occasionally, he'd take calls on the Red Phone – a direct line from Air Defence Great Britain – ordering him to switch transmitters in order to confuse German bombers. It was all 'heady stuff for a sixteen-year-old'.

What of the Memorial School boys who – with their headteacher's help and encouragement – joined up straight from school in the late 1930s? George Simpson enlisted with the Queen's Own Royal West Kent Regiment and had a frustrating and difficult war: he was in Malta during the siege of 1940–42 and the following year he was captured on the Greek island of Leros. He spent the rest of the war in military prison camps in Germany, enduring conditions that were at times much worse than those in the internment camps.

Food was very scarce. Believe it or not I used to go round the perimeter wire, pick dandelions and make a sort of soup with the root and eat the leaves. We had a clandestine radio in the pigeon loft and listened in to the Russian advance, plotting their movements. That's what kept you going.

Jerry Eaton and his brothers all entered the Services. Two went through the Army Apprentices School at Chepstow and joined the Royal Electrical and Mechanical Engineers; two joined the Royal Navy. One of them was among more than three hundred killed in 1942 when his ship, the light cruiser HMS *Curacoa*, was sliced in two by the *Queen Mary* as it escorted the liner, laden with American troops, through U-boat infested waters off the Irish coast – a disaster kept from the press at the time.

Jerry went on to live his dream of flying. After school, he left Belgium for RAF Halton to train as an aircraft technician. This changed him in more ways than he expected.

My name is actually Stanley. I was fifteen and had a strong Belgian accent when I arrived at Halton in 1936. We all lived in dormitories and next to me was a chap from Cornwall. We got talking and he said, 'Where are you from?', and I said, 'Belgium', so he said, 'Ah! You're one of those bloody Jerries, aren't you?' And of course I said I had nothing to do with the Jerries, but he decided he'd call me Jerry anyway, and for the next three years that was my nickname. After that it just stuck. The only person who ever called me Stanley was my Mum.

His three-year apprenticeship ended just as the war started but he really wanted to fly aeroplanes rather than tinker with their engines. Being caught in a Blitz raid one night only stiffened his resolve to get up there and fight back, so he immediately applied for pilot training. But at that stage in the war technicians who understood the sophisticated new aircraft then coming into service were more valuable to the RAF than pilots. This soon changed and Jerry was accepted for a basic training course in the empty blue skies of Oklahoma.

After a brief refresher in Britain's cloudier and more treacherous conditions, Jerry learned tactical reconnaissance on Mustangs and joined 4 Squadron as a 22-year-old Pilot Officer. But he was soon itching for something more exciting than reconnaissance. He had his eye on fighter-bombers:

Some of my friends were on Typhoons at Tangmere and I asked my CO if I could get a transfer but he refused point-blank. Anyway, I went down to Tangmere to meet my friends and that evening I met the Wing Commander (Flying), Denys Gillam. I explained my situation. He got a scrap of paper and took my number, name and squadron. Seven days later I was there. I had a couple of days learning how to fly this thing and then was operational straight away. It was only later I found out why he was so keen to get me there – at that point the casualty rate in Typhoon squadrons was one of the highest.

Jerry got on famously with 'Tiffies': 'a marvellous aeroplane, very tough, and more responsive than Spits', although when they were carrying their maximum payload of two 1,000lb bombs or eight rockets, 'the stick went like rubber' and the plane was difficult to control.

He saw at first hand the attrition of pilots, especially young and inexperienced ones: 'Some of them came and within two weeks they were gone. But you never thought of dying. We felt very much alive. There was a tremendous sense of excitement about going out and destroying the enemy's infrastructure. We were happy to be fighting for a good cause and doing damage to the enemy.'

Danny Quinn, the young pupil gardener who had managed to escape from Boulogne on a destroyer, was also desperate to fly. He joined the RAF soon after arrival in England and after a stint in the RAF Regiment, joined 547 Squadron Coastal Command as an Air Gunner in Liberators on U-boat patrols. His missions were long, dangerous and – when the patrols moved to the Baltic and North Atlantic – bitingly cold. 'Our aircraft had no heating and the gun turrets were as cold as a deep freeze. We wore three flying suits – one of cotton, one of silk and a top one of canvas – and three pairs of gloves, but we were still freezing cold. We kept going with sandwiches and flasks of hot Oxo.'

Danny lost many crew members and had some near-misses himself:

We were on standby for four days after coming off a ten-hour patrol in the Bay of Biscay – we were free. I went into town and when I came back they told me my crew was being called out on a training flight in the Irish Sea – we had to practise using the new Leigh Lights on a Navy sub. So I took my bike and went to look for them. Then someone said, 'Yes, they're just taking off'. So I chased them on my bike. I got to the end of the runway just as they were taking off. They never came back. They crashed in the Preseli Hills and six of my crew-mates died.

Danny and Jerry both played an airborne role in the 1944 D-Day Normandy landings. Coastal Command's job was to protect the invasion fleet from U-boats and prevent German shipping movements. Danny was proud to claim that 'not one life, nor one pound of equipment from the invasion fleet was to be lost as a result of U-boat activity – none of them got in'.

Jerry's squadron was based at Needs Oar Point near Lymington, in preparation for the planned invasion.

We knew there was going to be an invasion, but we didn't know when. It was an absolute secret. One of the ways we kept it – not only our wing but Spits and Thunderbolts as well – we smashed up all the radar stations along the French and Belgian coast. We attacked them day after day with rockets and bombs, so the Germans wouldn't have any radar support to see what was coming.

They were returning from a sortie in France when, just off the Isle of Wight, one of their squadron leaders had engine failure and went down in the sea. They saw his parachute open, so, after refuelling at Tangmere, twenty-three aeroplanes went out in a line to search for him. They didn't find him but on the way back they saw an awe-inspiring sight: . . . 'hundreds and hundreds of boats leaving all the ports. The whole coastal strip was just a mass of boats. Our Leader made us keep radio silence, not a single word, and when we were back in the briefing marquee he said, "As you've just seen, tomorrow is D–Day."'

Jerry was up at 5 a.m. the next day, 6 June, expecting to be called out early, but they didn't go in until that evening.

There were so many planes available to attack these German targets – something like thirty squadrons of Typhoons alone. The sky was full of aircraft – you had to be careful not to collide. When we finally went across, all we could see were fires burning everywhere, vehicles on fire, buildings on fire, and we had to go inland quite a way to find something to attack . . . We were looking for tanks or vehicles coming up towards the beaches. What we found was this very large column of horses towing these carriages full of German soldiers. And I remember as we attacked – we were using mostly 20mm cannon – we were con-scious of all these troops jumping off these vehicles, trying to take cover. We must have killed loads of them and unfortunately of course the horses too.

Jerry was more familiar than most with some of the areas he was sent to bomb: 'Our squadron went to attack the railway marshalling yards at Arras, where I used to live. We dive-bombed Arras. I didn't feel very happy about it – it used to be my home – but that was our job.'

Danny's targets were impersonal – often unseen beneath the waves – but his final operation brought him the closest he'd ever been to the enemy. They were on a photo-recce off the Danish coast late in the war, when they sighted two German warships, the *Prinz Eugen* and the *Nürnberg*. Much to Danny's amazement: 'They surrendered to us. They all stood on deck with their caps off. We circled round till the Navy came, going in close about thirty or forty feet. They knew the game was up, they must have been glad it was all over.'

Jerry captures the feelings of all those from the Ypres British community who fought from the earliest days of the war in the Services or as civilians, often risking their lives to defend what they had always been taught was their motherland:

You had to have a strong sense of doing something of value for your country. You had a job. You'd been trained for it and your duty was to do it. We weren't conscious of all the evils of the Nazi regime then, but we knew we were fighting a good war.

13

Secrets

I wasn't frightened. I didn't know what could happen to me. I think maybe I was too dumb to be frightened.

Elaine Madden, SOE agent, 1944

FOR THE CHILDREN of the British Memorial School who had made it back to England in May 1940, life was shaped by war. They had escaped from the occupying forces ravaging their adopted homeland to a Britain straining every sinew to keep those forces at bay. As soon as they were old enough they joined in the war effort. Their fearless and uncomplicated patriotism may have been dented by their initial reception, but it remained undimmed. They were fighting Hitler for Britain – and for Belgium too.

It took some time before anyone in authority realised what a potential asset they had in this cohort of young people. They were fluent in several languages and many understood German. They knew the flatlands of Flanders and swathes of occupied territory and could effectively disappear among their peoples. Some of them were even competent Morse operators. Was this asset exploited? Too often it was not. Sometimes it was even deliberately and perversely ignored. Though some didn't think to volunteer information about their skills or preferred to keep them hidden under a bushel, most recognised that they had something special and wanted it put to good use in the fight against Hitler.

Bob Simmons volunteered for the RAF on his seventeenth birthday. With his background in radio, he was trained in radar navigation and joined 400 Squadron in May 1944, just before the Normandy landings. 'I volunteered for France, telling them I knew the country and the language and all that. They posted me to Burma.'

John Osborne also volunteered to go back. 'I knew the language, the territory, who you could trust and who you couldn't. I wanted to do something, but I was rejected. I think because I had dual nationality, British-Belgian, they couldn't trust me.'

It wasn't until after VE-Day that Danny Quinn got to use his languages, when he was posted to Holland on an intelligence operation to root out former SS men and hand them over to the Dutch military police. Charlotte Dunn's twin brother Priestley joined the Royal Engineers and was on bomb disposal teams in the London Blitz before doing intelligence training. But he was dissuaded from going on to undertake missions in occupied Flanders because of fears for the safety of his Belgian wife, whom he'd had to leave behind in 1940.

Other evacuees managed to use their special skills in the war effort. After a brief period in the Navy, Ernie Batchelor joined the Green Howards in 1944. He worked behind enemy lines in Holland and Germany as a wireless operator before Operation Market Garden and the Battle of Arnhem, and was later attached to the Special Air Service (SAS). After the war he met and married a German girl, but his wartime experiences prompted mental health problems that blighted his family life.

Often their linguistic abilities came out quite by chance. Dorothy Charlton and her family left Poelkapelle with Danny Quinn's family in May 1940. Dorothy and her sisters had been used to a quiet life at home with their mother, but things changed once they got to England. To their mother's distress, Dorothy joined the Belgian section of the WAAF and her two sisters joined the ATS.

I was a meteorologist. I was sent to Pathfinder Command at Wyton, and I was there until I had a huge argument and was reported for swearing at an officer. I told him they'd given the wrong gen about cloud cover to the bombers going out – I went off the deep end! So I was hauled over the coals and then sent to Group Captain [Donald] Bennett. He told me to stand easy and then he said: 'I gather you've had a bit of a rumpus in the

Ops Room.' I said: 'You could call it that.' 'Well, what I'm interested in is the language you were being so rude to the officer in.' I was swearing in French, Flemish and everything – I can't swear in English, it doesn't mean anything to me.

After establishing that it could have been French, Flemish or Dutch, and was most likely a combination of all three, Bennett dismissed her with a warning. But, she says, three weeks later he called her back:

'We have an idea that you might like to be trained to be in another sector.' So I said, 'Why? Isn't my work good enough?' 'We wondered if you'd like to be trained to go back – to be dropped back in occupied territory.' I thought it sounded like fun, so I did.

If Dorothy was recruited for covert missions in this way, it would have been unorthodox. Potential recruits weren't usually told of the sensitive nature of the work until they were well into training in case they turned out to be unsuitable.

These days Dorothy prefers not to talk about what happened after that. She says she did 'quite a few' missions for SOE (Special Operations Executive) in northern France from the end of 1942 and in the past she has spoken of being betrayed, arrested and brutally interrogated. In any personal account of wartime exploits, it is difficult to establish the facts from this distance when the subjects are now elderly, in failing health, or have already lost their memories. And if, as in Dorothy's case, there is no surviving independent record of what they may have undertaken. Truth, never a straightforward commodity in oral history, is not easy to capture. Dorothy's secret war, if she had one, remains a secret.

In the middle of 1941 Sir Fabian Ware was approached by a mysterious Mr Wonnacott, 'one about whom one must know nothing'. Wonnacott asked him to compile a secret report on IWGC staff evacuated from France and Belgium for something called the Inter-Service Alien and Refugee Register. The report had to grade the men according to four categories:

1. Exceptionally intelligent and observant.
2. Intelligent and observant.
3. Moderately intelligent and observant.
4. No grading [irredeemably dim?].

Ware duly complied and the Ypres Area Horticultural Officer, Major Gill, who had been Haworth's right-hand man on the evacuation, made the assessments of the men in his area, adding unsolicited comments (Dorothy Charlton's father, for example, was 'very talkative') along the way. Ware wrote to Gill, thanking him for his efforts, adding: 'Some day I will tell you what they were wanted for.'

In fact, Wonnacott worked for NID6, the Naval Intelligence Division of the Admiralty responsible for gathering topographical intelligence and for maintaining a 'contacts index' of individuals who had detailed, specialised knowledge or expertise that could help in the war effort. Were any of the IWGC men from Ypres ever approached for their 'knowledge or expertise'? If they were, the Commission's files are silent on the matter.

After her dramatic escape from Dunkirk with the BEF, Elaine Madden found herself lodging in a flat off Fleet Street and working as a clerk for the British Relay Wireless Company. At night she was a Women's Voluntary Service (WVS) volunteer, supporting ARP wardens as they searched the rubble of bombed-out buildings for casualties.

> You felt you had to do something. There were all these posters saying 'Do Your Bit'. You couldn't just stand there and say, 'What are you doing for the war effort?' It just wasn't on. I wasn't brought up like that in my school. You were taught to do something useful.

But she felt this still wasn't enough. When she got to bomb sites and found injured people, all she could do was comfort them and alert the emergency services who then came to do the real work. So she studied for Red Cross certificates in Home Nursing and First Aid in order to lend more practical help until the ambulances came.

I don't know why I wasn't more scared of the Blitz. I used to walk around in it and even when I was off-duty I'd take flasks of tea out to the firefighters. Some people would say, 'Wait till it's quietened down, there are still bombs out there', but I'd say, 'Not to worry, if one has my name on it, OK, well, then I go.' So the Blitz didn't scare me much but those stupid little butterfly bombs – they looked like tin cans with wings and they used to get stuck in the trees and could fall on you and explode – they scared the life out of me. Of course sometimes you had to leave people who were dead or too badly injured to be helped – that was quite horrific. But I wasn't scared.

By the beginning of 1944, Elaine was twenty. She had already had two deferments from call-up to the ATS and had run out of reasons not to go. There was no choice, and she really didn't want to join the ATS. Perhaps it was the uniform, but she 'didn't want to be some-body stuck in the Army'. Surely she could do something better, more useful? After all, she spoke three languages. By now she was sharing a flat in Bayswater. She was grumbling about it one day with her flatmate, Susan, and a US Army officer they knew who used to take them out to dinner occasionally. A few days later the officer took her to lunch alone and asked her if she was serious about doing anything to get a better job. Yes, she said, she was.

He introduced her to someone at the American Embassy who was recruiting people for unspecified secret operations, but as she was British, he said he would have to check that the British authorities didn't want to lay claim to her first. As it happened, they did.

I met some people in south London somewhere who interro-gated me and decided that they would refer me to the Belgian section of SOE as Belgium was the country I knew best. I met Ides Floor [senior SOE staff officer with a direct link to the Belgian security service in exile] and he interrogated me for a long time, asking questions about my family. Then he said they would check them out and call me. So I said OK, although I didn't quite know why, I knew nothing about what I was supposed to do.

The Special Operations Executive was set up in July 1940 in response to the dirty tricks – disinformation, sabotage and infiltration by spies and Nazi sympathisers – that the Germans had supposedly employed in order to achieve their startlingly swift invasion of France and the Low Countries a few months earlier. In fact, Blitzkrieg's success owed more to old-fashioned surprise and superior strategy than to the efforts of a 'fifth column' – if such a thing ever existed. Nevertheless, it spurred Churchill to demand a new secret service to wreak havoc behind enemy lines. Specially trained agents would be sent under cover into occupied countries to organise sabotage and subversion. Churchill, as ever, put it more vividly. SOE, he said, would 'set Europe ablaze'.

After a wobbly start, some notorious disasters in the field, and open hostility from the Secret Intelligence Service (MI6), SOE began to achieve useful results – usually by unorthodox or illegal methods – sabotaging key infrastructure, knocking out German war production and supporting local Resistance networks. By the time Elaine met Major Ides Floor early in 1944, it had a well-oiled recruitment and training machine designed to weed out all but the fittest candidates for these 'special operations'. The recently confirmed head of T (Belgian) Section was Hardy Amies, who later achieved fame as the Queen's couturier.

> He became my superior officer. Very superior. He was a reasonably good looking man. He was tall, very very smart and very very pansy. There was something in his manner. His uniform was made-to-measure and everything about him was so immaculate. I saw him from time to time when he deigned to meet the lower orders.

In March the domestic security service, MI5, ran checks on Elaine. It reported no trace of her on its records but an intriguing footnote links her with her young aunt, Simone, with whom she had escaped from Poperinghe in 1940. This shows how MI5 agents must have been out and about in London, eavesdropping on other people's conversations:

She may be connected with one Simone DUPONSELLE, who in January 1941 approached a Private in the FFC [French forces] at Lyons Corner House in Coventry Street, and asked him how she could get letters through to relatives in occupied France and Belgium. Enquiries showed that her parents were the proprietors of the Palace Hotel, Poperinghe, and that she was anxious to hear from them as she had no news of them.

After she and her Belgian relatives had been cleared, Elaine was sent to Lillywhites department store in Piccadilly to pick up 'the most beautiful uniform' of the First Aid Nursing Yeomanry – the traditional cover for women SOE agents. Packing the trousers that had been specially provided, she set off for the first of a raft of assessments and training courses. These were all held in comfortable country houses specially requisitioned for the purpose, earning SOE the nickname 'Stately 'Omes of England' – though some were in Scotland.

In April 1944 Elaine went through the preliminary filter, the Students' Assessment Board (SAB), at Cranleigh in Surrey. Candidates were given a cover name and from now on within SOE she became Elaine Meeus (although, confusingly for all concerned, agents in the field had a variety of code names – Elaine was Imogen and also Alice – and a completely different set of names on their false papers). The SAB assessed intelligence, practical aptitude and psychological suitability for covert operations and identified the roles which candidates might fit best. Elaine's SAB report grades her as being of average potential as an agent, but of well above average intelligence, with good marks in Mechanical Aptitude and Instructional Ability. The course leader's assessment is astute:

This girl has a good intelligence, a confident manner, has a good imagination and is capable of taking decisive action . . . and there is no doubt about her disinterested desire to help the Belgian cause. She is neither a leader nor an organiser, but she is alert, efficient and methodical. At the same time, she is not above being helpless and feminine when the chance presents itself. She is sophisticated for her age and . . . her consciousness of her powers to attract is not likely to interfere with her application to the task in hand.

The so-called Group B training courses that followed were more practical and specialised, but Elaine was bewildered by some of the things they were asked to do.

I thought I'd ended up in a loony bin. We did stupid things like swinging from one tree to another and crawling under netting. I wondered what on earth this was for. Then we were sent to Scotland to learn how to do things like 'silent killing'. They thought I was too small, too light, too fragile to do the whole course, so they just showed me a few things, like how to slit a man's throat from behind . . .

Then things got even more bizarre. Professional criminals taught them how to burgle houses and crack safes. They had to break into a real house and find 'secret papers' hidden somewhere in the attic – and return to base within thirty minutes.

They learned German officer grades, uniforms, aeroplanes, tanks and weaponry by heart. They were taught how to handle Sten guns – shooting from the hip – and how to make sure the target was dead. Then on to SOE's 'finishing school' on the Beaulieu estate in Hampshire, where Elaine remembers being 'very well looked after'. Here they were introduced to the arcane world of coding and learned 'clandestine life' – the art of maintaining their cover over long periods and during interrogation.

Towards the end of those classes a 'German soldier' came into my bedroom in the middle of the night and said I was a prisoner and had to go to the interrogation room. A big room, dark except for a big headlight over the table and three 'German officers' sitting behind the table, and I was sitting there in my pyjamas. They started interrogating me about my alibi and then they made me stand on this chair with this big floodlight in my eyes. And then they made me take my pyjama jacket off and I was there on this damned chair, just in my pyjama trousers, thinking, what the hell are they playing at? Then they switched the lights on and I could see all the other students sitting round the room and they started clapping. I could have killed those people! It was ghastly!

By now, the nature of Elaine's job as an SOE agent must have been abundantly clear, but she was less well informed about the risks. She knew she would have to sustain an alibi for weeks, possibly months, at a time. However, her fate if she were to be discovered would be much worse than having to stand bare-breasted on a chair. She didn't know that T Section agents had a one-in-three chance of never coming back; that if they did survive capture, the best they could expect was to end up in a concentration camp. Either way, they would be tortured first to extract information, something that the gentlemen impersonating the Gestapo in English country houses were unable to simulate. Elaine concentrated on the task ahead. Naivety and ignorance protected her from dwelling on the downside.

She passed out of Beaulieu and her file notes record that she needed more practice in coding, having been taught the main techniques of the time: 'Innocent Letter based on Playfair, with conventions. Double Transposition. Letter One-time Pad and Mental One-time Pad with conventions and Mental Indicator'. At this point Elaine was told by T Section at HQ that she would be going on to RAF Ringway outside Manchester for the final stage of her training, parachute jumping.

Parachute jumping? I must have gone white in the face. 'Yes, of course. How do you think we get you to Belgium?' I must have looked scared. This chap flew into a filthy rage. 'How the hell did you get in here? After all that training and now you're too scared to jump!' He got me so angry, I was stamping my foot. I said, 'I *will* jump, I *will* jump, I *will* jump!' 'You'd better,' he said, 'or there'll be hell waiting for you!' So off I went to Ringway.

Elaine's first drop was from a balloon at 300 feet – low for a parachute jump – in a pattern called Slow Pairs. Agents didn't open their parachutes themselves; they were hooked up to a 'static line' attached to a bar in the aeroplane which opened the parachute automatically on their descent. From this first jump, her nerves melted in the euphoria of being in the air:

> It was a funny feeling, very quick before the parachute opened. But once you got down it was as if you'd conquered the world – the most wonderful feeling. Up top it was scary but once you'd come down the only thing you wanted to do was get up there again. The next day we went up in a plane and that was even better!

She had five training jumps in all. During one, a young Pole froze when he got to the opening and was unable to jump, so they unhooked him and sent him to the back of the plane to recover. 'When everyone else had jumped, including me – a girl – he suddenly ran to the hole, yelling in Polish, and jumped. But his parachute wasn't hooked up and didn't open. I saw him fall past me in mid-air.'

Elaine's passing-out report was kind: 'Miss Meeus was happy here in spite of natural nervousness . . . She showed no hesitation in the aircraft or balloon when the time came to jump and made safe landings.' She was now ready, as SOE put it, for 'service in the Field'.

It was midsummer 1944. Following the D-Day landings in June, Allied troops were finally starting to push through into France. But VE-Day wouldn't be celebrated in Britain for another nine months and Europe was still a dangerous place. Paris had yet to be liberated and much of Belgium was still in German hands.

André Wendelen was one of T Section's most able and distinguished agents. A 25-year-old Brussels lawyer at the time of the German invasion, he had managed to escape to England in May 1940 and joined SOE in 1941. Having passed through training with exceptional reports, he went back to occupied Belgium to help establish a ruthlessly effective Resistance network. He had already survived two dangerous four-month missions – something of a record – and was known to the Gestapo. His senior officers commended his 'dash and courage' but also his 'lucid and orderly mind'. Now he was about to embark on a third – highly sensitive and political – operation. His wireless operator was another SOE veteran, Jacques Van de Spiegel. His courier was a new recruit who went by the name of Elaine Meeus.

I was told I was to be the 'ears, legs and mouth' of André Wendelen. It was his third time out and the Gestapo were looking for him – they even had 'Wanted' posters up with his picture on. I had to do as much of his legwork – meeting contacts and so on – as possible, so that he didn't have to go out. Part of our mission was to find out if there were any V-1 or V-2 rocket launching sites in Belgium. That wasn't all, but I didn't know that at the time.

On the night of 4/5 August 1944, Elaine and her team were dropped into the Belgian Ardennes by a USAAF (US Army Air Forces) plane. She decided to jump ahead of Wendelen and van der Spiegel in case she got last-minute nerves.

The red light went on when we were getting near the dropping point. Then the green light went on when the opening was ready. The dispatcher opened the hatch and I got into position ready to jump. And then suddenly this American dispatcher said, 'Honey, I'm going to give you the last kiss you'll get in a long time' and he just picked me up by my harness, kissed me and literally dropped me in the hole, so I never had to jump, I was dropped!

Once in the warm night air, she was able to appreciate the extraordinary scene around her.

It was fabulous. As soon as the parachute opened, it was absolutely wonderful – there was a full moon and it was a beautiful summer's night. I saw André go past and then Jacques and there I was still floating. I wasn't going down! They'd given me a full-size parachute too big for my size and the heat was keeping me in the air.

She struggled to the ground, folded up her parachute tightly and buried it as she'd been taught; then she helped gather up their equipment – including civilian clothes, the radio and a large amount of cash – dropped with them. They went to the nearby farmhouse, as arranged, and slept. (The farmer later exhumed the parachutes and kept them, neatly marked with their false names, and they went back to recover them after the war.)

Was Elaine scared at the thought of what lay ahead? 'No, I just felt, I'm home, I'm back in Belgium. I didn't think about there being Germans about or hearing the plane. I wasn't frightened; I think maybe I was too dumb to be frightened.' But her lack of experience was a liability – and ignorance of local conditions by her T Section minders didn't help. The next day, they changed into the civilian clothes provided for them. When Elaine opened her suitcase she found to her delight: '. . . the most glamorous grey and white tweed skirt and jacket, a beautiful big black handbag and shoes with big crepe soles. I opened the handbag and there in gold letters was "Made in England"!'

Wendelen, who hadn't worked with a woman courier before, helped her scratch out the incriminating letters and they went to meet their first Resistance contact, a woman who ran a bar in the small town of Ciney. They took care to travel and arrive separately as they were never to be seen in public together. The woman immediately took Wendelen to one side: 'For God's sake, you can't let her walk about like that! She smells English! We haven't seen shoes like that in the past four years, and that *suit* . . .! If she goes around looking like that, she'll be arrested in no time.'

So Elaine was bundled into a local dress shop for something more befitting a Belgian hausfrau living under German occupation, and told to ditch the handbag. She kept the lovely clothes from London hidden for the rest of the mission.

They moved on to Brussels and the days were filled with meeting contacts, gathering intelligence and sending and receiving coded messages back and forth to London at prearranged times. It was thought safer for Elaine rather than Van de Spiegel to carry the radio transmitter in its suitcase, and she was charged with finding the safe houses where he could operate from. Helped by local Resistance people, she would organise a security barrier around the safe house, watching for German direction-finding vans that could pick up the radio signal and betray them.

She soon learned not to show her ignorance by asking for real coffee in shops: 'That was something they didn't tell you in training. That there was no coffee, no butter, no real soap. I don't suppose the men [at Beaulieu] ever did any shopping.'

The work went on. Wendelen had bribed a German soldier at a V-2 launch site with a great deal of money and was feeding back information to London, together with intelligence on troop and tank movements. Then a message from London confirmed their highly secret main assignment, code name Patron-Lysander. They were to look after a Monsieur Bernard and make preparations for his escape to England. Elaine returned to the Ardennes to meet their new charge at the château where he was in hiding.

I didn't know who Monsieur Bernard was, I just thought he was some top-notch Resistance man who was being hidden from the Germans and was important enough to go back to the UK. I hadn't the faintest idea who he was but he was the most charming man I've ever met in my life! I had a lovely time with him. His English was impeccable and he loved London and made me talk about which nightclubs were still open and what people were doing there.

They would play ping-pong and cards ('he always cheated') and go out for walks together. He was only forty but he suffered from sciatica and had to do exercises to stop his legs seizing up. On their walks they'd stop for a cigarette and a chat:

We talked about the King and Queen and then we got on to the Belgian Royal Family and what people in Britain were saying about them, and I said, 'That King Leopold, the damned traitor, with his German wife! [In fact she was Belgian.] And his brother Charles, what a useless so-and-so, where was he? He could have joined the Resistance and showed a bit of pluck, but God knows where he was – drunk in some brothel somewhere . . .' So he would laugh and say 'Yes, probably!'

When Elaine wasn't having a lovely time with Monsieur Bernard, she was recce-ing possible landing sites for a light aircraft to come and pick him up. She fed back to London the coordinates and complex technical information for potential sites in the difficult Ardennes terrain. The RAF kept rejecting her suggestions as unsuitable. Time was going on; they'd already been in Belgium for some weeks.

While she was minding Monsieur Bernard in the Ardennes, Wendelen and van der Spiegel were back in Brussels. One day she got a message asking her to return the radio to them urgently. The Resistance had blown up the rail link and she was anxiously wondering aloud how she would get back 'to her parents' in Brussels from her hotel in Ciney when she was offered a lift by a fellow guest, a German officer. Not hesitating, she gracefully accepted and he carried her luggage – the suitcase containing the radio receiver – to his staff car.

He picked up the case, and in quite good French, said, 'Heavy! What have we here? *Marché noir?*' So I fluttered my eyelashes a little – everyone was buying on the black market then – and I said, 'Just a little ham, butter, meat – for my family.' His driver put the case in the boot and we went on our way. The journey was perfectly pleasant, we kept the conversation light, nothing about the war, and when we got to Brussels he said he'd drop me off at my parents' house. I gave a false address near our apartment and he dropped me at the door, waiting for me to go in. I waved enthusiastically from the doorstep, hoping he would soon drive away, which thank God he eventually did.

Meanwhile the endgame in Europe was gathering momentum. By the end of August Allied troops were starting to overrun Belgium and Brussels was in sight of being liberated. But there was still danger for Elaine.

Near to our apartment was the SS headquarters and they were all outside in the street burning papers before the advancing British troops could get to them. I'd been decoding some important messages for André in the safe house with Jacques but they were tricky and they took me some time to finish. So I was out on the streets after curfew on my way to our apartment with these decoded messages stuffed quickly into my handbag – we were supposed to conceal them. When I got near to the SS headquarters I was stopped by this German soldier. He asked me for my papers, so I produced them and he said, 'You're from Coxyde' – this was part of my cover – so I said yes. 'Then you speak Flemish?' It turned out he was a conscript from Flanders and he started talking away to me in Flemish. I hadn't spoken Flemish for about five years, so I was surprised it came out so fluently. If I hadn't spoken Flemish I would have been in trouble. I kept praying, please God, don't let him open my handbag . . .

Almost a month after they had been dropped into Belgium, on 3 September, the British liberated Brussels. In the chaotic city where fighting was still sporadic, Wendelen and Elaine found themselves in charge of a British tank while the tank commander went off to relieve some of his men. They saw groups of German soldiers run past, making for the cover of nearby trees. Wendelen fired his revolver at them and Elaine got up into the turret and managed to get the gun firing, though she had no idea what she was firing at. Neither of them hit anyone but Elaine thinks she may have damaged a monument. It was while they were holed up in the tank that Wendelen told her that the plans for Monsieur Bernard had changed with the arrival of the British. And he revealed the charming cheat's true identity: 'André said, "Didn't you recognise Monsieur Bernard? He's Prince Charles, King Leopold's younger brother." I gasped. "But you don't know the awful things I said to him!" When I told him, André laughed his head off!'

The original plan had been to get Prince Charles to Britain, where he would lead the Belgian government-in-exile, ready to return after liberation and take over the throne from his discredited brother, then still in Germany. But, when all the preparations had been made, Charles refused to go, saying that it was ridiculous for him to 'escape' to Britain just as his country was being liberated – he would only have to come straight back. He was right. Belgium was now free and Charles was about to be installed as Prince Regent. Not long after this revelation, Elaine met him again at a celebratory dinner.

> I was very nervous about meeting him again. Especially after all those things I'd said about him and his family. And I didn't know whether to call him Sir, or Your Royal Highness, or Your Majesty, or what. Anyway, he was as charming as ever: 'I think you'd better just call me Bernard!'

Elaine describes her SOE mission in 1944 as a time of high excitement, comradeship, purpose – and fun. She laughs a great deal as she recounts her near-misses. She was lucky, certainly. It may have been near the end of the war in Europe but SOE agents were still being captured, tortured and put to death – four from T Section had been beheaded only weeks before. The official history of SOE records that, of 182 agents sent by T Section into the field, sixty-one died in action, in interrogation, or in prison; twenty-three survived arrest, many languishing in concentration camps until 1945. Elaine didn't ever think about using her standard issue cyanide pill; indeed, she forgot she had it. And she never thought about what might have happened had she been discovered or betrayed. 'I didn't think about the tortures I might have faced. I only found out about all that afterwards. A girl I knew who'd been dropped into France had all her nails pulled out, hands and feet.'

She also didn't know how exceptional she was. Only two women agents were ever dropped by T Section into Belgium during the war: Elaine was one; the other was Olga Jackson, a Belgian married to an Englishman, dropped on the same August night. Olga's extraordinary mission was to meet as many German officers as possible and demoralise them by convincing them that Germany was losing the war – a fifth columnist for the Allies. Elaine heard later that she was dropped in the wrong place, panicked, and went into hiding until the liberation.

For Elaine, this was a time of special significance for another reason. 'I fell in love with André. We were living together in Brussels, I mean he was my boss and it was normal. I lived with him and we became lovers. He was a wonderful man, the love of my life.' For a short euphoric time following liberation, she lived a 'fairy tale' in which anything and everything seemed possible, including her dream of a life with André Wendelen. But her war work wasn't finished, and her love life became more complicated. Elaine's story continues after Belgium's liberation but, looking back on her brief but intense part in the secret war against Hitler, she insists she was nothing special: 'I was just young and excited and willing to do anything except join the ATS! Not a heroine. Still, at my age, I'm glad of my life. I can still look in the mirror and feel proud.'

14

Resistance

We were in far bigger danger than the SOE people because they had a back-up. They used to come out and after three or four months have a rest in Switzerland or bugger off back to England in a Lysander. We were there all the time.

Stephen Grady, Voix du Nord/Sylvestre-Farmer
Resistance networks, 1941–4

THE *DÉPARTEMENTS* OF Pas de Calais and Nord, close to the border with Belgium, were among the most heavily and consistently populated with Germans during the war; they were also the most perilous for those who sought to subvert the efforts of the occupying forces. Resistance here – as in the rest of occupied France – was slow to start. General Charles de Gaulle's famous call to arms of 18 June 1940, courtesy of the BBC from London, may have signalled the start of his formidable tenure as leader of the Free French, but it had little immediate impact in France.

When something resembling a Resistance movement finally got going in 1941, it lacked organisation, materials and professionalism. But it had some exceptionally brave and able volunteers and eventually grew, with arms and expertise supplied by the British, into an effective 'secret army' on the ground, hindering the German war effort, disseminating propaganda, protecting Allied airmen from discovery and eventually preparing the way for liberation. Stephen Grady was among them and he started his Resistance career early.

In September 1941, after his 'miraculous' release from imprisonment for sabotaging the Messerschmitt, sixteen-year-old Stephen was recruited into a nascent group – the term Resistance wasn't used at that stage – started by Jules Houcke, the mayor of Nieppe, his brother Marcel, and the local headmaster. They were looking for a fluent English speaker who could interrogate Allied airmen shot down in the area and decide whether they were genuine, or German spies.

> I had to ask them questions like 'Where's the statue of Eros in London?' Out of about a dozen airmen that I assisted, there was only one occasion when I had any doubt. He couldn't reply to my questions, and he had a sort of German accent. I let my Resistance people know . . . I think they shot the chap, but I'm not sure. With Americans it wasn't so easy because some of them had German names.

Minor acts of sabotage – they had no access to explosives for anything more effective – and helping British, Canadian and American airmen continued in a haphazard and amateurish way until the following year, when the occupation became increasingly oppressive:

> They were very cruel, shooting people for nothing – hostages everywhere for nothing . . . I was called into a meeting some time in early 1942 and told that I would now belong to the Resistance movement; there was still no name to it. The question was, how were they going to get arms? I said I had arms – we'd kept the rifles and the machine gun and the grenades from 1940, buried in a Bren gun case, well-oiled, and also some pistols.

Stephen and his friend Marcel had had the foresight to create a useful cache from arms left behind by retreating Allied troops. But this display of initiative was spoiled when the headmaster in the group took fright, dumped the recovered arms in his school toilets, and disappeared shortly afterwards. The weapons were retrieved from the cisterns and dried out but they still weren't much use as 'we hadn't more than a couple of dozen rounds for any of them'.

Apart from hiding Allied airmen and helping them to escape, the group's other main task was to distribute the clandestine newsheet, *La Voix du Nord*, established in Lille in 1941 as 'the Resistance organ of French Flanders', which printed news based on BBC bulletins and Allied war reports. 'I took part in distribution of the early numbers of *La Voix du Nord*. Everything was done by bicycle in those days. I used to cycle to Béthune, Lens, and deliver small packets of the *Voix du Nord* sheets for onward distribution. It was already a highly dangerous thing to do.'

Nor was assisting airmen a safe or straightforward operation. Many of them came down between Saint-Omer and Béthune, where there were German fighter interception centres. Local spotters alerted their Resistance leaders and Stephen would be dispatched with two bicycles, civilian clothes and his testing questionnaire. They were hidden in people's homes, moving from house to house, village to village, their hosts often not knowing where they had come from or where they were being sent on to. Many were saved from capture and helped to England via established escape chains. They never forgot their French hosts. Stephen recalls two Canadian airmen, shot down in their Marauder in early 1943:

> They stayed for a month or so, moving around, and then eventually they were passed on by people whom I didn't know; because during the Resistance the idea was that one got to know as few people as possible. Contacts were strictly limited for the sake of security. As we found out later, they got safely back to England through the Spanish frontier – because one of them, Curly, a Squadron Leader – came back twice after the war to visit us.

Security was paramount to avoid the network being compromised, but not all the contacts were reliable, people tended to know each other's business in rural communities, and there was a constant fear of betrayal.

> You were at the mercy of somebody being caught by the Germans before you knew anything about it. This was hanging over your head all the time. It wasn't a question of being caught for what *you* did; it was a question of being caught for somebody else talking about you. That's why you weren't supposed to keep

any notes and all these airmen that I helped, I didn't know their names. I didn't know where they came from and I didn't want to know.

On one occasion, over a period of a week Stephen took the crew from a downed Flying Fortress one by one by bicycle to a safe house nearly 40 kilometres from the crash site, but the day after he delivered the last one: '. . . the Germans got the lot! The silly buggers, they let them out at night so somebody must have talked. The man sheltering them, his wife, kids – all shipped to Germany. Never seen again. Fortunately, they didn't track it back to me because I hadn't given them my name. That's how you were caught.'

Stephen had reason to be especially careful not to draw attention to himself. His IWGC gardener father was still in hiding at their home in Nieppe to avoid internment. The whole family depended on what little the *mairie* paid Stephen to tend the British cemeteries in the commune. Discovery meant not only certain imprisonment for his father and the prospect of forced labour or possibly capital punishment for Stephen, but reprisals on the rest of the family – his blind mother, three siblings, grandmother and aunt. To make matters worse, their house on the rue de Sac, just outside Nieppe, was right on the Belgian border:

One particular nuisance was the presence of a German customs officer at the end of our street. He was in military uniform and patrolled with an Alsatian dog. He knocked on our door a couple of times to see if we had any eggs. There were occasional flaps when German patrols descended following acts of sabotage, or to catch defaulters from the STO [Service du Travail Obligatoire, compulsory labour in Germany]. On these occasions my father had to leave the house and stay with neighbours or friends off the beaten track – he 'evacuated' a dozen or so times. The remarkable thing was that although my father was the only British national living in Nieppe – at the time a small town of about 6,000 inhabitants – and although people knew that the family was still there, no one throughout the four years of occupation did anything to denounce us to the Germans.

It was during this 'amateur' period of resistance that Stephen was told about Lillian and Joyce Wilkins living alone in Ypres in difficult circumstances after the internment of their mother. He knew them from the Memorial School and decided to cycle to Ypres – a dangerous cross-border expedition in itself – to see if he and his Resistance friends could help them.

> I remember going there – it must have been early on in 1941. I knocked on the door and Lillian said, 'Don't come in, the Germans are everywhere', and she shut the door. She was absolutely petrified. I can't remember now who told me about them but I thought if they came to Nieppe the Mayor would look after them.

But Lillian was not to be persuaded, and he cycled all the way back to Nieppe.

With the arrival of SOE agent Michael Trotobas in Lille, the scale, scope and impact of Stephen's Resistance network changed dramatically. Trotobas – Stephen knew him only as Capitaine Michel – was born in Brighton of a French father and an English mother. Bright and effortlessly bilingual, he was educated in Britain and northern France and in 1933 joined the Middlesex Regiment, where his ingenuity and leadership abilities were quickly recognised. He fought with distinction in the early months of the war and earned a Mention in Despatches for his part in the retreat from Dunkirk. He was just the kind of man Maurice Buckmaster, the head of SOE's French section, was looking for to support the emerging but desperately under-resourced Resistance movement.

When Trotobas was dropped outside Lille in November 1942, it was his second attempt to complete a mission first started in September 1941. That went badly wrong when his Jewish wireless operator, André Bloch, was denounced by a neighbour, captured, tortured and executed. Trotobas managed to stay undetected until he was arrested in the unoccupied zone and sent to Mauzac, a concentration camp in the Dordogne run by the Vichy government on behalf of Berlin. In July 1942 he escaped with ten other *résistants* across the Spanish border. Still only in his twenties, he reported for duty at SOE HQ and was promptly dispatched back to France. He resumed his code name, Sylvestre, and his brief: to create a sabotage circuit – code name Farmer – to impede German war production around the industrial hub of Lille.

As a junior activist in the Voix du Nord network, Stephen had direct contact with Capitaine Michel on only a handful of occasions during 1943, but he learned his Resistance skills from the SOE man and, as a result, became involved in increasingly dangerous missions. One of Trotobas' priorities was to arm and train local networks and supply the means to carry out sophisticated, large-scale sabotage operations. In October 1943, he took Stephen and three others to collect a consignment of arms parachuted in by the RAF in seven containers just outside Arras.

On the way there we had a 6.35 pocket pistol, which is just about big enough to kill a wasp, and about three rounds of ammunition. At least on the way back we had a few Sten guns! We went there in two hired lorries without travel permits. The lorries were propelled by these gas machines, as fuel was so scarce in France in those days, and we collected these containers, which were hidden in a beet silo. On the way back, the second lorry – in which I had taken a place in the rear – broke down on a steep hill outside Arras.

The stationary lorry containing Trotobas, four Resistance men and a consignment of explosives, grenades, Sten guns and revolvers barely concealed under a pile of turnips threatened to attract unwelcome attention. Trotobas abandoned them to their fate – the risk of arrest was too great. But 'by some miracle' the driver was able to get the truck going again and they made it back to the farm in Nieppe where the arms were to be unpacked. Trotobas returned the following day to open up the containers. He gave Stephen tea and chocolate for his father from a container of NAAFI supplies, and then it was on to the serious business of death and destruction. He passed over to Stephen one of the few precious Luger pistols in the consignment and showed him how to use it. Next came instructions in bomb-making:

I was trained by Trotobas himself to make up the packs of Nobel 808 explosive, and how to prepare the detonators and the primary charge and the timing devices. I was the artificer, as it were. And I used to make the bombs and then the targets were decided by, I suppose, Trotobas and Marcel Fertein, who was his number two as far as we were concerned.

The targets were bridges, railway lines, waterways, factories – anything necessary for German war production and distribution. They were told how to place the explosive for maximum effect but Stephen recalls that the results were mixed. 'A lot of the sabotage on the railway lines, for instance, was good for its effect on the morale of the local population, but in fact the Germans were usually able to repair the damage in a couple of hours. Most of it was just fireworks. Mind you, it annoyed the Germans intensely.'

One attempt to blow up sluice gates on the River Lys was a case in point.

I made this fairly large bomb with plastic explosive and four or five of us went down at dead of night. The first thing was to neutralise the guard, who happened to be a poor old boy living with his wife in a little house nearby. So we got hold of him and he asked to be tied up so that the Germans would know that he offered some sort of resistance. We yanked the telephone wires off the wall, dumped this explosive charge against the shut sluice gates, ran off and waited. There was an explosion, but apparently the damage was almost nil, because the bomb hadn't been placed properly. A few weeks later, we went back again, and this time we opened the sluice gates and jammed the bomb between the gate and the wall – the gate was blown open and we disrupted the traffic for months.

Concealing the consignments of arms and explosives was a problem; it was too dangerous to hide them in garden sheds or cellars, so Stephen brought the 1940 hiding place he and his friend Marcel had made in one of his father's war cemeteries, Pont-d'Achelles, back into service:

We'd dug this pit in the centre of one of the two bastions in the cemetery and covered it with corrugated iron sheets and soil, then made a narrow access shaft under the foundations. We stored the arms here for distribution to three or four local Resistance groups, taking them round at night by handcart with an armed guard.

He never mentioned any of this to his father or other family members. He was in the Resistance. That was all they needed to know, and they never discouraged him.

Stephen's association with Capitaine Michel was action-packed but short-lived. Audacious sabotage successes during the summer and autumn of 1943 infuriated the Germans and led to a one-million-franc price on his head. Trotobas was betrayed by a colleague under torture and tracked down to the safe house in Lille where he was living with his girlfriend and fellow activist, Denise Gilman. At dawn on 27 November 1943 a Gestapo raiding party armed with machine guns sealed both ends of the street and surrounded the house. In the gunfight Trotobas managed to shoot the leading officer dead at his front door and was still firing his revolver as he fell, mortally wounded. Standing behind him, Denise Gilman was shot dead.

Afterwards, some of his comrades made a covert visit to the house to remove any incriminating material. They found nothing but Trotobas' black cat. From then on, a black cat's head became the symbol of the Farmer circuit.

Their inspirational leader was dead but the work continued. Stephen was now a junior officer and Section Chief leading ten men. Until now his group of three sections had been involved in a couple of sabotage operations a month. From spring 1944, with Allied preparations for an invasion of France, activity intensified. One of their favourite and most effective 'sabotage tricks' was to incapacitate German convoys with nails soldered together in the shape of a cross; however they were thrown, they always landed upright.

They caused havoc. On one occasion we put 200 or so of these on the road at night and waited for the convoy. This ammunition convoy arrived and as we left we could see sparks coming off the cobblestones as they went over them. They were there for about a week – all the tyres were ripped. We didn't know this till later, but the Germans went absolutely mad, hauling out local people from their homes, with torches, trying to pick up these nails. They stopped about two houses down from us, where we'd gone back to bed with our Sten guns thrown in the rabbit hutch and another supply of nails in the back. We were very lucky.

Stephen carried out this particular operation with a USAAF airman, Conrad Kersch, who had baled out with the rest of the crew before their Flying Fortress blew up in mid-air over Saint-Omer in March 1944. After being sheltered by the Resistance in Nieppe, Kersch made up his mind to stay on and help them. He spoke no French, but he was fluent in German.

He refused to be passed on to the escape chain as he said that even if he made it back to England via Spain it would be too late to take part in any future action. So we gave him French identity papers and he became Albert de Groote. He was game and fearless and constantly pushing for action. He was a member of my section, as I was the only one who could communicate with him.

In April 1944, Stephen took on his most perilous mission. The Resistance group in the neighbouring village of Steenwerck was threatened with exposure. A woman who ran a bar there with her mother had a German captain for a boyfriend; he was stationed at rocket sites on the coast and spent his off-duty weekends with her. He had noticed local Resistance activity and threatened to shop them. Marcel Fertein decided that the German had to be disposed of, but they couldn't use local men for the job, so Stephen and three others were deputed to do it. Trotobas had given him the Luger; now he had to use it.

They went to the bar two Saturdays running but the officer wasn't there. On the third Saturday, Stephen arrived and met one of the team who said he'd act as lookout. The other two failed to turn up.

He went into the bar and asked to see the officer on the pretext of wanting a job 'on the coast'.

> He came in just in his shirtsleeves and said, 'What do you want?' and I shot him in the chest at point-blank range, twice, just as Trotobas taught me. I was supposed to get the mother as well – she was thought to be a bad patriot – but the Luger jammed after two shots. We didn't have the proper ammunition and I was using Sten ammo. So I left quick, with the old girl shouting, 'Murder! Murder!' and a few people starting to come after me. My lookout had run off as soon as he heard the shots and I was on this old bike that kept breaking down, the chain kept coming off.

Stephen hid in a chickenhouse in a wood for three weeks until it was clear that he hadn't been recognised. He was extremely lucky to get away with it, and with hindsight, he sees that his action was foolhardy and put not just his own life in danger:

> When I think about it now, my hair stands on end. I mean it was a hell of a risk. I could have been recognised, I didn't know if there'd be any other Germans in the kitchen or something. It wasn't only a risk to me. My whole family could have been deported and disappeared. I went and did it because I was told to do it. Mad. Crazy. I was eighteen and I did what I was told. I never thought about it.

Stephen has other regrets too. He has always hated the Germans, but he believes the assassination of this officer 'wasn't cricket': the man was off-duty and had no chance to defend himself, though it might have been much worse for Stephen if he had. There was another troubling consequence: 'At the time the penalty for such an act was decapitation. It was said that the SD [Sicherheitsdienst – SS Intelligence] had arrested someone – the girlfriend suspected a Pole of having a grudge against him – and charged them with the act. God knows what happened to him.'

Unavoidably, Stephen took part in actions that resulted in inno-cent people being deported and executed by the Germans. He wasn't alone: every *résistant* was in the same boat. It was one of the human costs of the secret war.

With the Normandy landings in June 1944, Resistance groups were mobilised, ready to support the invasion, and told to expect a massive influx of Allied paratroops in the Pas de Calais region. Stephen and his group went off 'to a lonely farm' to train for the imminent action. 'But nothing much happened so we went home with our tails between our legs and threw our Sten guns back in the rabbit hutch.' They returned to business as usual, blowing up railway lines and planting nail traps. In July they raided Nieppe town hall and stole a consignment of ration cards to distribute to young Frenchmen in hiding from the STO. In the safe they also found 10,572 francs which they appropriated for Resistance funds. (Fifty-five years later, Stephen wrote to Nieppe's mayor apologising for the theft and enclosing the postal order receipt he had kept as evidence that he'd passed the money on. He was given a post-hoc pardon by Monsieur Le Maire and the receipt was placed in the town museum with other Resistance memorabilia.)

But Stephen's group, under the direction of Lieutenant Jean Sonneville, 'a tough professional smuggler', was itching for action. The Battle of Normandy was still raging but the secret war was over: it was time for direct engagement with the enemy. In Nieppe, this started on 27 August when one section shot up a German motorcycle and captured its two riders. Stephen's section topped this the following day when they surprised a jeep, killed one of the occupants, captured the rest and commandeered the car. Others ambushed a dozen soldiers in a farm with their horses and carts. Over four days they had taken about twenty German prisoners and secured sundry means of transport. So far, it was all going their way.

On 1 September, they received an urgent message to go to Pont d'Nieppe to reinforce Marcel Houcke's group as they fought to defend the bridge over the River Lys. Sonneville took Stephen and his section off to respond, leaving the growing number of prisoners in the charge of a few volunteers. One of them, armed with a pistol, was Stephen Grady senior.

For the next three days, they battled to save the bridge. At first it went well. They attacked an eight-wheeled troop carrier with grenades and threw two Germans out – but lost two of their men in their own gunfire. They attacked a convoy with trucks towing three 88mm guns, destroying the guns, killing some Germans and taking more prisoners. One night, Stephen, Kersch and a few others captured seventy-five more men when Kersch, in his perfect German, convinced their commanding officer that they were surrounded. He surrendered them all to what he was 'extremely annoyed' to discover were only a handful of lightly armed Resistance men. But there was a problem.

What was now obvious was that there was no discipline in our ranks. We'd started out with about twenty Resistance men but we'd been joined by forty or so more volunteers who'd been given German rifles. No one listened to orders. We were a rabble. So when the SS came, we didn't last five minutes.

Stephen and Houcke's son Jean had taken a breather in a nearby house for something to eat when they saw through the front window:

. . . files of Germans in camouflage jackets on each side of the road, advancing towards the bridge. They were pushing some civilians in front of them. There must have been a couple of hundred – they were SS we discovered later. They rushed the bridge, set up machine-gun positions and within minutes had overrun the Resistance positions.

Looking to escape from the back of the house they found more SS setting up machine guns nearby, so they vaulted over the garden wall where a neighbour hid them in a half-full cistern in his garage. They stayed in there motionless, armed only with a grenade, for much of the following night, listening to gunfire and with Germans only yards away. The shooting went on all night. When they came out in the quiet of the following morning the SS had gone, but forty Resistance men and volunteers lay dead.

Having helped to pick up the dead, five of us decided to chase the Germans into Belgium and get our own back. We set off in the captured jeep and as we drove towards Comines we passed an advance post held by British troops. We went on in spite of a warning and were suddenly fired on. The jeep stopped. I jumped into a ditch. Sonneville shouted to me to get back to the British lines and get help. Two of us ran until we were out of range of the rifle fire, commandeered bicycles from a farm and cycled to the British outpost to tell our story.

There, the British promised a rescue party and Stephen and his companion were sent off in the opposite direction, escorting a dozen German prisoners. The three Resistance men – including Conrad Kersch and Jean Sonneville – were finally rescued but the British lieutenant leading the party was killed outright on arrival by a bullet through his helmet. It soon became clear that there were more than two hundred Germans positioned on the bank of the Comines Canal with machine guns and mortars. Had the five Resistance men driven on another fifty yards, they would have entered a death trap.

It was 5 September 1944 and the end of Stephen's unusually long and distinguished Resistance career. He was still only nineteen.

Stephen believes that Churchill's risky investment in supporting the French Resistance movement paid off. He saw its achievements first hand over four years of occupation: it discouraged collaborators; it helped hundreds of Allied airmen to escape and thousands of young Frenchmen to avoid the hated STO; and it provided vital intelligence to the Allies, for example on the location of V-1 and V-2 launch sites.

De Gaulle said France liberated itself. That's rubbish. They couldn't have done it without the Allies, but the Resistance did contribute militarily. It was a good investment . . . Yes, I was proud. I used to feel very thrilled when the results were positive. I enjoyed putting nails on the road. I enjoyed seeing the Germans go down with all their tyres flat. I enjoyed hearing them screaming because they couldn't proceed any further. I enjoyed blowing up the railway lines. I enjoyed blowing up the sluice gates. What I wouldn't have enjoyed was being caught in the act. But I wasn't.

Like Elaine Madden, Stephen Grady was lucky. He was young and fiercely patriotic. He took risks and did things he says he would never do again.

> I was very, very lucky. I was stupid, I was too patriotic really, I thought it was the right thing to do . . . You're very callous when you're young. You don't care. You kill or be killed . . . The Germans were absolutely despised and hated in the north of France. They were torturing people in the First World War, they occupied Lille for four years and it was full of atrocities. People were naturally anti-German.

He thinks about it more now than he did then. Sometimes, unexpectedly, he wakes up in a cold sweat, thinking the Sicherheitsdienst are chasing him for shooting the officer in the bar in Steenwerck. But he was never scared of Hitler:

> I felt about Hitler like I feel about the Devil. Hitler to me was just the name of the chap who was responsible for all the evils that had befallen us. The main enemy to me was the German police, never mind Hitler. I knew Hitler wouldn't catch me, but I was afraid the German police might.

15

Liberation

*We could hear the shooting . . . I'd already gone out to buy some
Allied flags.*
John Parminter, aged thirteen at the liberation of Ypres,
6 September 1944

AFTER FOUR LONG years of occupation and several months of
anticipation following the Normandy landings, the people
of Ypres were more than ready to celebrate liberation. Before it
finally came in early September 1944 there were unpleasant reminders
of what they had gone through in May 1940: pockets of fierce fighting, the destructive instincts of a retreating army, and mass movements of weary and dispossessed people passing through the town.
This time, though, most of those in transit were Germans – in uniforms less pristine than in 1940 – and they were fleeing east not west.

John Parminter had lived with his mother at the Hôtel de la Gare
throughout the occupation. He recalls the excitement of those late
summer days after weeks of sporadic gunfire and growing signs of
withdrawal. By mid-August the Germans had blown up the nearby
landing strip and disabled vehicles not needed for the retreat. Local
people then finished the job by picking them clean of usable parts.
Among the retreating soldiers were refugees from the fighting in
Normandy.

We had the Germans all coming back from France in farm carts,
together with the smallholders. It was a really sad sight. I still
remember them – the broken-down cart with this little wizened

old peasant reluctant to abandon his horse. Some of them, their feet were bleeding because they'd walked all the way from Normandy.

Keenly as it was anticipated, liberation wasn't as straightforward as people had hoped, nor were the liberators quite who they expected. It wasn't the British or the Americans who came to set Ypres free, but the Poles. The 1st Polish Armoured Division, having chased the Germans back from the Channel coast, got to Ypres on the morning of 6 September. There wasn't an immediate welcome and it wasn't a walkover.

Nenette van Bost, twelve, and her family were sheltering from street fighting in the large cellars of a convent, together with its elderly residents and many other families. Above them in the convent were German soldiers determined not to surrender to the Poles and threatening to detonate a mine in the grounds. Occupied and occupier were holed up together and both risked being sacrificed in a futile gesture, so there was immense relief when the soldiers finally gave themselves up. 'I can still see them all coming out. My mother crossed them on the forehead, to bless them, saying "You must be pleased it's all over."'

There were further alarms and misunderstandings. At first people had tried to speak English to the liberators and panicked when some of them spoke German. The rumour quickly spread that these weren't liberators at all but Germans in English uniforms. The confusion was understandable: John remembers two Poles – friends from the same town – greeting each other; one was with the Free Polish Army, the other conscripted into the Wehrmacht.

Celebrations had already started in the market square, but they were premature:

We went out, thinking everything was over and some white flags came out from a side street when the Poles were very near us and the shooting started again. The Germans had put these white flags out and started to shoot as the Poles went towards them. So we were back to the stage where there was some intense fighting going on.

By the end of the day the street skirmishes had ceased and prisoners were rounded up. The celebrations could start in earnest. Every bar and café was packed, long-hoarded bottles were opened, and something of the riotous atmosphere of 1919 returned to Ypres. 'We had some bad weather but it didn't stop us. It went on for days. There was general euphoria. People were buying rounds and drinking champagne and calling people in from the streets to have a drink!'

John Parminter flew the Stars and Stripes from his mother's hotel and buglers from Ypres' fire brigade formally resumed their nightly observance to the memory of British Empire war dead at the Menin Gate. Before long, local craftsmen set about repairing the battle-scarred memorial. The massive stone lion looking out over the Menin Road towards the old battlefields of the Salient had suffered shrapnel damage to his rear end. The three stonemasons in charge of his restoration couldn't resist their own bid for posterity: they put their names on cloth in a bottle and embedded it in the lion's new backside.

On the coast at Ostend, RAF flight mechanic George Sutherland was part of a forward party sent in to repair airfields sabotaged by the retreating Germans. Chosen in part because of his knowledge of the terrain and local languages, he moved on to Amiens, making sure that he stopped off in his native Poperinghe to see old friends and neighbours on the way: 'I promised I would come back when I ran away, eh!' But he wasn't back for good quite yet. It would be another eighteen months before he was demobbed and back working in Lijssenthoek cemetery.

In newly liberated Brussels, Elaine Madden's first thought was to ask for her FANY uniform to be sent from London. When it arrived she was thrilled to see that it now bore the wings that proved that she *had* jumped for her country and for Belgium. As 'the only British girl in uniform' in Brussels, let alone one who had demonstrably played such a daring part in its liberation, she was mobbed in the streets by well-wishers and admirers. 'I was feted. I was champagned. I was proposed to and I was asked out. It was an uproar. It was fabulous!'

Over the next two weeks, she enjoyed every minute of the celebrations and her own celebrity, until she learned that she was to be given another SOE mission.

The war in Europe was far from over. Much of Holland was still in German hands, from where V-1 and V-2 rockets were launched daily into Antwerp, Liège and Brussels; together they received more V-1 hits than the whole of England. Hardy Amies had set up a forward HQ, SPU 47, in Brussels to support the work of the Special Forces and Dutch Resistance organisations in regaining Holland. Here he oversaw the work of the Verstrepen Group – T Section's only major post-liberation operation. Since D-Day it had been responsible for facilitating secure wireless communications between the Belgian secret army's HQ outside Brussels to its five operational zones. In the chaotic and potentially lawless months immediately after liberation, the Group provided the same service for the returning government to communicate with its provinces.

Late in 1944, the Group extended its work into the occupied western Netherlands, providing tactical intelligence for the Canadian First Army. It was led by Flemish-born radio expert René Verstrepen and its wireless operations were the responsibility of a successful young agent, Michael Blaze. Still only twenty-four, he'd had an eventful war, seeing active service with the Belgian Army and spending time in French prisons and in the Foreign Legion before joining SOE as a wireless operator on missions to Tunisia and Belgium.

They needed a competent coder, and Elaine joined the Verstrepen Group to work with Blaze. Her parting from André Wendelen was unhappy; the affair was foundering. The exceptionally able and well-connected Wendelen had been offered an Ambassadorship in Vienna by the new Belgian government. She had hoped they would marry, but his career ambitions came first. The end of Elaine's 'fairy tale' was bleak:

In those days to be an ambassador you needed money and André didn't have any money, or not much as his father was a General and I suppose they had a nice house, but they didn't have a fortune. I had no money – even less than he did. So he married a girl with money . . . and I married Michael Blaze out of spite.

This wasn't quite the end of the affair. Soon after his marriage, and on the eve of Elaine's own wedding in March 1945 after the Verstrepen mission ended, Wendelen came to see her in London with a proposition:

> He tried to convince me not to get married. I could go to Vienna with him to the Embassy and he'd find a job for me and we could still be together although he was married. I said, 'No, I'm not going to be your mistress. If you'd really wanted me that much, you could have married me.' I couldn't see me living with him as a mistress and having to hide all the time. I couldn't stand that.

Elaine married Blaze, a strikingly attractive man with jet-black hair and green eyes and, as it turned out, a serially unfaithful husband. Even then, she knew she had a rival for his affections.

> Hardy Amies was in love with my husband. They were very close friends. When we came back to London – this was just before we were married – we were at a luncheon and Amies was there, and that's when I found out . . . He was all over him. Michael went to introduce us – of course we already knew each other although he was very senior to me. And he looked me up and down and said: 'Don't tell me you're going to marry this stupid girl!', as though I was a bit of dirt sticking to the floor . . . He never admitted it, but I'm practically certain that they were more than just good friends, not only by the way they behaved together but how jealous of me Amies had seemed at the time. And that's why he'd been so awful to me.

Certainly the stink of animosity still rises from the note on Elaine's personal file, where Amies writes: '. . . Madden [has] frankly been a bloody nuisance ever since the liberation. [She] did some quite good work when she was first with the Verstrepen Group, but caused trouble later on, which ended in both she and Blaze being sacked.' As far as Elaine is concerned, they weren't 'sacked', they were recalled to London after the work of the Verstrepen Group finished early in

1945. And she doesn't know what 'trouble' she caused – unless it was to marry Michael Blaze.

After fighting the liberation battle for Nieppe, Stephen enjoyed a brief but intense period of rejoicing with his Resistance colleagues. His father, in hiding for more than four years, could at last break cover and join in the celebrations. But Stephen soon hankered after new excitements.

I'd had enough of France and managed to get a passage in a Dakota back to England in November 1944. I volunteered for the British Army. I'd been advised by Colonel Buckmaster [head of SOE's French Section] to join the Intelligence Corps, but when I walked into the recruiting station in Euston, not knowing much about anything, the Recruiting Sergeant lost no time in putting me in the Royal Fusiliers.

In the brutally random way of the British Army in wartime, in January 1945 a perfect candidate for intelligence work found himself square-bashing in Glasgow as a private with the Royal Fusiliers. After four months and an exchange of correspondence with Buckmaster, he was finally transferred to the Intelligence Corps, 'just before my outfit was sent to Burma, where most of them got knocked off'.

After training at the Intelligence Corps depot at Wentworth Woodhouse, near Rotherham, Stephen was posted to the Middle East as a lance corporal in the 28th Field Security Section. Cairo and Beirut were 'like Butlins' after the danger and privations of occupied France: 'It was a holiday camp. I enjoyed every bit of it. We didn't do much, really. I was on frontier control, trying to stop emigration to Palestine, and keeping track of the French political office – because they were still in Beirut – and what they were up to in Greece, where there was a civil war going on.'

Within eighteen months he had won a commission and seemed set for a promising post-war career in Intelligence. But by the autumn of 1946 he was back in France. A tragic accident would set him on a completely different and unexpected course.

★

Bob Simmons, the young RAF radar specialist, had volunteered for France after D-Day but found himself in Burma, where his squadron's job was to drop supplies to the 14th Army – the so-called Forgotten Army – racing to beat the monsoons to Rangoon and fighting a sticky jungle war with the Japanese. 'We finished up entering by boat – the first into Rangoon. We knew the Japs had left when the British POWs wrote on the roof of the prison in large white letters: "Extract digit – Japs gone."'

The POWs may have kept their sense of humour, but they had lost much else. Bob saw some pitiable sights in Malaya when, after liberating Penang, he was involved in the repatriation of those former inmates of Singapore's notorious Changi Gaol who were fit enough to fly. 'We'd arrive and these gaunt men would shuffle out. We would lead them to the mess, sit them down, give them lunch, take them to the loo, lead them back. We could hardly talk to them, they seemed to be like zombies. They were stunned and hadn't quite realised . . .'

It was the autumn of 1945 and Bob was still only nineteen. What he saw then he still finds too upsetting to talk about.

Thanks to Hardy Amies, Elaine's SOE career was over but she had one more important war mission. As a trained parachutist, she volunteered for a newly formed unit, SAARF, the Special Allied Airborne Reconnaissance Force. Early in 1945, when the defeat of Nazi Germany looked inevitable, Allied planners turned their attention to the plight of the thousands of prisoners of war still in captivity there. In the chaos and violence that often accompanied liberation, POWs were, it was thought, particularly vulnerable to reprisals and needed special protection. Though the Allies had known for some time about the existence of German concentration camps, their full horror had yet to be discovered. The extermination camps, on the other hand, were an abomination as yet unimagined.

SAARF was created by Supreme Headquarters, Allied Expeditionary Forces, to drop small teams near the camps, just ahead of the liberating forces, to negotiate with camp commanders a safe and speedy evacuation of their prisoners. It was to use the SOE field model – two officers and a radio operator in each team. They knew conditions in the camps were bad but they had no idea how bad, and they were unsure how Hitler – increasingly manic and unpredictable – would respond in the final stages of warfare, threatened by the British and Americans from the west and the Russians from the east. It was a bold humanitarian mission but, as its code name – Operation Vicarage – unwittingly suggested, also an exceptionally naive and potentially dangerous one.

On 2 April Elaine joined 350 Vicarage trainees at Wentworth golf course in Surrey. Among her colleagues were other former SOE agents, and men from airborne and special forces – a mix of French, British, American, Belgian and Polish volunteers. With news that some camps were being evacuated and prisoners force-marched in appalling conditions to avoid the Russian advance – Edwin Tester at Kreuzberg was among them – the nature of the mission rapidly changed. The role was now based on reconnaissance and intelligence rather than direct intervention. And after the first airborne mission in late April ended with SAARF teams being captured and imprisoned, parachute drops were abandoned; subsequent teams were sent in by air transport and used trucks and jeeps on the ground.

The Allies and the Red Army were moving fast and camps were being overrun sooner than expected. One of the first was Auschwitz, liberated by the Russians in January when few details emerged; it wasn't until much later that its scale and role as an extermination camp were fully understood in Britain. During April, even as SAARF operatives were being trained in England, the Allies moved into Germany, and many camps – Buchenwald and Bergen-Belsen among them – were liberated by American and British forces. The nature of the mission changed again.

Elaine went into four camps with SAARF, just behind British and American troops. She thinks Buchenwald was the first and Flossenberg the last. Dachau and Bergen-Belsen were the others. Their mission in each was to identify and repatriate any surviving Belgian political prisoners – SOE agents and those imprisoned for Resistance activities. They managed to find two. Her recall of what she saw is clear, but she can no longer distinguish exactly when and where she saw it.

They'd asked us to take photographs. When I got back to the UK I went to stay with an aunt near Bolton. I had nightmares every night for six weeks, from what my aunt told me. She took the pack of photographs and burnt them. She said that I was in such a bad way that she just couldn't bear to think of me looking at them, and having it all come back. I didn't want to think about it. There are no words to explain the horror of those camps. Unimaginable. I've never talked about it. How could I explain to my daughter about the horrible things that happened? Those of us who saw it don't talk about it.

Talking is difficult, but Elaine knows what she saw. The mute and motherless five-year-old running around among the dead and dying, unable – or unwilling – to speak. Roads made of human cinders. The emaciated man who told them how he had been castrated with a twisted dinner napkin. The sunken eyes and fleshless faces. Piles of bodies in the crematoria waiting to be burned. So many bodies, dead or barely alive.

I think it was Flossenberg, but some of the last people there who'd been killed had been hanged and there were about ten of them hanging there dead and they hadn't had time to take them down when we got in there. One of the women was at least seven or eight months pregnant and not only had she been hanged but thank God – maybe thank God – they'd shot right in her belly and killed the child . . . Atrocious things.

Among the atrocious things she saw was the infamous lampshade made from the tattooed skin of prisoners. Some doubt this ever existed, but Elaine has no time for the revisionists and the deniers. 'The thing that makes me mad is people like Le Pen who say it didn't happen, or it wasn't so bad. When I hear people like that I could kill them. They didn't see it. I saw it.'

SAARF's work lasted barely three months; it was disbanded on 1 July 1945. By then the war in Europe was over. Hitler was dead. At the end of April he had shot himself rather than face the Red Army, and Germany surrendered a week later. Elaine doesn't recall a debriefing. There was no counselling and post-traumatic stress disorder wouldn't be recognised for another fifty years. She was thanked, given the money owed to her and 'that was that'.

On VE-Day, 8 May 1945, almost exactly five years after the Germans invaded France and the Low Countries, Jerry Eaton was celebrating back in Britain: 'We went to the pub and had a good party with the locals. On the way back we passed a couple of WAAFs, one wheeling a bike. Our car was already full, but we opened the sunshine roof, picked these girls up, and I stood up through the roof, holding the bike with the WAAF on it, and the other one squeezed inside.'

Life after liberation would continue to be extraordinary – and difficult – for some time yet. Now, though, those who had come from Ypres were determined, just as their fathers had been in 1919, to put the experiences of the past five years behind them. The naïve teenagers of May 1940 had grown up. The world had changed, just as all the children on the evacuation had changed. After everything they had been through, would they want to return to the flat fields and scattered villages of Flanders?

16

After

Ypres is part of me. It's right in me, you know.
   John Gabriel, who left Ypres in 1940 aged fourteen

IN SEPTEMBER 1945, Reginald Haworth went back to Ypres for the first time since his heroic evacuation feat in May 1940. He was there to report to Sir Fabian Ware on the extent of the damage to the British Settlement and to talk about its future now that the war was over.

The fabric of the church and school buildings hadn't fared too badly. An Allied bomb had caused superficial exterior damage to St George's but the interior had been respected: there were even reports that services had been held there during the occupation. Local schools had made use of the Memorial School and the Presbytery had been a German officers' club. Now, though, furniture and precious memorials were gradually coming back from wartime storage. Nenette van Bost's father returned St George's regimental flags from their hiding place in the bottom of his wardrobe:

> I went with him to give them back. And they weren't very pleased with him. He hadn't told them immediately after Liberation that he had them and they'd been looking all over the place for them and were despairing. He was peeved: 'And I've kept them all these years for you!'

On the surface at least, things were getting back to normal. The Revd. Dye had moved back into the Presbytery and the British Settlement's long-standing Secretary, Lieutenant Colonel Poole, was 'anxious to restart the Settlement's work'. But this was not 1929, or even 1939. There was no money to pay the chaplain's stipend and few people to attend his infrequent services. The Settlement had no resources of its own and the Commission, though willing to play its part, had more pressing priorities.

The casualties of the recent war may have been half those of 1914–18, but there were still 370,000 new dead to bury and 250,000 new 'missing' to commemorate, this time scattered across 24,000 sites all over the world. The cemeteries and memorials of the old Ypres Salient had suffered the ravages of war and five years of neglect. Despite the voluntary efforts of local people – and the communes like Nieppe which had employed Stephen Grady in its British cemeteries – many were overgrown, in poor repair and in some cases mined and bomb-damaged. The Imperial War Graves Commission had to start work all over again.

Gardeners were gradually returning, but demobilisation was slow and war casualties, retirements and men deciding not to come back meant that the number of British families in Ypres wouldn't be anything like pre-war levels. This had serious implications for the British Settlement, and in particular for the British Memorial School. In his report for Ware, Haworth noted that only thirteen British children under the age of fifteen were likely to be living in the Ypres area in or after the spring of 1946, and that there would be few Protestant families. Though there was never any doubt about the need to secure the future of St George's Church – it was a national war memorial as well as a place of worship – he had to conclude that any attempt to run a school could not be justified.

For Haworth, this was the second trip down memory lane that year. At the end of April he'd had an unexpected letter from the Mother Abbess of the Wisques convent where his party of women and children had found sanctuary in May 1940. She had come to their aid then; would the Commission now help her? There were seven elderly and disabled Sisters, 600 kilos of luggage and 'some precious objects' that all needed to be brought back to Wisques from the mother house in Solesmes where they had been sent for safety in 1940. It was an arduous two-day journey at a time when travel was difficult because of damaged roads and railways, and fuel shortages. Could the Capitaine possibly provide a vehicle or some petrol?

Haworth didn't hesitate. With some difficulty, he arranged for a three-ton Commission truck to pick up the Sisters, their copious amounts of luggage – and what he suspected was the convent's entire wealth in unspecified valuables – and personally escorted them on the uncomfortable 425-kilometre journey back to Wisques. It was a debt he felt honoured to repay, but that wasn't the end of it. Haworth never forgot Wisques: he later arranged to donate the interest on his War Bonds to the convent and, in the year before his death, he asked the Commission to deliver 'a simple bunch of roses' to the Mother Abbess on each anniversary of their fateful visit, 'ad infinitum'. Senior staff from the head office in Arras did so, faithfully and in person, every year until the 40th anniversary in 1980.

The gardeners who had been evacuated to Britain had a difficult choice to make after the war. By now, many of them were in their fifties and didn't want another move. Though their harrowing evacuation experiences were rarely spoken of, they had had a profound and unsettling effect. The families now craved security and certainty, commodities not easily come by in post-war Europe. If life in Britain was austere, it was no easier in France and Belgium: food was in short supply; Commission wages barely covered the essentials; former homes and belongings had been looted, damaged or lost. The threads of former lives would be hard to find, let alone pick up.

For those like Jack Fox with French or Belgian wives, the decision was easier. The women missed their families and were anxious to return. Jack took up his old job with the Commission and Adrienne Fox and nine-year-old Jimmy went with him early in 1946, leaving their four girls – Betty, the youngest, was by then nearly sixteen – in England. They settled in the border village of Le Bizet and Jimmy, after five years at school in suburban north London, was plunged back into a Flemish culture he barely remembered.

For the men with British wives, the decision was more problematic. Being a Commission head gardener in Belgium was Harry Wilkins' 'whole life', but he had promised Lily while she was interned in Liebenau that they wouldn't go back after the war. Harry broke his promise, but Lily refused to make the move permanently and lived half the year in a flat in London with Joyce and Lillian, who recalls:

> My father loved being out in Belgium. He loved the work, he loved the people. I think he was determined to go back. But Mother would only live with Dad six months of the year because she was frightened of it all happening again. She was dead scared of it happening again. And she never forgave my father for leaving us in France with Brigadier Prower. Not for a long, long time.

Harry Wilkins retired in 1955 but never really settled to life in England. He had been a stalwart of St George's but 'never went inside a church again' once he was back. Though he had never had a day's illness in his working life, Harry contracted lung cancer and died in 1962. Lily, despite her nervous disposition and wartime experiences, lived to see her hundredth birthday.

Betty Parker's father didn't want to go back, but he returned to Belgium temporarily to train new, local, staff. Like everything else, the Commission was changing. The first generation of gardener-caretakers – the 1914–18 veterans – were now approaching retirement. Young men who had survived the recent war were looking for different opportunities. They were less inclined to live abroad, and the emotional pull of trench comradeship was no longer there. It was now right to recruit local labour.

None the less, a strong thread of continuity ran through the Commission's work in Flanders. The pre-war pupil gardeners like Danny Quinn and George Sutherland who had followed their fathers into the IWGC now returned to carry on their work. After demob from the RAF, Danny went back to Poelkapelle in 1946 as a gardener-labourer. Priestley Dunn, another former pupil gardener, returned to his Belgian wife and his old job as a gardener-caretaker at Bedford House Cemetery, then moved on to create new cemeteries for the recent war dead, first in Belgium and then in the desert battlefields of North Africa. This was very different from the work his father had done.

I had fifteen cemeteries to look after but they were all far away from each other, so I'd set off on a tour on a Monday morning and not get back home for a month. The Commission wanted beautiful green lawns like in Belgium – of course it wasn't possible – we had to find special grass to grow and native trees and shrubs, and work out how to get a water supply in. We were there three years and made it our home-away-from-home.

Those who went back often found they had to start again from scratch, but some were luckier than others. John Osborne and his parents returned to find that their home had been a billet for German officers. It was much as they had left it, except for a large inkstain on the dining table and an apologetic note from the officers saying they'd had it replaned but couldn't get the stain out. Margaret Dupres' English parents had 'wonderful Belgian friends', who stored all their belongings in a room in a building subsequently requisitioned by the Gestapo as its Ypres HQ. Despite the occupiers' suspicions, the English family's possessions were never disturbed. After nursing training in England, Margaret chose to return with her parents to Belgium as a district nurse.

One of Margaret's childhood playmates in the cemeteries was John Gabriel, the son of gardener Bert Gabriel, whom she remembers as 'a lovely man'. The Gabriels didn't return to Belgium. In retrospect, John sees how difficult this was for his father and how his decision had an impact on the whole family.

He wanted to go back, to be with his friends, but my Mum didn't, so we stayed in England and Dad worked as a caretaker. He didn't like what he did. I think he really missed the cemeteries. We never had a proper house and nice things after we left Belgium. Although we had a council house, we never managed to assemble a nice way of life.

The loss of his pre-war career and the supportive circle of friends in Ypres had tragic consequences. Some years later, severely depressed, Bert Gabriel took his own life by stepping off the platform at Baker Street Underground station into the path of train.

★

After the war Elaine Madden and Stephen Grady at last received official recognition for their efforts fighting the enemy in occupied territory. In October 1945 King George VI was 'graciously pleased' to confer on Elaine a Mention in Despatches for 'fearless devotion to her many and varied duties' during her 'valuable work' for SOE. The Belgians honoured her with the Croix de Guerre, which she received personally – with a wink – from 'Monsieur Bernard'.

Stephen was awarded the United States Medal of Freedom for 'courage, bravery, and exceptional devotion to the common cause of freedom, undertaking . . . hazardous duties, knowing the price to be paid if apprehended'. He too was Mentioned in Despatches and awarded the Croix de Guerre with Silver Star. The citation notes:

> He is a British subject with a perfect knowledge of the French language and rendered sterling service to the Voix du Nord . . . he successfully accomplished several dangerous missions [and] . . . took a heroic part in the fighting to liberate Nieppe.

Stephen was enjoying his time in the Middle East with the Intelligence Corps and looked forward to making a career in the Army. His father, in hiding throughout the war, had gone back to his work as a head gardener in the cemeteries around Nieppe. He was driving on Commission business one day in 1946 when he swerved to avoid a child and ended up in a ditch. He would have survived the accident but he was given two anti-tetanus injections by mistake, which killed him. Stephen's mother, blind for many years, was ill with cancer by this time and his younger brother and sister were still at home. Stephen was now the family's only breadwinner. He did his duty, got himself released from the Army on compassionate grounds, and went back to France. 'I found myself back in Nieppe and what could I do? There was no other employment with any prospects other than with the Commission. So I started as a gardener's labourer.'

It wasn't what he'd imagined or hoped for and the first years were hard. In 1949 his younger brother, a pupil gardener, also died in a road accident. He was twenty-one. By now Stephen was married to a girl from Rotherham he had met when he was training at Wentworth, 'so I had somebody to do the cooking and look after the family, so that I could make a home'. But he knew he had to better himself. Albert Roberts, the IWGC head gardener who had set up horticulture classes at Tost and helped build the famous Giromagny rock garden, was an old friend of his father's. Albert gave him some sound advice:

> He said, 'Look, Steve, you're wasted. You've got to do some-thing. Study horticulture. If you get the Senior Certificate, you're made in the Commission. I'll lend you some books to get you interested.' So I started reading books and gradually I got interested. I got a correspondence course and I sat for this exam. I did it all on my own and I got a First – the top grade!

Stephen caught the learning bug. As a former army officer, he qualified for retraining and won a place to study for the prestigious Royal Horticultural Society National Diploma at Wisley. It was a year's course and the Commission made him resign to do it, with no guarantee of re-employment, but he took the risk. After qualifying, he went back to the Commission to ask about a job:

> There was an old chap there called Major Gill who was head of the Horticulture Department during the war. I had an interview with him and the man in charge of staff. I asked about the pros-pects for re-employment with my new qualification – no one else in the Commission had it at that time – and he said: 'Prospects? Until you've had ten years under a good head gar-dener, you've got no prospects!' So I said thanks very much and walked out.

Gill, one of Haworth's escort officers in the 1940 evacuation, was old-school IWGC where rank, class and loyalty counted for more than talent. A forward-looking organisation could ill afford to turn down young people of such potential. The 'man in charge of staff' called Stephen back, apologised for Gill's behaviour, and offered him a job as a head gardener. It was the start of a distinguished 37-year career with the Commission.

Much of it was spent in the Balkans and the Middle East dur-ing troubled times, where he had regular contact with foreign governments and Embassy defence attachés. He spoke fluent Greek and 'a bit of Bulgarian'. He had the perfect cover. Was he ever approached to spy for Britain? 'No. Nobody ever asked me to do any intelligence work. Had they asked me, I would have done it, but they didn't ask me.'

In his final job before retirement, as Director of the Commission's operations in France at its Arras headquarters, Stephen found himself in a position to pay a last tribute to his wartime Resistance leader, Captain Michael Trotobas. After his death at the hands of the Gestapo, Trotobas had been buried with hundreds of French Resistance fighters in a communal grave under a memorial in Lille. 'I said: "This is wrong. This is a war grave. He's entitled to a Commission headstone and the grave should be recognised." So now he has a separate Commonwealth headstone as part of the memorial. I was able to do that for him at least.'

There was something else Stephen was able to do. He delivered the final bouquets to Madame Jacqueline de Villepin, Mother Abbess at Wisques, before this small act of remembrance instituted by Reginald Haworth ended, at her request, in 1980.

Things would never be the same again for the British in Ypres after the war. There were no longer enough of them to call a colony and their Settlement was in jeopardy. A rescue package from the British Legion and the IWGC secured the immediate future of St George's Memorial Church in 1948 but the financial situation was always precarious and the Presbytery and the Pilgrims' Hall were later sold off to raise funds. Hopeful noises about reopening the school came to nothing and the building was turned into a social club for British Legion members and Commission staff. The British Memorial School existed for just eleven years, but its impact on the hundred or so children who passed through its doors lasted a lifetime. It had done its job.

The old order passed. The Ypres League, inactive since 1939, filed for bankruptcy and was wound up in 1946. Sir Fabian Ware, seventy-eight and an ill man, finally retired as Vice Chairman of the IWGC in June 1948 and died ten months later. The Commission's Imperial associations, honourable but unfitted for the new world, took a little longer to dislodge. After finding these an increasing impediment to its work overseas, the Commission belatedly changed its name to the Commonwealth War Graves Commission in 1960.

The work carried on. The pupil gardeners progressed to greater things. Danny Quinn worked his way up through the ranks, becoming a Horticultural Supervisor in the Middle East and earning the British Empire Medal. Three generations of Sutherlands worked for the Commission over a period of more than eighty years. George Sutherland followed his father Walter as a gardener-caretaker in Lijssenthoek cemetery and his son Alex followed him. In 1923 Walter Sutherland planted a young Blue Atlas cedar in Lijssenthoek. His son and grandson have watched it grow to maturity. Now a magnificent backdrop to the Stone of Remembrance, it is a fitting symbol of the continuity of the Commission's work and the dedication of its gardeners. Their lasting achievement – under Ware's inspired leadership – has been to create order from unspeakable chaos, to make places of beauty, dignity and calm for the bereaved, and to remind succeeding generations that war comes at great cost.

The aftermath of the Second World War was very different from that of the First. Millions of non-combatants had been directly affected; Britain was too war-weary and too focused on survival to devote much time to practical expressions of remembrance. Ypres went quiet for many years. The Last Post was attended at times by barely a handful of old soldiers, at others by nobody at all.

Nearly a century after Ypres entertained the first pilgrims in its temporary bars and shack hotels, the crowds have returned. Remembrance has a new importance in people's lives and the cemeteries and memorials have visitors again. Interest in family history, fuelled by digitisation of records and information; the two world wars on the National Curriculum; continuing fascination with how ordinary people cope in war as combatants and civilians: all have contributed to the latest regeneration of Ypres as a centre for learning about events of personal and universal importance before they slip out of living memory.

Some things have changed. Dutch has replaced French as the official language of West Flanders: Ypres is now Ieper. Pilgrimages have taken on a different form. The Ypres League charabancs conveying impoverished widows and nostalgic military men to still-scarred battle sites have given way to air-conditioned coaches on their way to Tyne Cot Visitors' Centre, In Flanders Fields Museum, Hill 60's preserved trenches and the other sacred sites – and sights – of the old Salient. The British Legion is still in the pilgrimage business, now cleverly rebranded as Poppy Travel.

At the Menin Gate, buglers from Ieper's fire brigade still faithfully perform the Last Post ceremony as they have done – bar the occupation years – every evening since 1928, whether there was anyone there to watch them or not. Now the crowd gathered under Blomfield's vast vaulted roof can be counted not in handfuls but in hundreds. Since the millennium, the ceremony has attracted 250,000 people a year. Many are British schoolchildren, in Ieper to learn about the consequences of war. This means laying wreaths in the German cemetery at Langemark as well as on British war graves.

At eight o'clock the traffic stops. Giggling and texting teenagers quieten as the buglers take their places. The Last Post sounds for the war dead, not just of the Ypres Salient in 1914–18 but of every conflict since, and it is impossible not to be moved. The scale of the memorial and the enormity of the event it marks overpower everything, if just for those few moments. Solemn young people lay wreaths, there is a brief pause, then the crowd disperses to the bars, restaurants and entertainments of the town. Ieper, responding as it did in 1919 to the mood of the times, reveals its ambiguous charm: as willing servant to the tourist trade and as a place to reflect, remember and learn.

St George's Church, though off the main tourist track, welcomes more pilgrims and visitors than ever. On Remembrance Sunday the church could be filled many times over with those who want to come and pay their respects in a unique national memorial. Behind it, in the comfortably furnished social club that was once the school, the original board still bears witness to the 342 Eton men in whose memory it was built. Photographs from the school's brief history remind regulars and inform visitors that the building once had another life.

The 'children' of the British Memorial School are now a diminishing band. They have lived different lives since 1945. For some, the war determined their future careers: Jerry Eaton DFC stayed in the RAF for another thirty years, rising to the rank of Wing Commander; after call-up to the RAF in the last year of the war, Sidney Harper went on to a 37-year career in civil aviation, flight-testing aircraft for BEA and British Airways; Bob Simmons moved into television after his wartime experience in BBC radio and became a BAFTA award-winning lighting director on major dramas and light entertainment.

Some never came back to live permanently in Britain. After many years in what was then the Belgian Congo, Elaine Madden divorced Michael Blaze and found happiness with a new partner. After his death she settled in the south of France.

> I often say the war years were the best years of my life . . . You had to make the most of every moment of every hour of the day and night, because there was always this thought that you might not be there tomorrow. So there was no limit. You lived . . . oh, to the end!

Stephen Grady OBE retired to the house he built overlooking a wild headland in mainland Greece where, he says, 'these days I'm a servant to the animal kingdom'. He lives a self-sufficient life among his olive groves with his chickens and rescue animals. In 2007 he and his wife Jean celebrated their sixtieth wedding anniversary but she chooses to live in Rotherham. Sustained by his Greek Orthodox faith, Stephen makes annual pilgrimages to nearby Mount Athos to paint, meditate and see friends in the monasteries there.

> I believed in the Almighty then and I still do. Perhaps the Resistance and its dangers helped me to do so. Those years of the occupation seem to have been half my life. The intensity of feeling during that period takes precedence over the succeeding

years. I've had 24 years in retirement here. It's gone like that – feeding chickens and cats and dogs.

Some years ago Lillian Wilkins went back to visit Liebenau, now restored to purposeful use as a residential home for children. A memorial in the chapel commemorates those asylum inmates murdered to make Hitler's Germany a purer place. 'There was a very eerie feel. I found it was very, very strange, standing in the garden. When I knew it, it was full of women. Now there was nobody there and the children were all indoors. There was still something there, you know . . .'

In 2008 Lillian made what she told everybody would be her last visit to Ypres. Now in her mid-eighties and the sole carer of her severely disabled daughter, Susan, she can no longer manage the annual pilgrimage to see old friends and to walk in familiar places. Even though the town holds some unhappy memories, 'it always draws me back, I have to go back'. Like John Gabriel, who returns every year and revisits the cemeteries where his father loved working so much. He has written with pride in the visitors' book in each of them: 'My father tended this cemetery from 1920 to 1940'.

Good memories will always outweigh the bad. As Betty Fox says: 'They were happy times. Ypres is special to us all, to our family certainly. Ypres is home to me, even though I feel English. I think it's because we had to leave it so quickly, it was as if you had to leave a bit of yourself behind.'

Jimmy Fox, perhaps unknowingly inspired by his early contact with the photographer James Jarche at the Memorial School, had a long career in professional photography. He became editor-in-chief with the Magnum photographers' collective in New York and Paris, where he worked with some of the twentieth century's greatest photojournalists: Henri Cartier-Bresson, Eve Arnold and Don McCullin among them. War photography was his stock-in-trade.

In my life in photography, I've spent thirty years looking at images of war – battle zones, dead bodies, fleeing refugees. I was always struck by how many soldiers and civilians had family

photographs with them when they died. These 'visual memories' bind us to our past and tell us who we are, what made us.
They are among our most treasured possessions. Looking at
photos of my own childhood started me on this long journey
to rediscover how we and our parents lived in Ypres between
the wars.

Jimmy has learned many things from his journey of discovery. He
now has a deep respect for the IWGC fathers, the men who tended
the war cemeteries in all weathers, quietly preserving the memory of
those who weren't as lucky as they were. But he also now understands how formative this early experience was for the children who
had to fight Hitler.

We were brought up to be British in a place shaped by the greatest man-made tragedy the world had ever known. When we
were caught up in the horror of another war, we realised the
true meaning of those cemeteries we'd played in. It was our
coming of age.

Acknowledgements

It isn't usual for one co-author to thank the other, but my biggest debt of gratitude is owed to Jimmy Fox, whose years of research on the men of the Imperial War Graves Commission in Flanders and their families forms the basis for this book. Jimmy is credited as co-author because the story could not have been told without his work. Though he entrusted the telling to me, Jimmy provided almost everything else, including an extensive contacts list, his photographic archive and firm guidance throughout.

I am particularly grateful to the 'children' of the British colony who talked to me and allowed me access to their family archives and photograph albums: Lillian Betts (née Wilkins), Sam and Dicky Boucher, Betty Bryant (née Parker), Charlotte Dunn, Margaret Dupres, Jerry Eaton, John Gabriel, Nina Garnham (née Pitt), Stephen Grady, Sidney Harper, Betty Haynes (née Fox), Arthur Jones, Yvonne Jones (née Lane), Elizabeth Kelly (née Boucher), Rene Lord (née Fletcher), Dorothy 'Coco' MacLeod (née Charlton), Elaine Madden, Lilly Morrice (née Boucher), Francis Murphy, John Osborne, Louise Over (née Francis), John and Nenette Parminter, Danny Quinn, Robert Rolfe, Bob (Claude) Simmons, George Simpson, George Sutherland, and Jacqueline Warsop (née Fox). Herman Hauge and Lucy Hayton gamely grappled with Flemish place-names in transcribing the interviews.

Jimmy also wishes to acknowledge the valuable contribution of memories, photographs and documents given to him over the course of his research by other former members of the colony (some of whom, sadly, have since died) and their families. They include: Joan Abrams (née Simpkins), Hedley and Alfred Batchelor, Jack Blake,

Leslie Cain, Judith Clowe, Lucy Denholm (née Knox), Priestley Dunn, Robert Eaton, June and Barbara Edis, Blanche Friend (née Rolfe), Joyce Gadd (née Dawson), Jane Garcy (née Boucher), Jeanette Gibb, Isabelle Gordon, Edward Harper, Mildred Hendricks (née Brown), Arthur, Albert and Richard Jones, Georgette Lee (née Piper), Joan Mauret (née Collick), Doris Miller (née Batchelor), Jack Oxenbridge, Georgette Restell (née Davis), Celia Richmond (née Batchelor), Kenneth Rolfe, Barbara Ruffle (née Haley), Georgette Samois (née Hoyles), Mary Setchfield (née Haley), Dorothy Smith (née Cuthbert), Norman Thomson, Diana White (née James), and Walter and Alfred White.

Servaas Heirman and his team on the Belgian television documentary *Heilig Grond: Ieper en de Britten* unearthed important new footage, and former Popperfoto archivist Petrina McNeill tracked down contact sheets for James Jarche's photographs of the Memorial School. Dr Eric Anderson, lately Provost of Eton College, provided background on the Etonians in whose memory the school was built. For important contributions to our understanding of the events of 1940 and of life in the internment camps, Jimmy also wishes to thank: L'Abbaye Notre-Dame de Wisques, George Bailey, Jeaninne Becue (née Robitaille), Harry Fisher and family, Marija Fueg of the ICRC Archives in Geneva, Odette Golder, former Commonwealth War Graves Commission archivist Shirley Hitchcock, Reggie Lewis and family, André MacDonald and family, and Emily and Roland Wells.

Descendants of key players in the evacuation and what followed were most helpful. In particular: John Duncan for permission to quote from his father William's camp memoir; Mildred Coucke-Goddard for permission to quote from her father Alfred's internment diary; Mandy Gadd for access to her grandfather Lawrence Dawson's escape account and wartime correspondence; Elizabeth Haworth for permission to quote from her father Reginald's memoir of the evacuation; and Sonja Tibber for her account of her father Edwin Tester's internment.

In Ieper/Ypres, Dominiek Dendooven at the Documentation Centre of the In Flanders Fields Museum provided fascinating source material and answered my many questions; the Revd. Ray Jones and

Senior Churchwarden Rita Hawkes explained the history and treasures of St George's Memorial Church; and Philip Noakes, Director of the Commonwealth War Graves Commission, Northern Europe, guided me to some of the area's most evocative cemeteries. Maria Choules, Peter Francis, Roy Hemington and Ian Small at the CWGC's headquarters in Maidenhead were unfailingly helpful in supplying archive material, photographs and information; Philip Longworth's excellent official history, *The Unending Vigil*, is a principal source for the chapter on the Commission's origins and early development. Penny Hatfield at Eton College Library and the staff at the Imperial War Museum's Reading Room and Guildhall Library's Manuscripts Section were also most helpful in providing source materials.

Colonel David Benest, formerly of the Parachute Regiment, and Lieutenant Colonel Alan Jones, formerly of the Army Air Corps, advised on military matters and I am particularly grateful to Professor Mark Connelly of the School of History, University of Kent, for reading drafts of the chapters on post-1918 Ypres. For information about the composition of the British colony I am indebted to Bert Heyvaert for his original research.

Extracts from the diaries, letters and Berlin broadcasts of P. G. Wodehouse are copyright © P. G. Wodehouse, reproduced by permission of the Estate of P. G. Wodehouse c/o Rogers, Coleridge & White Ltd, 20 Powis Mews, London W11 1JN. The writings of Edwin Lutyens, from which extracts are taken, are part of the Drawings and Archives Collection, RIBA British Architectural Library at the Victoria and Albert Museum. The quote by Pat Beauchamp is from her book *Fanny Goes to War*, published by John Murray in 1919. *The Immortal Salient* by William Pulteney and Beatrix Brice was published by John Murray for the Ypres League in 1925. *The Pilgrim's Guide to the Ypres Salient* was published by Herbert Reiach for Talbot House in 1920. Every reasonable effort has been made to trace copyright holders. Any errors or omissions may be rectified in future printings or editions.

Lizi Cosslett and Steve Humphries of Testimony Films have been a constant source of information, encouragement and good humour throughout this complex project; I have Steve to thank for telling me about the colony and the British Memorial School in the first place, and for introducing me to Jimmy Fox. Working on the stories of the people in this book – and meeting many of them – has been a privilege and an education. My partner Bevan Jones shared in some of these horizon-expanding expeditions but also put up with the less appealing aspects of my total immersion. I thank him for his forbearance.

Sue Elliott

Illustration Acknowledgements

Page 1 above and below: © In Flanders Fields Museum, Ieper. Page 2 above: Charlotte Dunn; below: Renee Matton/Proven. Page 3 above left: John Gabriel; above right and below: Fox family. Page 4 above: © Commonwealth War Graves Commission; below: Edis family. Page 5 above: Barbara Ruffle; below: Joan Mauret. Page 6 above: Edis family; below: Fox family. Page 7 above: Jerry Eaton. Page 7 below and page 8 above and below: © Getty Images (photographs by James Jarche). Page 9 above: Elizabeth Haworth; below: Photo Collection Dehaecke F34, Town Archives, Ieper. Page 10 above: Bundesarchiv Bild 1011-383-0337-22/Bocher; below: Wells family. Page 11 above: Sonja Tibber; below: MacDonald family. Page 12 top, middle and below: Lillian Betts. Page 13 above left, above right and below: Elaine Madden. Page 14 above left, above right and below; page 15 above and below: Stephen Grady. Page 16 above: © In Flanders Fields Museum, Ieper; below: Bob and Sheryl Simmons.

Every reasonable effort has been made to trace copyright holders, but if there are any errors or omissions, John Murray will be pleased to insert the appropriate acknowledgement in any subsequent printings or editions.

Sources

Much of the material for this book came from interviews given to the authors and to Testimony Films by former members of the British colony in Ypres, and from photographs and documents in their possession. The following sources were also invaluable in piecing together the history of the colony and what happened to its people during and after May 1940.

Post-1919 Ypres, the British colony, Settlement and School

The Private Papers of Maj. Gen. R. Briggs CB. IWM Department of Documents 8109 99/1/2

Commonwealth War Graves Commission archive. Correspondence, Papers and press cuttings.

The Documentation Centre of the In Flanders Fields Museum, Ieper, has an extensive collection of materials on the British Settlement, including British Memorial School Annual Reports and copies of the *Ypres Times*.

Hawkes, Gillian. *St George's Memorial Church; a short history*.

Heyvaert, Bert. *De Britse kolonie in Ieper tijdens het interbellum (1919–1940)*. Unpublished Masters thesis. University of Leuven, 2003.

Captain P. D. Parminter's recollections of post-1919 life in Ypres, written in 1964 for *The Beacon*, the magazine of the Brussels British Community Association.

The Pilgrim's Guide to the Ypres Salient published by Herbert Reiach on behalf of Talbot House, 1920. IWM Department of Printed Books 2140.

The Private Papers of J. M. Prower. IWM Department of Documents 11666 01-51/1.

Pulteney, William and Beatrix Brice. *The Immortal Salient*. Published by John Murray for the Ypres League 1925. IWM Department of Printed Books 12064.

Ypres British Settlement Minute Books of the Trustees 1925–48. Guildhall Library Manuscripts Section.

The *Ypres Times*, journal of the Ypres League, 1921–39. Complete collection held by the IWM.

May 1940 evacuation

Commonwealth War Graves Commission archive, Correspondence and reports.

Dawson, Lawrence. Undated (probably autumn 1940) 21-page personal account written for Captain Grinham of the IWGC.

Haworth, Reginald. *Flight from Flanders*. Unpublished memoir, 1941.

Horton, Roger. *Les Civils Britanniques Internés en Europe entre 1939–45*. Published by the author, 1995.

Occupation and Internment camps

CEGES-SOMA Centre for Historical Research and Documentation on War and Contemporary Society, Brussels.

Department of War Victims, Brussels.

Duncan, William Crawford. *Camp Leader*. Undated (probably written between 1946 and 1949). Unpublished manuscript.

Feuerheerd, Anitha Sophie. *You had to be Lucky! A record of my war reminiscences 1939-45*. Undated. Unpublished manuscript held by the Liebenau Foundation, Meckenbeuren, Germany.

Inspection Reports of ICRC delegates to Tost, Kreuzberg, Giromagny and Liebenau camps. International Red Cross, Geneva.

The Private Papers of B. A. Parsons. IWM Department of Documents 6526 79/2/1.

Debrief written by Albert Roberts for the IWGC, 1944. Commonwealth War Graves Commission archive.

The Tost Times and Advertiser camp newspaper 1, 16 and 30 June editions, IWM Department of Documents 704 Misc 153(2369).

Unpublished internment diaries: Alfred Percy Goddard, Jean Scott, Edwin Tester and Alfred Wells.

SOE

Elaine Madden's personal SOE file HS9/973/7. The National Archives.

Further Reading and Reference

Cemeteries and Memorials in Belgium and Northern France. Commonwealth War Graves Commission.

Ypres in War and Peace. Pitkin Guides, 1992.

Bardgett, Suzanne and David Cesarani (eds). *Belsen 1945: New Historical Perspectives*. Valentine Mitchell, 2006.

Chapman, Paul. *A Haven in Hell: Talbot House, Poperinghe*. Leo Cooper, 2000.

Cooksey, Jon. *Calais 1940: a Fight to the Finish*. Leo Cooper, 2000.

Coombes, Rose E. B. *Before Endeavours Fade: a Guide to the Battlefields of the First World War*. After the Battle, 2006.

Debaeke, Siegfried. *Ieper Before, During and After the Great War*. De Klaproos.

Deighton, Len. *Blitzkrieg: from the Rise of Hitler to the Fall of Dunkirk*. Pimlico, 2007.

Dendooven, Dominiek and Jan Dewilde. *The Reconstruction of Ieper: a walk through history*. Openbaar Kunstsbezit in Vlaanderen.

Donaldson, Frances. *Yours, Plum: the Letters of P. G. Wodehouse*. Penguin, 1992.

Foot, M. R. D. *SOE in the Low Countries*. St Ermin's Press, 2001.

Franks, Norman. *Typhoon Attack*. Grub Street, 2003.

Hanson, Neil. *The Unknown Soldier*. Corgi Books, 2007.

Helm, Sarah. *A Life in Secrets*. Abacus, 2006.

Holt, Tonie and Valmai. *My Boy Jack? The Search for Kipling's Only Son*. Pen & Sword Books, 2007.

Lloyd, David W. *Battlefield Tourism*. Berg, 1998.

Longworth, Philip. *The Unending Vigil: the History of the Commonwealth War Graves Commission*. Leo Cooper, 2003.

McCrum, Robert. *Wodehouse: a Life*. Penguin, 2005.

Miller, Russell. *Behind the Lines: the Oral History of Special Operations in World War II*. Secker & Warburg, 2002.

Neave, Airey. *Flames of Calais*. Pen & Sword Books, 2003.

Thorpe, Adam. *Nineteen Twenty-One*. Vintage, 2002.

Vinen, Richard. *The Unfree French: Life under the Occupation*. Penguin, 2007.

Winter, Jay. *Sites of Memory, Sites of Mourning: the Great War in European Cultural History*. Cambridge University Press, 1995.

Websites

www.aftermathww1.com

www.bbc.co.uk/history

www.cwgc.org   The Commonwealth War Graves Commission website offers information about its work worldwide, a search facility for its Debt of Honour Register, and useful histories produced in collaboration with the Imperial War Museum, including one dedicated to the Ypres Salient.

www.fany.org.uk

www.firstworldwar.com

The Great War Forum at www.1914-1918.invisionzone.com/forums/

www.inflanderfields.be   The website of the In Flanders Fields Museum, Ieper.

www.insigne.org/SAARF-I.htm   Background to the Special Allied Airborne Reconnaissance Force.

www.iwm.org.uk The website of the Imperial War Museum.

www.lastpost.be The website of the Last Post Association, Ieper.

The Long, Long Trail at www.1914-1918.net/

http://netministries.org/see/churches/ch00278 St George's Memorial Church.

www.pgwodehousebooks.com/berlin.htm Transcripts of Wodehouse's Berlin broadcasts.

www.testimonyfilms.com

www.visitflanders.co.uk/go/destinations/ypres-history.html

The Web Genocide Documentation Centre, University of the West of England, at www.ess.uwe.ac.uk/genocide/mord/htm gives background and original documents on Nazi 'medical killing' programmes.

The Women of the Special Operations Executive. www.64-baker-street.org

Index